CEAC

D1521065

"Have To" History: The Boring Parts

Stuff You Don't Really Want to Know (But for Some Reason Have To) About the Most Boring Events, People, and Issues in American History

~ ~ ~

Dallas Koehn

INTRODUCTION STUFF

Let's be honest: if you find history boring, the problem usually isn't the history – it's *you*. History is inherently fascinating. Any belief to the contrary indicates a severe character flaw and suggests numerous poor personal choices in your life.

And yet… there certainly are bits here and there which simply don't stir the ol' imagination the way the colorful parts do. It's one thing to explore the motivations and strategies of those who fought on each side at Gettysburg; it's another to fully appreciate the implications of the federal land management policies being debated while they did. Sometimes those boring bits are pretty important, however. They impact the interesting parts we *do* care about. They reflect larger issues we *should* understand. They keep coming up on state tests and APUSH exams.

I know that last part sounds rather lame, but it suggests that lots of presumably smart people think this stuff *really does matter* or they wouldn't keep forcing it into curriculum maps and study guides year after year. That leads us to the first official purpose of this introduction – persuading as many people as possible to buy this book. Yes, it's intended for students trying to brush up on the parts they probably glazed over or slept through. Yes, it's also intended for the informal lover of history who genuinely wants a better understanding of this wacky collective history of ours.

In other words, YES – of *course* you should buy this book. Maybe several copies so you can talk about it with friends. And don't forget Granddad. He loves this stuff.

I'm an educator by trade, so naturally I'd like to encourage and assist anyone focused on "passing" something (although it's always nice to think they might genuinely want to *learn* something along the way). But I'm also a realist, and teenagers aren't known for coughing up their own money to add yet another tome to the "good intentions" pile. Besides, I love a good recreational history book unhampered by the need for legislative approval or wrapped in feigned "neutrality" about everything that's ever happened. Hopefully, this compilation can satisfy both needs. (Yet another reason to purchase multiple copies. It also makes a great gift for those folks you never know how to shop for!)

This book can be read sequentially or by jumping around to whatever topics interest you most. You may notice occasional overlapping between chapters in order to ensure appropriate context for the topic at hand. Nothing in history exists in isolation from everything else, and part of why some stuff strikes us as "boring" or (perish the thought) "unimportant" is that we often lack the context and connections to think otherwise.

In order to keep this volume as accessible and (hopefully) enjoyable as possible, I've tried to minimize the use of school-specific language. The glaring exception is the final segment of each chapter ("Making The Grade") which specifically targets likely exam questions of various formats. If you're in school, you should pay particular attention to these. If not, you can safely skip those bits – or browse them anyway while thanking the pedagogical gods that you're past all that.

Observations and examples used in these segments have been drawn from an extensive survey of practice materials and released state exams from around the country as well as the College Board's Advanced Placement U.S. History course (APUSH). It is not my intention to claim anyone else's work as my own; by definition, however, these materials are created by the same folks who literally decide what's likely to be "on the test." It's impossible to avoid emulating their language or echoing their priorities when preparing students for those same exams.

Finally, part of what sometimes makes history *seem* so boring is the scrubbing away of anything approaching "bias" or "point of view." Textbooks and other institutionally approved sources dance around or brush over issues and questions that would make any number of subjects *relevant* and *engaging* for they'll offend some vocal group or other. Readers of this work will quickly discover my own biases and assumptions leaking through in every chapter. This is not a bold act of defiance so much as a shameful lack of self-discipline, but it may prove beneficial nonetheless. History *should* provoke us, and other people's interpretations and assertions *should* annoy us from time to time. It forces us to rethink our own assumptions and drives us to learn more in order to better crush them on social media like the flotsam they are.

Personal convictions are never an excuse for sloppy history, however. Everything covered herein is accurate to the best of my understanding. Some events may be streamlined or simplified, some interpretations subject to debate, but that's part of how history works. If we refused to prioritize or synthesize information for fear of creating subjective narratives, we'd never get past Columbus. Heck, we'd never make it *to* Columbus.

A major thank you to my infinitely patient wife for tolerating this laborious process once again and for smiling politely every time I promised I'd take a break from writing once this book was finished (even though we both know that's unlikely). Thank you to Christine Bond Custred for her suggestions and encouragement along the way and to Jarrod Gollihare for his brilliant cover art despite my constant last-minute tweaks and conflicting requests. Finally, a very special thank you to the many readers of Blue Cereal Education who offered feedback and warm fuzzies in response to the various drafts posted there over the past eighteen months. You light up my life and fill my nights with song.

Resetting now.

--Dallas Koehn, BCE@BlueCerealEducation.com

HISTORY SURVIVAL SKILLS:
THE FIVE BIG QUESTIONS
If You Know The Answers, You're Doing It Wrong

Introduction

It's sometimes helpful to think of history in terms of "guiding" or "essential" questions. While this may seem like one more thing teachers have come up with just to make our lives difficult, that's not always the case.

See, most history classes attempt to cover some fragment of a larger story without sufficient time or perspective. It can sometimes feel like a blur of names, dates, and places, drawn together only by happenstance – or the next quiz. Recognizing a few overarching themes or guiding questions can help *connect* that information, making it easier to understand and to remember. "Big Picture" questions help those names, dates, and places become "stickier" by making them part of an endless narrative or ongoing debate. They help us consider more clearly how things have changed, how they've stayed the same, and why it matters.

If you're currently a student, your teacher may have already introduced their own "essential questions" to guide you. If you're in Advanced Placement U.S. History (hereafter referred to as APUSH, with all the usual disclaimers about how nothing in this book is officially affiliated with the College Board or its myriad manifestations), you've already been introduced to eight sacred, interconnected "themes." It still wouldn't hurt to check out the versions presented in this chapter, but if your priority is surviving a class somewhere, stick to the language and priorities of whoever hands out the grades.

Don't worry – if you care about the actual *learning*, any decent set of "guiding questions" will help you get there. On the other hand, if you're just trying to pass the class and move on, why make it harder for yourself? Keep looking back at those themes or "big picture" questions at each step and ask yourself how whatever's being covered this week connects to one or more of them.

Trust me on this. It totally works.

For those of you who've moved past formal education, these guiding questions still offer their love and guidance. (Plus, it would feel awkward to start skipping ahead this early in the text, no?) In addition to helping you *feel* smarter, they're handy frameworks for stretching your own thinking, guiding your own learning, or bluffing and blustering your way through social media arguments with people who clearly *haven't* read this chapter.

Automatic win for *you*, Captain Deep-Think.

Question #1: Who's In Charge? (And How Much Power Should They Have?)

This is one of the easiest to see in action – any time period, any topic, on any scale.

In any given family, who makes the decisions? Does Mom run certain things by Dad while deciding other stuff by herself? Can older sister manipulate certain situations without repercussions while you're held accountable for everything? There are as many power dynamics in families as there are families. The same is true of your local Board of Education, your favorite major corporation, and all the way up to the White House.

In any school, who's really in charge? Is it the building principal? Their secretary? The math department? The teachers' union? The angriest parents? And how much sway do each of them really have? In any classroom, who's in charge, and how in charge are they? Does the teacher guide confidently or hang on for dear life? And how much power should classroom teachers have anyway? Or, if they are in control, how much of that power should they exercise, and in what circumstances? What less-obvious sources of power and influence are in play in some classrooms, and how can you tell?

In early American History, who was in charge, the Colonies or England? The Federalists or the Anti-Federalists? The States or the Central Government? The Executive, the Legislative, or the Judicial – and in what mixture?

What about the North or the South? The wealthy, the educated, or the daring? The God-fearing or the Godless? The soldiers, the hippies, or the industrialists? The police or the protestors? Who has the power? How much power do they have? How much power *should* they have? And who *wants* that power or may be perceived as a *threat* to that power?

You get the idea. Once you start thinking about it, this question is everywhere – and it *always* matters.

Question #2: Who Gets To Be A "Real" (or "Full") American?

When Jefferson first wrote that "all men are created equal, and are endowed by their Creator with certain unalienable rights," it was widely assumed that "all men" actually meant "all rich, white, educated men."

Over time, that definition evolved to include those who aren't so wealthy and may not be all that educated. After the Civil War, citizens no longer even had to be white to exercise political power (at least on paper – reality may have taken a while to catch up). Eventually, even *women* could vote and run for office and such. "All men" gradually came to mean "all adult citizens of whatever race or gender."

And yet, over 200 years later, we're still trying to figure out exactly who those "all men" really are.

Are undocumented immigrants "all men"? Does the whole "pursuit of happiness" bit apply to them as well? Should we educate their kids? Provide emergency medical care? Let them get a driver's license? What are the pros and cons of each scenario?

Are people of color "all men"? Like, even if they're suspected of something untoward? Are they still "endowed by their creator with certain unalienable rights" even if an officer or other white person feels uncomfortable as a result?

Do poor people deserve the same levels of medical care or personal dignity as those who've demonstrated "moral superiority" by making "better choices" (as evidenced by their inherited wealth)? What about same sex marriage? Are these couples entitled to a wedding cake or should they simply be thankful we let them marry at all? And Muslims - are they "all men" (the kind who are "created equal"), even if we're pretty sure they're not even Christians?

Our founders argued about it in various forms before declaring independence, and we're still arguing about it today. Once you become aware of it, you'll see this question everywhere as well. You may also notice that some people are mighty touchy about possible answers.

Question #3: What Is The American Dream?

Americans have always had a sense of purpose or calling – a conviction that their trudge through this broken world *must* mean more than a paycheck and a few messy relationships. But what *is* that calling, and how has it changed (or stayed the same) over time?

Is it about a set of ideals by which men should live - a chance to prove that a government founded on the proposition that all men are created equal can, in fact, long endure?

Is it about land and opportunity? Westward expansion? Forty Acres and a Mule?

Is it about freedom or other basic protections? Access to health care, education, or personal safety?

Is it about power? Sex? Wealth? Notoriety? More sex? YouTube followers? Even more sex?

Maybe just a little 3-bedroom house with a dog and a white picket fence? True love? Netflix? Being the first to own the iPhone13?

Legislators promote a lot of what they do as protecting, restoring, or otherwise promoting the "American Dream." We argue about whether or not everyone has an equal shot at it. Most of us are expected at some point to care about it, chase it, or come up with a pretty good reason for rejecting it.

Seems like at some point we should have some idea just what *it* is.

Question #4: How Far Should America Reach?

There were a number of provocations leading to the American Revolution, but the Proclamation of 1763 – "Don't you dare go past those mountains" – was certainly among the most irritating.

Manifest Destiny. Indian Removal. War with Mexico. Imperialism. Walking softly but carrying a big stick. The Monroe Doctrine (and Roosevelt Corollary). Isolationism. WWI. WWII. The Cold War. The Korean Conflict. Whatever we were doing in Vietnam. The "War on Terror." The G8 Summit. The Paris Climate Accords. Human rights in China, or Russia, or…?

It was a difficult question two centuries ago, and a shrinking world has only increased its complexity. Every election, every news cycle, every world event simply stirs it up further. How far should we go to explore, help, control, or recreate in our own image? (Seriously – we'd be doing them a *huge* favor… they're a mess!) Is it even possible in the twenty-first century to *not* be involved? The entire world practically lives in the same tenement.

There are no *easy* answers to any "big picture" question. On this subject, there are rarely even *good* ones.

Question #5: How Do We Balance Freedom & Security?

This one might be the most important of all. Its ramifications are obvious when discussing the "War on Terror" or protest marches or any of the dozens of ways our government spies on us "for our own good" without due process or practical limits. The question is just as important, however, when applied to economic policy, or society and culture.

Somewhere between laissez-faire capitalism (served on a bed of fresh Social Darwinism) and "you have nothing to lose but your chains!" lies an ideal balance of economic freedom and government regulations aimed at equity and general prosperity. Finding it, on the other hand, has proven both tricky and controversial.

It's not any easier when it comes to society and culture. If we believe that *some* unity has to be maintained in order to promote stability, why pretend we believe in "unalienable rights" to begin with? (Maybe we should start calling them "only-partially-alienable-in-certain-circumstances rights" to give ourselves a little breathing room.) On the other hand, if people are free to maintain their own language, sexuality, religion, culture, political ideologies, shoe size, or crappy taste in music and entertainment, what exactly is left to hold us together? Puritan stricture is clearly undesirable, but so is complete cultural anarchy.

How do we give people the freedom to be whoever they feel the need to be while still maintaining workable communities or a cohesive society?

Government at all levels is constantly confronted with the question of what they should or shouldn't regulate. Smoking. Drinking. Wearing your seatbelt. Various drugs. Vaccinations. Public nudity or obscenity. What counts as food and what's cruelty to animals. What counts as religion and what's a dangerous cult. Too much freedom and we self-destruct. Too little and we become just like every other wannabe empire throughout history.

If you've ever owned a pet, you may have wrestled with this same issue. Outside, they're able to do the kinds of things animals like to do. They might also pick up a weird disease or get hit by a car. The *safest* place for them, realistically, is a small kennel, placed in the tub, inside a central bathroom with the door closed, 24/7. There *is* a small trade-off in terms of their happiness, however.

Parents confront a similar dilemma. Should they step in or let their kids resolve their own problems at school? What about curfews, chores, cell phone usage, or choosing their own friends? Helicopter too much and they grow up useless. Govern too little and they might self-destruct or do long-term damage to their own future. For that matter, they might not grow up at all. The *safest* place for them, realistically, is a small kennel, placed in the tub, inside a central bathroom with the door closed, 24/7. You'll want something to muffle any noise so neighbors don't call the police, however.

You'll easily recognize infinite variations of this one in the world around your or in pretty much any historical setting; you just have to pay a little attention – even if you don't really want to.

CHAPTER ONE: THE THIRTEEN COLONIES

Three (or Four) Regions – Three Types of Charter –
Three Approaches to Religious "Freedom"

Three Big Things:

1. The thirteen original colonies are often discussed in geographical chunks – New England, the Middle Colonies, and the South (which is sometimes split into Chesapeake and the Lower South). The cultures and economies of each region were shaped by the circumstances in which they were founded and the natural features of the land itself.

2. There were three basic types of charter – corporate (or "joint-stock"), proprietary, and royal. Most colonies began with corporate or proprietary charters but were later taken over directly by the crown.

3. The colonies tried different approaches to religious "freedom" in the centuries before independence. Some allowed great latitude of belief, and most attempted a degree of tolerance – at least relative to what was common in Europe at the time. The remaining few inspired a new word in the American lexicon: "puritanical."

Introduction

Most state curriculums allow three or four weeks to get from Columbus sailing the ocean blue to the colonists declaring independence – a period of nearly 300 years. Educators then have the rest of that year to take students through the Civil War (another 100 years) and a second full year to get from Reconstruction through Making America Great Again (around 150 years). If you're a student (or used to be) and you find some of this colonial stuff to be a bit of a blur, don't worry – it's practically planned that way.

So, unlike many subsequent chapters, this one won't be pushing specific individuals or moments you simply "have to" remember and understand. Instead, we're going to focus on general schemata – mental structures into which you can organize the important individuals and events emphasized by your teacher or your personal research. You'll find no stories about Pocahontas or the "First Thanksgiving" here and no excerpts from that "City on a Hill" thing ("The eics of all people are uponne us...") Those are the *interesting* bits, after all.

Instead, we're going to categorize the original thirteen colonies in three distinct ways – by region, by charter, and by how they handled religion.

Buckle your capotains... it could get bumpy.

Three (or Four) Regions

Most texts chunk the colonies into three regions; APUSH and a handful of others prefer four. Under either system, the regions are basically the same. In the "Hey, look at us – we're more specific than you!" version, Virginia and Maryland are separated from the rest of the south and treated as special. (Given that it's Virginia and Maryland, both are no doubt quite comfortable with that distinction.)

The New England Colonies – Massachusetts (including what later became Maine), New Hampshire, Rhode Island, and Connecticut. The economies of New England centered around small farms, livestock, fishing, whaling, furs, lumber, textiles, shipbuilding, and rum. While it was possible to grow crops, the rocky soil, short growing seasons, and all those darned mountains made large-scale agriculture impractical.

The religious climate was largely Puritan (with Rhode Island being the notable exception). Dissent was not tolerated and consequences could be severe. Religion shaped local governance and impacted economic choices as well. The Puritans didn't use the term "Protestant Work Ethic," but they certainly typified it. Self-discipline, frugality, and due diligence were *spiritual* as well social or economic values. New England would have preferred to remain entirely insulated, had it been practical, and did less business with the outside world than any other region.

The Middle Colonies – New York, Pennsylvania, New Jersey, and Delaware. The economies of the Middle colonies centered around wheat, corn, livestock, textiles, paper, and iron (plows, kettles, etc.) Middle colonies closer to New England exported lumber and did a little shipbuilding, while those further south grew tobacco or other cash crops.

Their ethnic mix was limited by today's standards but the most diverse in the colonies. In addition to English settlers came Dutch, Germans, Scotch-Irish, French, and even a few Swedes. Quakers, Mennonites, and Lutherans shaped the culture and theology of the region, with a healthy smattering of Presbyterians and other Calvinists just to keep things interesting. Members of the same faith would typically congregate in their own communities; religion was often supported by local government and individuals were expected to adhere to the norms of whichever theology ruled their neighborhood.

The Southern Colonies (three-region version) – Maryland, Virginia, North Carolina, South Carolina, and Georgia.

The Chesapeake Colonies (four-region version) – Maryland and Virginia. Flat land and long growing seasons were ideal for large-scale agriculture, although numerically most citizens lived on plots small enough to work themselves (subsistence farming). The commercial economy of the Chesapeake region was based almost entirely on tobacco and required maintaining reliable commercial networks both with sister colonies and abroad. Tobacco was wildly profitable, but it exhausted the soil quickly, encouraging rapid expansion and periodic massacre of the locals in order to claim more land. It was also labor-intensive.

Very labor-intensive.

Originally, indentured servitude was implemented and promoted as a win-win. Landowners were provided with free labor and the indentured were promised freedom and land or other fun prizes after a certain number of years in the fields. It doesn't take much in-depth analysis to notice that this system strongly encouraged landowners to drive laborers mercilessly, allowing them as little sleep, food, or freedom as possible. Maximizing profits meant squeezing every possible bit of labor out of the indentured before their time of service expired. Ideally, of course, they'd die shortly before you had to actually give them anything.

If you're wondering, there's little indication anyone felt badly about treating their workers this way. Indentured servants were considered slothful and corrupt, as evidenced by their tendency to get sick or collapse from exhaustion. Some even ran away – and after all you'd done for them!

Indentured servitude was soon replaced by slavery. There was no need to promise the slaves *anything*, and it was harder for them to run away because they didn't look like anyone else in the colonies... except for other slaves.

Religion in the Chesapeake colonies was largely Anglican (the American version of the Church of England), although anything overtly Protestant could usually find some form of toleration. Direct government support was generally reserved for Anglican churches, but members of the other faiths could form their own communities and live by their own rules as long as they weren't perceived as "radical." Maryland was at one point intended as a haven for Catholics, but they weren't actually a majority and at different times lost even nominal protections. Overall, however, it was usually possible to lay low and get by.

The "Lower South" (four-region version) – North Carolina, South Carolina, and Georgia. The economy of the Lower South was (no shocker here) largely based on cash crops – tobacco, grains, corn, rice, etc. (There was some cotton production as well, but this wouldn't truly take off until the invention of the cotton gin in the late eighteenth century.) This gave the Lower South the same thirst for expansion as the Chesapeake region and eventually the same reliance on slave labor.

The most common religions were Anglican, Baptist, and Presbyterian, although anything Protestant and not too adventurous was generally fine. Government support was largely reserved for Anglican churches, but members of the other faiths could form their own communities just as in the Chesapeake region.

Three (Evolving) Formats

ALL English colonies were established via special charter from the King. A

13

charter described in some detail the "rules" for how a colony would be run and the specific relationship between that colony and the King. There were no "independent" colonies prior to the Revolution. The differences between colonies in this sense were primarily structural.

Corporate Colonies (sometimes called "Joint-Stock" or "Self-Governing") – Joint-stock colonies were financed by pools of investors, allowing them to raise substantial capital without severe risk to any one individual. If the company proved profitable, everyone gained. If not, the loss was dispersed. Anyone able to afford investing in a joint-stock venture, of course, was probably doing well enough that they had no reason to leave their established lives and move to the New World. On the other hand, the system allowed folks without resources to move overseas and experience their own grand adventure – a new beginning, a chance to rebuild civilization from scratch, and mass starvation if they weren't massacred by the locals first. And hopefully they could do it all *profitably*. Surely they owed the stockholders *that* much, at least?

Corporate charters actually gave colonists more relative freedom and control over their own lives and communities than either of the other options. As long as they could send a little something back, few investors cared *how* they did it.

Virginia (obviously) began this way, as did Massachusetts, Connecticut, and Rhode Island in the New England region and Georgia in the South/Lower South.

Proprietary Colonies – These colonies were governed by charters granted to individuals who in turn reported to the King. (This usually included some form of annual "tribute" or payment.) This system was particularly popular in the late seventeenth century after the British "Restoration" of King Charles II and the Stuart Monarchy. Charles II granted land in the Middle and Southern colonies to individuals who'd supported and financed him during the fray.

Proprietors held an authority not so different from nobles under feudalism. Each proprietor organized his territory as he wished, established trade or businesses, chose who could live there and under what laws, and determined the official religion.

New Hampshire began under a proprietary charter, as did *all* of the Middle Colonies, Maryland, and Carolina (which eventually split into North and South Carolina).

Royal Colonies (sometimes called "Provincial") – These were under the direct rule of the King of England via his on-site representatives. While this didn't entirely eliminate the "middle man" (there was still a pretty big ocean between the colonies and the crown), this was the system we typically envision when singing along with *Schoolhouse Rock* cartoons.

None of the colonies *began* as royal colonies, but by 1775 all but two (Delaware and Pennsylvania) had been taken over directly by the throne – usually long before the stuff we think of as leading to the Revolution. That's part of what makes the whole "charter" issue so messy – very few colonies retained the same legal structure over their entire existence. In some cases, it's possible to categorize the same charter in different ways, depending on who's doing the sorting and which time period they have in mind.

So good luck with that.

Three Approaches To Religion

Categorizing colonial approaches to matters of faith is largely an artificial convenience applied after the fact to make history a tiny bit easier for normal people. There weren't preprinted labels or anything – just general patterns which evolved over time. With that disclaimer, let's look at three basic approaches:

Puritanical – Religious belief and behavior were dictated by religious leaders and their understanding of scripture. These men were often economic and political leaders as well, giving them secular power in addition to religious authority. There was little or no room for "dissenters" and punishments could be severe. This approach, not surprisingly, was most dominant in New England (minus Rhode Island). As time passed, this approach became less and less prominent. For some reason, the majority just didn't seem to enjoy it.

Pragmatic – Different religious groups found ways to accommodate one another out of necessity or practicality. Communities developed around shared faiths (mostly Christian and primarily Protestant). There were clear expectations for behavior and belief within each community, but they weren't generally as rigid as further north. People had other things to do and lacked both the time and the inclination to cut off ears or burn holes in anyone's tongue. (They might scowl at you a bit, however.) This approach was commonly found in the Middle colonies (minus Pennsylvania) and eventually across parts of the south as well.

"Kumbaya" – Most common belief systems were welcome as long as they agree to play nicely with one another. Man's relationship with the Almighty couldn't be dictated by statutes or improved by punishment. Rhode Island and Pennsylvania (with all those wacky Quakers) were the only colonies to really give this a shot early on, although New York moved this direction eventually as well. By the Revolutionary Era, most colonies were somewhere between the Pragmatic and the Kumbaya approach. When the U.S. celebrates "religious freedom" in the modern sense, it generally means this approach. At the time, it was thoroughly unique.

General Trends and Elaboration

As you've probably picked up on by now, the concept of "freedom of religion" wasn't nearly as prominent in colonial times as popular history would have us believe. For many, the idea that an individual could simply *choose* how to understand or serve the Lord Almighty made about as much sense as letting a toddler *choose* whether or not fire was hot or wolves were friendly. To most

Puritans (including the Pilgrims), "freedom" was the ability to break away from the oppressive wrongheadedness of the Old World and set up things the "right" way in the New – as God clearly intended. Catholic or Jewish communities in the Middle colonies, on the other hand, mostly just wanted the "freedom" to establish their own little enclaves and be left alone.

Of course, many colonists came for reasons unrelated to their religious beliefs – economic opportunity, a fresh start, escaping poverty, political upheaval, etc. Religion may have played an important role in their lives (socially, personally, or both), but it wasn't at the top of their agenda when they booked passage.

Nevertheless, despite the celebrated efforts of a few individuals, Protestantism was both *dominant* and *demanded* in a majority of places. Most colonies, whatever their charter, had an established church which was supported by tax dollars. For much of the colonial period, church attendance was required by law and deviations from religious norms could be severely punished by local authorities. Those unwilling to at least recognize the virgin birth and resurrection of Jesus and the basics of personal salvation (whether predetermined or chosen) were often driven out of their communities – if they were lucky. Rhode Island and Pennsylvania were the only colonies which provided sustained efforts towards true religious tolerance.

There was no universal public education system, but you could find local efforts supported by tax dollars and reinforcing whichever religious flavor held sway in that colony or community. In the New England colonies, literacy was essential to properly read and understand the Bible and other religious writings, as well as to participate meaningfully in society and politics. As you looked further south, education became less and less predictable, often depending on your social status and the whims of your community.

Evolving Circumstances & Shifting Perspectives

Over time, as immigration increased diversity, those belonging to different Protestant denominations were sometimes excused from directly supporting the established faith and allowed to instead funds their own religious institutions. After the Great Awakening of the 1730s and 1740s (and especially after its sequel nearly a century later), denominational authority began to weaken dramatically. Christianity became more "democratic" and the idea of "free will" gained increased influence in how faith was understood by many. The Awakenings also marked a shift away from Calvinistic theology towards a faith more compatible with American ideals.

While Calvinism and the doctrine of "predestination" provoked plenty of deep theological *thinking* and spiritual *consideration*, a man with the "free will" had the power to change his own destiny (by accepting the grace of God). He could go forth and *get things done*. He could transform his family through his faith. He could impact his community through his actions and his choices. He could, given the opportunity, help shape the direction of a nation – all while the Calvinists were still debating supralapsarianism vs. infralapsarianism.

In short, the Old Lights (think Puritans) were *educated*; the New Lights (think Methodists and Baptists) were *empowered*. Cotton Mather (history's favorite Puritan) wrote books. John Wesley (founder of the Methodist church) held revivals.

The whole "all men are created equal and endowed with certain unalienable rights" would have made little sense to Calvinist hearts and minds. The whole premise ran counter to most of Christianity's foundational teachings in the previous two millennia. The Great Awakening gave Christianity a complete makeover and a whole new mission. The children of God were no longer put on this earth to serve the church and merely await the Second Coming in fear and trembling; they were here to get involved and build a nation. (If need be, they'd show everyone else how to get on the right path as well.) At the same time, the faith preached by the Great Awakening distinguished between institutional authority and one's personal relationship with the Almighty – laying the groundwork for formal separation of "church" and "state."

But we're getting ahead of ourselves a bit.

Making The Grade: What You're Most Likely To Be Asked

When it comes to the Colonial Era, anything goes. You'll most likely encounter some curve balls, but you can at least be prepared for the obvious stuff. Expect questions about Jamestown (especially the whole "no work, no food" rule instituted by John Smith), the Pilgrims (particularly the Mayflower Compact), and anything teasing what will come to be thought of as "freedom of religion" (Anne Hutchinson, Roger Williams, the Quakers, etc.) Questions may be phrased in terms of "firsts" – the first permanent English settlement in the New World (Jamestown, 1607), the first example of self-government in the colonies (Plymouth, 1620), or the first colony to grant broad religious freedom (Rhode Island, 1636).

Expect at least a few multiple choice questions related to the initial purpose of various settlements, ways in which geography shaped the economies and lifestyles of each region, or early manifestations of representative government:

1. Which two American colonies were settled largely as an attempt to escape religious persecution? (A) Virginia and South Carolina, (B) Pennsylvania and Maryland, (C) New York and New Jersey, or (D) Vermont and Connecticut.

2. Which of the following colonies was *not* established primarily for economic reasons? (A) Virginia, (B) South Carolina, (C) North Carolina, or (D) Georgia.

3. Why did most colonists settle near the Atlantic Coast or along major rivers? (A) Access to navigable water made it easier to trade and communicate. (B) Most charters prohibited settlements in other locations. (C) British ships were the colonists' primary defense in case of Indian attacks. (D) Drinking water

was difficult to find in the New World until wells could be dug.

4. What was the primary reason large plantations developed in the South but not in the Middle Colonies or New England? (A) Large mountain ranges and limited water access made it difficult for the south to industrialize or conduct commercial trade. (B) Colonial charters prohibited slavery in most colonies due to religious reasons, but not in the corporate colonies of the south. (C) Longer growing seasons and fertile soil encouraged the cultivation of cash crops like tobacco, wheat, corn, and rice. (D) Relations with local Native American tribes made the acquisition of land easier than with warrior tribes further north.

5. New England town meetings and the Virginia House of Burgesses were both examples of... (A) early revolutionary movements promoting independence from England, (B) local representative government in the colonies, (C) public events in which women were allowed equal participation, or (D) the dominance of religious leadership in colonial politics.

6. Which of the following best describes local government in the colonies from 1607 – 1763? (A) Most practiced some form of democracy, although participation was limited compared to later centuries. (B) Local governments were dominated by religious leaders everywhere except Rhode Island. (C) Local governors appointed by the King acted as chief executives with local representatives whose roles were largely advisory. (D) Most colonies practiced some form of direct democracy in which people voted on most legislation publicly in mass gatherings.

If you live in one of the original thirteen states, you'll probably see specifics related to your "colony" as well.

Short answer questions or essay prompts are actually a bit easier to anticipate and tend to be phrased more broadly:

7. Discuss different reasons people came to the colonies. (A common variation: compare the reasons for settlement in {one region} with motivations for coming to {another region}.)

8. Discuss the economies of each region of colonies – what they grew, made, or sold. (Same idea on variations – compare the economy of this region to the economy of that region, etc.)

9. Discuss the role of religion in the colonies (usually with an emphasis on the Pilgrims / Puritans, Massachusetts, and the relative freedom offered by Rhode Island. This one also often appears as a comparison question between two specified regions).

10. Identify key interactions with Amerindians (the natives), whether positive or negative.

If you're in APUSH or anything else "advanced" (or if your teacher is simply feeling gung-ho about things), you should be prepared for a cut'n'paste prompt asking you to explain how some specified factor (geography, natural resources, cultures, motivations for colonization, etc.) impacted some other factor (economics, politics, cultural norms, etc.) in two or three selected regions. I know, I know – but it's not as bad as it sounds. Sometimes you'll even get to choose one or more of the cut'n'paste elements!

The trickiest prompts are those demanding somewhat more extensive knowledge of specific topics related to the era:

11. Discuss the growth of representative government and institutions during the colonial period. (This lays the groundwork for declaring independence.)

12. Explain why/how slavery came to the colonies. (Discuss indentured servitude, efforts to enslave Amerindians, and the general roots of the slave trade in Europe and Africa, etc.)

I could go on, but I don't want to frighten you this early in the timeline.

Don't panic if you encounter colonial questions you have no idea how to answer. Take a breath and ask yourself if they're actually a variation on one of the prompts above. Consider what you do know and how it might relate to what's being asked. Then, give it your best shot and move on. It's done.

Hang in there. Most of this stuff ends up foundational to everything else covered in U.S. history – so that helps. Also, it all gets a bit easier after independence. (Not necessarily *easy*, but *easier*.) And way less boring. Except for about twenty other things – all of which we'll cover next.

Colony	Region	Founder(s)	Original Charter / Charter (1776)	Primary Religion	Economic Focus	Associated Events	Notable Individuals (Pre-Revolutionary)
New Hampshire	New England	Captain John Mason, Sir Ferdinando Gorges	Proprietary (1629) / Royal (1776)	Puritan	Shipbuilding, Textiles, Rum, Lumber, Furs, Fishing, Whaling	King Philip's War	John Wheelright
Massachusetts	New England	Mass. Bay Company / John Winthrop	Corporate (1629) / Royal (1776)	Puritan (Pilgrims were Puritan Separatists)	Shipbuilding, Rum, Lumber, Furs, Fishing, Whaling	Mayflower Compact, "City On A Hill," Pequot War, King Philip's War	Myles Standish, William Bradford, John Cotton, Anne Hutchinson
Connecticut	New England	Thomas Hooker	Corporate (1662) / Royal (1776)	Puritan (Pilgrims were Puritan Separatists)	Shipbuilding, Rum, Lumber, Furs, Fishing, Whaling	Fundamental Orders of Connecticut, Pequot War, King Philip's War	John Winthrop, Jr.
Rhode Island	New England	Roger Williams (and Others)	Corporate (1636) / Royal (1776)	Mixed / Relative Freedom	Shipbuilding, Rum, Lumber, Furs, Fishing, Whaling	xxxx	Anne Hutchinson, William Coddington
New York	Middle	xxxx	Proprietary (1664) / Royal (1776)	Mixed / Relative Tolerance	Wheat, Corn, Furs, Livestock, Lumber, Furs, Iron Products	xxxx	***
Pennsylvania	Middle	William Penn	Proprietary (1681) / Proprietary (1776)	Quaker / Relative Freedom	Wheat, Corn, Hemp, Flax, Shipbuilding, Iron, Paper, Tanning	xxxx	***
New Jersey	Middle	Sir George Carteret & Lord Berkeley of Stratton	Proprietary (1664) / Royal (1776)	Mixed / Local Variety	Corn, Wheat, Rice, Livestock, Indigo, Iron Products	xxxx	***
Delaware	Middle	It's... Complicated (William Penn?)	Proprietary (1664) / Proprietary (1776)	Quaker / Local Variety	Tobacco, Corn, Wheat, Rice, Livestock	xxxx	***

Colony	Region	Founder(s)	Original Charter / Charter (1776)	Primary Religion	Economic Focus	Associated Events	Notable Individuals (Pre-Revolutionary)
Maryland	Southern (3 Reg.) Chesapeake (4 Reg.)	Cecil Calvert (Lord Baltimore)	Proprietary (1632) / Royal (1776)	Catholics / Mixed / Relative Tolerance	Tobacco, Wheat, Tobacco, Corn, Tobacco	Maryland Toleration Act	***
Virginia	Southern (3 Reg.) Chesapeake (4 Reg.)	John Smith	Corporate (1607) / Royal (1776)	Church of England (Anglican)	Tobacco, Tobacco, Tobacco, Wheat, Corn	Colonial Charter, House of Burgesses, Bacon's Rebellion	Sir Walter Raleigh, John Rolfe, Pocahontas
North Carolina	Southern / Lower South	The Lords Proprietors	Proprietary (1663) / Royal (1776)	Church of England / Local Variety	Rice, Tar, Pitch, Turpentine	Roanoke (the lost colony), Culpeper's Rebellion	***
South Carolina	Southern / Lower South	The Lords Proprietors	Proprietary (1663) / Royal (1776)	Church of England / Local Variety	Cotton, Rice, Tobacco, Indigo	***	***
Georgia	Southern / Lower South	James Oglethorpe	Corporate (1732) / Royal (1776)	Church of England / Local Variety	Indigo, Rice, Sugar	***	***

CHAPTER TWO: THE ARTICLES OF CONFEDERATION (1777 – 1789)
BFF4Eva – We Pinky Promise!

Three Big Things

1. The Articles of Confederation was the first constitution of the new United States. Its provisions reflect a loose alliance of states determined to avoid the sort of overbearing centralized government from which they'd just broken free.

2. The unicameral legislature established by the Articles was the only "branch" of central government created by the Articles. It had very little actual authority and few resources with which to implement its decisions.

3. Eventually the Articles were replaced by the U.S. Constitution, much of which was clearly designed to correct the problems of its predecessor.

Context

The thirteen colonies which had just broken away from Mother England considered themselves to now be thirteen distinct free and equal states. While we've come to think of "states" as shorthand for "geographical subdivisions of a country," that's not what the term indicated at the time. Athens, for example, was an independent city-state of ancient Greece. Athenians spoke the same language as Corinth, Rhodes, or Sparta, but the concept of "Greeks" was fleeting and inconsequential unless there were Persians storming the shores. "Greece" was more akin to "the Allies" or "NATO" than to the modern understanding of "U.S.A."

The Articles of Confederation, then, were a rather loose agreement between what we might think of as city-states. They were willing to cooperate in matters of collective security and basic commerce (sort of) but were otherwise quite touchy about their independence – from one another as much as from anyone overseas.

In prioritizing the independence of the states, the Articles failed to provide for a central government strong enough to get anything done. No one was in charge – or, at least, there were so *many* in charge that they cancelled one another out. Either way, it wasn't working the way they'd hoped.

It's unlikely you'll ever stumble into a dinnertime conversation about the pros and cons of utilizing the legislature as a court of appeals or need to come up with "A Committee of the States" on a quiz, so we'll stick with a few highlights here.

Read It For The Articles

Article I. The Stile of this confederacy shall be, "The United States of America."

Despite its capitalization here, in the rest of the document (and for a century thereafter) it was written as "the united states." The phrase wasn't typically used as a title, but a description. You wouldn't capitalize "our leftover lasagna" or "my clinically depressed goldfish." It's not until after the Civil War that it became common to capitalize the term, which simultaneously transitioned from plural ("the united states are having trouble agreeing about tariffs") to singular ("the United States is experimenting with protective tariffs again, because *that* always works out well").

As a grammatical issue, this is a minor curiosity. As a reflection of big picture American history, however, it's paradigmatic.

Article II. Each state retains its sovereignty, freedom and independence, and every Power, Jurisdiction and right, which is not by this confederation expressly delegated to the United States, in Congress assembled.

This is the Tenth Amendment on steroids and after a few beers. The Tenth Amendment (which came later) added an interesting "or the people" at the end which opens up all sorts of room for discussion, but that's for another chapter.

Article III. The said states hereby severally enter into a firm league of friendship with each other, for their common defence, the security of their Liberties, and their mutual and general welfare, binding themselves to assist each other, against all force offered to, or attacks made upon them, or any of them, on account of religion, sovereignty, trade, or any other pretence whatever.

This "firm league of friendship" was the political equivalent of "pinky swears" among middle schoolers or friendship bracelets handed out to grandparents. It's a sweet thought, but it turned out to be a shaky foundation basis for running a country.

Article IV. The better to secure and perpetuate mutual friendship and intercourse among the people of the different states in this union,

No, that's NOT what "intercourse" means here. Stop snickering. What are you... 12? (OK, actually you might be – sorry about that. No offense.)

the free inhabitants of each of these states, paupers, vagabonds and fugitives from Justice excepted, shall be entitled to all privileges and immunities of free citizens in the several states; and the people of each state shall have free ingress and regress to and from any other state, and shall enjoy therein all the privileges of trade and commerce, subject to the same duties, impositions and restrictions as the inhabitants thereof respectively...

In other words, "no border checks between states." Notice there's an exception for criminals or poor people – basically the same class in the minds of the founders. If you're a student, keep this in mind when you get to "Jacksonian Democracy" or other efforts to extend full citizenship to marginalized classes. It's a fun detail to throw in, and if you play your cards right ("But even our Founding Fathers recognized that poverty was a moral failure as much as an economic condition..."), it might start a huge argument and distract the teacher enough that you don't have to take that quiz after all.

Article VI. No vessels of war shall be kept up in time of peace, by any state... nor shall any body of forces be kept up, by any state, in time of peace, except such number only as, in the judgment of the united states, in congress assembled, shall be deemed requisite to garrison the forts necessary for the defence of such state...

No State shall engage in any war without the consent of the united states in congress assembled, unless such State be actually invaded by enemies...

Relations with foreign countries should be handled at the national level, by the legislature. No treaties, no tariffs, no wars, no side deals by individual states or groups of states. On the other hand, the nation didn't keep a standing army. Americans weren't interested in maintaining a heavily armed force sitting around in peace time with nothing to do. They feared such a body would eventually be used domestically to discourage dissent or enforce the wishes of corrupt leadership.

So, instead...

{E}very state shall always keep up a well regulated and disciplined militia, sufficiently armed and accounted, and shall provide and constantly have ready for use, in public stores, a due number of field pieces and tents, and a proper quantity of arms, ammunition, and camp equipage.

The Second Amendment would later echo this phrase with a similar intent in mind, but over time we've come to read it as primarily protecting the rights of white males to hunt animals or kill burglars. While the number of gun deaths in the U.S. dwarfs every other civilized nation in the world, it's not all bad news. States have seen *huge* savings in field pieces and tents as the federal government began to rely more and more on a permanent professional army.

Article IX. The united states, in congress assembled, shall also be the last resort on appeal, in all disputes and differences now subsisting, or that hereafter may arise between two or more states concerning boundary, jurisdiction, or any other cause whatever...

All controversies concerning the private right of soil claimed under different grants of two or more states, whose jurisdictions as they may respect such lands..., shall, on the petition of either party to the congress of the united states, be finally determined...

Like Moses and Aaron, the national legislature created by the Articles of Confederation would resolve any cases involving representatives from two or more states or conflicts between the states themselves. Given that there was no executive or judicial branch, they'd be the only ones who could.

Article XII. All bills of credit emitted, monies borrowed, and debts contracted by or under the authority of congress, before the assembling of the united states, in pursuance of the present confederation, shall be deemed and considered as a charge against the united states, for payment and satisfaction whereof the said united states and the public faith are hereby solemnly pledged.

This one would prove to be a problem. Paying your bills requires having a source of income, and the government under the Articles didn't give them much to work with. In theory, all states were supposed to contribute. If they didn't, the Articles authorized the legislature to... ask them nicely again later, maybe.

Article XIII. Every State shall abide by the determinations of the united states, in congress assembled, on all questions which by this confederation are submitted to them. And the Articles of this confederation shall be inviolably observed by every state...

Or what?

It's a fair question. What are the consequences if they don't observe them? As it turned out, the answer was "Or shame on them! Now we have to ask nicely again later!"

Article XIII: ...and the union shall be perpetual...

This phrase was referenced when the southern states attempted to secede in 1861. President Lincoln and others pointed to it as evidence they weren't allowed to do that. The U.S. Constitution, which replaced the Articles of Confederation in 1789, didn't address this issue directly, but the very first thing listed in the Preamble was the new Constitution's intention "to form a more perfect union." More perfect than "perpetual" doesn't leave much room for taking your ball and going home anytime you're worried you might not be allowed to enslave your fellow man forever and ever.

Why The Articles Of Confederation Failed

Shays' Rebellion (1786) was the trigger for the Constitutional Convention, but it wasn't the sole cause – more of a "last straw" kinda thing. There were numerous reasons the delegates who met in Philadelphia to revise the Articles chose to simply toss it and start over, but you're good if you can remember these five:

1) Congress lacked the power to tax. Just like individuals or businesses, without income, the government couldn't accomplish much. It couldn't even pay its existing debts.

2) Congress lacked meaningful authority over commerce. In an effort to protect state autonomy, the Articles allowed minimal regulation of trade between the states or between the states and other nations. States taxed and tariffed and toll roaded one another until no one could make a decent profit or accomplish anything. Sometimes water needs a hose. Sometimes horses need a track. And sometimes commerce needs a standardized national system.

3) Most states had governments with distinct legislative, executive, and judicial departments – three branches, as it were. There's a reason that worked so well for them. It's theoretically possible to utilize a table with one leg or ride a cycle with one wheel, but it rarely works as well as having several. A national government needed specialized branches, each with its own designated role to play.

4) There was no national military. Any military action required calling up the various state militias and hoping they'd be OK with whatever leadership Congress appointed. There's a reason football teams practice together before a game instead of trusting the various players to study plays and work out individually at home. The same is true of marching band, drama, or any other organization. Even weddings go better if you rehearse first. So it is with war.

5) The one branch that did exist – the legislature – was largely impotent. Each state got one vote, regardless of its size or how many delegates were seated on its behalf. Laws required the support of nine out of thirteen states to pass – a nearly impossible number to achieve on most issues. Even when a law did pass, there was no provision for enforcing it.

Making The Grade: What You're Most Likely To Be Asked

With multiple choice questions, the most likely thing you'll be expected to know about the Articles of Confederation is that they failed because they didn't give the central government enough power. (This is a common short answer or essay topic as well.) You'll probably be expected to identify Shays' Rebellion as the trigger for tossing them and writing the Constitution. You'll also want to remember that the only "branch" of government under the Articles was the legislature. Here are a few common variations:

1. One major weakness of the Articles of Confederation was that…? (A) Legislation required only a simple majority of states to pass. (B) It was difficult for the central government to raise money. (C) The chief executive was given too much power. (D) It lacked a mechanism for amendments.

2. All of the following were weaknesses of the Articles of Confederation EXCEPT…? (A) Congress lacked the power to tax. (B) There were no separate branches to perform different functions. (C) It did not establish a national military. (D) It gave Congress too much control over trade and other commerce.

You get the idea.

For short answer or essay prompts, there are a few classics you should be prepared to encounter:

3. Why did the Articles of Confederation fail? (See? I told you.) Try to offer more than "not strong enough" when writing your response. Check out the five reasons above and see what you can do with that.

4. Compare the Articles of Confederation with the U.S. Constitution. (Sometimes this will specify "in terms of X." If you get caught off guard and don't

actually know what's in the Constitution yet {shame on you}, you can build a passable response simply by using the same list of weaknesses referenced above. The Constitution "fixed" each of them. Some Americans at the time argued that it actually fixed them a little *too* well – that the central government was too strong and some sort of "Bill of Rights" would be necessary to protect basic rights.)

If you're in APUSH or any other advanced class, you should also be ready for these:

5. Why did the delegates to the Philadelphia Convention decide to replace, rather than repair, the Articles of Confederation? (Hopefully this has been addressed in class or somewhere in your assigned reading. If you have no idea one way or the other – there's a reason you're reading *this* book, after all – you can treat this as a variation on Question #1 above. Just add stuff like "it was simply *too* broken" every few paragraphs.)

6. Discuss some of the successes of the Articles of Confederation (or accomplishments of the U.S. under the Articles of Confederation).

This last one is a fun twist, since most of what we remember about the Articles are its shortcomings. You'll want to discuss the Northwest Ordinance, putting down Shays' Rebellion, and winning the Revolutionary War, despite the many challenges associated with each.

And all while operating under a pinky-promise.

CHAPTER THREE: THE U.S. CONSTITUTION
We Could Be Using Pirates

Three Big Things

1. The U.S. Constitution is a surprisingly concise document which outlines the basics of the Legislative, Executive, and Judicial Branches, as well as a few ground rules for how states interact with one another and a handful of other miscellaneous laws.

2. The Preamble introduces the overall goals and purpose of the rest of the Constitution, something to which we should all probably pay more attention.

3. Everyone should be familiar with the Constitution (including subsequent amendments). Because many of us are not, however, here are a few boring bits you should still absolutely know.

Disclaimer

We're not going to go through the entire Constitution, nor will I be including any little triangles showing "checks and balances" between the three branches. That stuff is in any decent textbook and most online sources as well. Besides, the Constitution isn't boring – not most of it, anyway.

On the other hand, for such a short little thing it can get a bit tedious, or even bewildering. What we're going to do here is start with an overview, then point out a few things you really must know about it... even if you don't really want to.

The U.S. Constitution has eight basic sections – the Preamble and seven Articles.

The Preamble: "Pre" (before) + "Amble" (to move smoothly and calmly)

A "preamble" is a traditional tool for introducing or clarifying the purpose and goals of a document. The Constitution's preamble is not technically law, but if something about the law isn't clear, it may be referenced in order to better understand what was intended.

The Preamble to the U.S. Constitution is familiar to anyone who grew up watching *Schoolhouse Rock* during Saturday morning cartoons. It joins the Pledge of Allegiance and the Twenty-Third Psalm ("The Lord is my shepherd; I shall not want...") as prime examples of recitations so familiar that we hardly even consider what they mean anymore. It's worth slowing down to think about – especially since teachers love asking students to rewrite it in plain, simple English.

"We the People of the United States..." – Notice the focus on individual citizens rather than states. The Constitution created a federalist system balancing power between state and federal government, but it was done in the name of the people making up those states and that nation – not the states or federal entities themselves. It's easy to overlook that the whole point was to create something that worked for *everyone*, not just those who "earned" it or "deserved" it.

"in Order to form a more perfect Union…" – The phrase "more perfect" may sound awkward to modern ears, but in the legal traditions of the time it was perfectly clear. Most colonists hadn't rebelled because they wanted *new* rights; they wanted their existing rights as English citizens to be *properly protected*. The Framers of the Constitution didn't reject the *ideals* of the Articles of Confederation; they simply wanted those ideals to work more effectively in practice. These were men whose worldviews and rhetoric were shaped by the Enlightenment – it was all about ongoing learning, progress, and growth. They'd run a few experiments (state governments, the Articles of Confederation, etc.), learned from them, and adjusted. The goal hadn't changed.

"establish Justice…" – This one could be interpreted several ways, but the most obvious emphasis is on "rule of law." The U.S. was formed in a time when monarchs still controlled much of the world. While it wasn't quite the Middle Ages, "justice" still often depended more on the will of the powerful than on clear, objective guidelines. Written law doesn't change based on who's being accused or who's doing the accusing. It strives to create a system all can agree is "fair" and transparent. In practice, the legal system is far from perfect, but it's an *ideal* essential to freedom and democracy – and one deserving of far more attention than it usually receives.

"insure domestic Tranquility…" – One of the side effects of justice is domestic tranquility – relative peace and calm at home (as in "within the United States") The Constitution sought to accomplish this by improving relations between the states as well as by empowering an Executive Branch to enforce the laws and a Judicial Branch to evaluate possible transgressions. A government in which more people feel they have a voice encourages the pursuit of peaceful, legal resolutions to disputes. Even the Supremacy Clause (Artice VI) serves the cause of "tranquility," since a stronger central government has the power to address disruptions like Shays' Rebellion. It might even prevent them in the first place.

"provide for the common defence…" – National defense was one of the few functions of a unified national government outlined in the Articles of Confederation. That didn't change with the update. It's interesting that this comes fourth in the Preamble's list of goals and priorities. That may have been purely rhetorical; perhaps it just sounded better here. Or perhaps it reflected a shift in focus; most of the new Constitution addresses internal matters, not international conflicts.

"promote the general Welfare…" – This references one of the most foundational functions of government – to do whatever helps the *most* people live the *best* lives possible with the resources and technology available. The means by which this may be accomplished should not be confused with the goal itself. Capitalism, for example, may be the best economic system for promoting general prosperity alongside personal opportunity. If so, it serves the goal of promoting the general welfare. But capitalism is not the sanctified ideal in and of itself – at least not according to the Constitution. We must be careful not to become so dedicated to the system or methodology (like our preferred flavor of capitalism) that we sacrifice the higher purpose (like promoting the general welfare) in its defense.

(It's just an example – don't get your free-market panties in a wad.)

"secure the Blessings of Liberty to ourselves and our Posterity..." – One of the ironies of strong central government is its potential for protecting individual liberties when states do not. Remember that "King Andrew" cartoon, with Jackson dressed like a monarch? The image was meant to disparage President Andrew Jackson, but it highlights his self-appointed role as defender of the little guy against corruption and wealth. (More recently, Donald Trump capitalized on a very similar theme.) Under the Articles, state authority was protected, but individuals were not. The stronger central government created by the Constitution here proclaims its intention to defend fundamental rights of the sort celebrated in the Declaration of Independence.

A few years later, a "Bill of Rights" would be added to fill in the details.

Article I – The Legislative Branch

Congress makes the laws (duh). You should already know why it's designed to be "bicameral" and what that means. It wouldn't hurt to revisit that "I'm Just A Bill" song, either.

Article I is the longest section of the Constitution. It outlines the general structure and powers of the Legislative Branch. The length suggests that this was the branch about which the Framers had the most to say, as well as implying that of the three "equal" branches, this one might be a tad more "equal" than the others.

The House was initially the only part of the federal government directly elected by the people. Its members are up for reelection (or not) more often than *any other part of government,* meaning they ~~can literally never stop campaigning~~ must remain responsive to the needs of their constituents. Remember all that stuff about how the Founding Fathers didn't really trust the masses to make good choices? Senators were chosen by the states. The President was elected by the Electoral College. The consolation prize for the little people was the House of Representatives. In keeping with the whole "no taxation without representation" theme, all bills involving the raising of revenue (taxes, tariffs, etc.) must begin in the House. The Senate gets input before final passage, but they can't initiate them.

The Senate was supposed to balance out the House, not only in terms of big states and small states (every state gets two Senators regardless of size) but as a wiser, calmer body (*snicker*). While the people elected Representatives, states appointed Senators using whatever method they chose. The House represented the people; the Senate represented the states. Since the ratification of the Seventeenth Amendment, Senators are directly elected by the people as well.

You want to spark a nice debate in class or at your next dinner party? Take a strong stand *for* or *against* direct election of Senators, the President, Supreme Court Justices, or any other federal role you like. It's always good times.

All Those Compromises

You may remember that there were several famous "compromises" enshrined in the original Constitution. The bicameral legislature, the 3/5 Compromise, and the bit about Congress not banning the slave trade for at least twenty years... they're all in Article I. Well, except for the "Electoral College." That bit of madness is *almost* in Article I; it was created in the very first section of Article II.

Rules About How Stuff Is Done

Most of the rules governing the House and the Senate are made up by politicians as they go. Maybe the filibuster is a good idea or maybe it's not, but it's not required, protected, or prohibited by the Constitution. Same for all those committees, rules for introducing legislation, or how to handle violent efforts to overthrow the government. The Constitution lays out a few general guidelines, then trusts those elected to office to figure out the details themselves.

In retrospect, that was either brilliant and a large part of why the nation has been so successful for as long as it has or a huge mistake which doomed us all from the start.

Artice I, Section 7, does lay out some specifics in terms of how a bill can get through both houses of Congress and the President's role in approving or vetoing it. Politicians have seriously complicated this over the years, but the basics are laid out in the actual Constitution and thus merit at least some attention.

Article I, Section 8

This section lists the majority of Congress's duties and powers. Even if you don't read the entire Constitution (although you should; it's not like it's all that long), you should read through this part.

You'll notice that while Congress is granted pretty extensive powers compared to what they had under the Articles of Confederation, there's lots of stuff not mentioned here that Congress seems able to do anyway. Investigating rock'n'roll lyrics, mandating pledges of loyalty and patriotic observation at sporting events, renaming highways or declaring holidays, promoting PBS and NPR, trying to prevent collective bargaining by workers' unions – you'll find none of these in Article I, Section 8.

On the other hand, Congress is given the explicit right to deputize mercenaries (i.e., pirates) to pillage and burn on behalf of Uncle Sam – and yet they hardly ever take advantage of it! How many problems could be solved if we were just willing to break out the pirates more often?!

Where does Congress derive the "authority" to regulate social media, set public education policies, or panic parents over violence in video games? Check out Section 8, around the third line, and you'll see this phrase:

> To regulate Commerce with foreign Nations, and among the several States...

That's the Commerce Clause, which has been there since the beginning but didn't do much for the first thirty years or so. Then, in 1824, the Supreme Court (led by Chief Justice John Marshall) heard and decided a case remembered as *Gibbons v. Ogden*. In that decision, Marshall and the Court made it clear that the Commerce Clause gives Congress authority over *any* trade or services which cross state or national borders, or anything which *might* impact trade or services which cross state or national borders.

In the modern era, that means Congress can regulate, well... almost everything. Look around you right now, wherever you are. If you can see it, touch it, think about it, or plan on doing it, Congress has the authority to regulate it under the Commerce Clause. When people complain about "big government," this is usually a major part of what they mean.

Now, keep reading Section 8 (no skipping!) until you get to this bit:

> To make all Laws which shall be necessary and proper for carrying into Execution the foregoing Powers, and all other Powers vested by this Constitution in the Government of the United States, or in any Department or Officer thereof.

That's the Necessary and Proper Clause, and arguably the source of most major political conflicts for the next hundred years.

You may be familiar with the never-ending conflicts between the Jeffersonian-Republicans (as represented by Thomas Jefferson) and the Federalists (as represented by Alexander Hamilton) over the appropriate size and power of the federal government. If not, go watch the musical *Hamilton*. They carry on about it incessantly, particularly in the second act. Basically, Jefferson and his ilk believed that any powers not specifically granted to Congress (or the rest of the federal government) by the Constitution were prohibited – that the Constitution sets strict boundaries on national authority. Hamilton and his peeps believed that anything not strictly prohibited by the Constitution was probably OK, as long as it in some way supported a clear function of government.

Imagine that the Constitution specified that you, personally, were responsible for borrowing money and allocating tax dollars. It would seem reasonable to allow you to run to Staples for a few legal pads and some ink pens to better keep track of everything, yes? As things get busier, you might deem it "necessary and proper" to hire a few bureaucrats to help manage the workload. You may even decide to create a National Bank. Those bureaucrats and bankers will need desks, and chairs, and office supplies, and a custodial service, and maybe a break room with cold drinks and a popcorn machine. It's all logically necessary and proper in fulfilling your designated constitutional role.

Naturally it's only a matter of time before you're investigating steroid use in baseball. Otherwise, how could you do your job as outlined in Article I, Section 8?

If that all sounds reasonable to you, you're quite possibly a Hamiltonian Federalist. If you think the scenario flew off the rails somewhere after you picked up a few office supplies, you might be a Jeffersonian Republican. If you still don't see how any of this gives Congress the right to grill Silicon Valley types about search engine algorithms, well... let's just say you're smarter than most politicians, whatever their party.

Article II – The Executive Branch

Article II outlines the role of the Executive Branch – primarily the President's duties and powers. The primary purpose of the executive is to enforce the laws of the United States. (I know, ironic – right?)

Writing this part was tricky because the young nation was still smarting from the oppressive monarchy of George III. The shortcomings of the Articles of Confederation had made it clear that a stronger central authority was necessary, and most state governments had separated legislative and executive functions. Article II attempted to give the president enough power to be effective while making it difficult for him to become an actual tyrant.

The actual role of POTUS has evolved well beyond that described in the Constitution. That, however, is a conversation for another day... so let's move on.

Article III – The Judicial Branch

Imagine you're doing one of those projects where you create your own country or form your own government and you have to explain how it all works. You have some pretty solid ideas about several of the sections, but while you're sure there should *be* a national court system of some sort, you're not really sure how it will work or even exactly what it should do. Still, you have to turn in something, so you fake your way through a few things that seem like they should be handled by the Judicial Branch then gloss over the rest and hope for the best.

Congratulations – you've just composed Article III of the U.S. Constitution. Now you just need to stall for a few years until John Marshall becomes Chief Justice. He's like that kid in any group project who takes everything home and just finishes it himself so you don't hurt his grade.

Despite its brevity, there are a few things worth noting about the Judicial Branch as created by the Constitution.

(1) Judges serve for life or until they retire of their own free will. This makes them virtually untouchable once seated. Sure, many have clear political pref-

erences, but there's not much politicians (even presidents) can do to pressure or cajole a federal judge. This has been the case since Day One, but nevertheless continues to surprise and frustrate whoever's in the White House.

(2) Federal courts do not generally deal in criminal law. If you murder someone or steal their dog or burn down a building or two, you'll typically be tried in a state or local court for violating state laws against those things. Federal courts primarily deal with stuff directly related to the Constitution and federal law. These cases might originate in a state criminal court, but they bump up to federal court if one party can show that a constitutional issue is involved – usually by claiming a fundamental constitutional right has been violated.

Just to make things messier, criminal actions which impact federal property or cross state lines suddenly become federal crimes as well. If you decide you simply must burn something down and take a few hostages, make sure it's locally owned and don't take anyone over state lines. (Just to be on the safe side, perhaps it's best to avoid burning things down or taking hostages altogether.)

There are a handful of scenarios in which a case begins and ends in the Supreme Court. They're uncommon and not that important except in very specific situations.

Article IV – Playground Rules

Article IV was largely an attempt to make the states play nicely with one another. It gives Congress the power to decide when and how new states could be added and requires all states to have a "republican" (small 'r') form of government. There's even a "fugitive slave act," although like everything else in the Constitution which dealt with slavery, they didn't call it that. In practice, however, escaped slaves were to be treated just like escaped criminals and returned promptly to the appropriate authorities. Most of Article IV was clearly a direct reaction to the weaknesses of the Articles of Confederation.

Article V – It's A PDF (Not A DOCX)

Article V explains how the Constitution can be amended. The process was not intended to be impossible (they're not homeowners' association bylaws) but it *was* intended to be difficult. The Framers wanted to discourage wacky, impulsive changes. They knew better than anyone else how difficult it was to write good law and worried that impulsive alterations might completely fubar the whole thing.

Article VI – "Oh, By The Way..."

For what is essentially the "miscellaneous" section, there are two pretty important bits in Article VI.

The first is a prohibition on "religious tests" for holding office. This is the only time religion is mentioned in the Constitution – directly or indirectly – prior to the First Amendment, and it involves separating religious beliefs and political power. (There is no "America is for Jesus" section in the U.S. Constitution.)

The second is the "Supremacy Clause." While the Constitution created what would later be called a "federalist system," giving some powers to the central government and leaving others to the states, this clause clarifies that in case of future conflicts, real or perceived, between the two, the federal government wins. Period. The only way around this is to either (a) change the federal government's mind about the issue at hand, or (b) persuade the Supreme Court that the federal government's actions are unconstitutional on some other basis.

Article VII – Ratification

Article VII: "The Ratification of the Conventions of nine States, shall be sufficient for the Establishment of this Constitution between the States so ratifying the Same." That's it. That's Article VII.

This cute little conclusion is official notice that the adoption of this new Constitution to replace the Articles of Confederation requires the approval of any nine of the thirteen states. Realistically, however, that might not have been enough to hold the young nation together – particularly if the holdouts included major players like Virginia or New York. Several states insisted on a Bill of Rights, which was soon added, so that helped. Rhode Island held out the longest, but no one cared because... well, no offense, but it was Rhode Island.

The Bill of Rights & Other Amendments

The Bill of Rights was added shortly after ratification of the Constitution. It's composed of the first ten amendments and certainly *looks* manageable enough. In reality, there are something like eleventy dozen distinct rights covered in those ten, and you should probably know them all. That's the bad news. The good news is, absolutely *none* of them are boring.

Making The Grade: What You're Most Likely To Be Asked

At the bare minimum, you should know the Preamble and what each of the seven Articles cover. Any questions about the "purpose" of the Constitution are probably looking for information from the Preamble or something about addressing weaknesses in the Articles of Confederation. We're not covering the Bill of Rights here (far too interesting), but state-level "end of instruction" type tests love asking about specific amendments therein. More generally, you'll almost always see some variation of this:

1. What was the primary objection to the new constitution? (Some worried it didn't do enough to protect individual liberties from this new, stronger central government; the solution was to add a Bill of Rights. I realize you probably already know this, but I felt compelled to mention it anyway.)

Beyond that, any of the following are fair game for multiple choice questions, short answer questions, or essay prompts with minor variations in phrasing.

2. Identify major compromises made during the Constitutional Convention. (The big three are typically the Three-Fifths Compromise, the Connecticut Compromise (setting up a bicameral legislature), and using the Electoral Col-

lege to elect a president. It's probably best if you have a general idea of the debate behind each and how these compromises addressed the wishes of both sides.)

3. Identify the three branches and what each does. (I won't insult you by explaining these here.)

4. Give examples of "checks and balances" between the three branches. (This one can be pretty basic or get rather involved, so be prepared. Your textbook almost certainly has a triangle diagram in it with the Legislative, Executive, and Judicial branches at each point. Arrows show one or two "checks" each branch has on the other. You should be able to fill out one of these in your sleep.)

5. Compare the Articles of Confederation with the U.S. Constitution. (This one was discussed in the previous chapter. Remember that the Constitution was largely an effort to "fix" the shortcomings of the Articles of Confederation. Consider framing both in terms of "Who's in charge?" and "How much power should they have?")

6. Explain the balance of federal and state authority under the Constitution (aka "federalism"). (This requires that you know what powers the Constitution specifically gives the federal government; the rest were technically left up to the individual states. It wouldn't hurt to include the debate over the need for a Bill of Rights and the inclusion of the Tenth Amendment. Even after ratification, the debate continued in the form of "strict construction" vs. "loose construction.")

Questions about specific articles or clauses are less common, but you may be asked about the Commerce Clause (Article I, Section 8), the Elastic Clause (same place), or the Supremacy Clause (Article VI, Section 2). It probably wouldn't hurt to brush up on those anyway.

In APUSH or other advanced classes, any of the above are still likely (but with bigger words and stuff). You should also be prepared for...

7. Identify and briefly explain three compromises in the Constitution involving slavery. (This one can be tricky for several reasons, including the fact that the Constitution never actually uses terms like "slaves" or "slavery." As Lincoln would later point out, the Framers danced around the issue as if they were ashamed to call it what it was. Nevertheless, it's there – the aforementioned Three-Fifths Compromise, the provision prohibiting Congress from outlawing the slave trade for at least twenty years, and even a fugitive slave act in Article IV, Section 2).

8. Evaluate the major arguments of the Federalists and Anti-Federalists during debates over ratification.

Obviously in an American Government class you'd be expected to dive a bit deeper and come up with more details. In American History, however, there's still nearly a century to cover before the end of the school year and there's simply no time. We've got to get to Andrew Jackson by Christmas!

CHAPTER FOUR: THE XYZ AFFAIR
Bribes and Prejudice

Three Big Things

1. France was mad because the U.S. was making nice with England. (Wasn't it only yesterday France had gone to so much trouble to help them get *out* of that relationship? We're they supposed to be hating England *together*?)

2. U.S. efforts to make nice with France led to serious drama when French representatives (code names "X," "Y," and "Z") made demands (including bribes) which the U.S. contingent found offensive – hence the catchy nickname for the entire mess.

3. The resulting kerfuffle led to a "Quasi-War" abroad and more pronounced divisions between political parties at home before being resolved by a new round of diplomacy and yet another new treaty. The dispute also prompted the Federalists to push through the infamous Alien and Sedition Acts (which didn't turn out all that well).

Background

If you've seen *Hamilton* (or at least listened to the soundtrack), you might be surprised to learn that many of the characters and events portrayed were based on *real people and events* in American history. Seriously, there should have been a note on the program or something to that effect. It would have added a whole other dimension to the experience.

In any case, I refer you to one of the highlights of the second act, "Cabinet Battle #2":

> *The issue on the table: France is on the verge of war with England. Now do we provide aid and troops to our French allies, or do we stay out of it? ... Secretary Jefferson, you have the floor, sir...*

Jefferson, as you may recall, thought it was a complete no-brainer that the U.S. should jump in and assist France. French aid had tipped the balance in the Revolutionary War and their rhetoric was rooted in the same Enlightenment ideals that inspired the colonies to rebel in the first place. Hamilton thought getting involved was a *horrible* idea, particularly since the folk with whom they'd actually signed a treaty (the King and Queen) were dead at that point, beheaded by French revolutionaries. President Washington agreed with Hamilton, and in the very next number ("it must be nice... it must be nice... to have Washington on your side...") the nation's first two political parties were formed – right there on stage.

It wasn't the *beginning* of tensions over how the new nation should be run, but it certainly helped clarify and solidify the sides.

The Federalists (think Alexander Hamilton) were pushing for a strong central government and a more unified nation. Despite the recent Revolutionary War, Federalists still tended to see the world through English eyes. It was the Federalists who'd pushed for the Constitution (which replaced the much looser Articles of Confederation) and who relied on the "three branches" system to keep the government checked and balanced. If taken to the extreme, their approach to the Constitution was that anything it didn't strictly *prohibit* was probably *OK*.

The Anti-Federalists, better known as the Democratic-Republicans (who didn't officially include "Southern M*****-F******" as part of their title), were less enthused about strong central government. They worried that the young nation would fall back into the same patterns and problems they'd had under King George. Democratic-Republicans loved the revolutionary fervor of the French and believed that an agrarian economy and local control were the keys to extending and strengthening the enlightened, independent nature of their new country. The Constitution gave the central government specific functions and powers, and anything beyond that was a leap into corruption and self-destruction. Historians often refer to this group as the "Jeffersonian Republicans" because, you know... *Jefferson.*

How to handle France wasn't the ONLY issue dividing these emerging parties, but it was pretty high on the list.

Jay's Treaty (1794)

Right after giving France a promise ring during the Revolution, Uncle Sam** slid right back into making goo-goo eyes with his ex, England. Washington and other Federalists were more pragmatic than they were idealistic; they had little interest in endless conflict with the world's most powerful nation. They signed a treaty resolving several points of contention: the British agreed to pull out of the Northwest Territory and to leave American shipping alone (although that one didn't exactly last) while the U.S. paid off some outstanding debts to British merchants. Both sides compromised a bit on shared boundaries. Perhaps most importantly, the treaty laid the groundwork for a positive trading relationship with England.

It's amazing how many things can be worked out when there's money to be made.

France saw this as a betrayal of all they'd thought they meant to the U.S., particularly after they'd sacrificed so much to help the young nation win its independence... *from the very nation it was now making all cuddly with!* France and England had been in recurring conflict since roughly the Neolithic Era, so Uncle Sam's insistence that they were just friends (albeit with benefits) rang hollow. France began attacking American shipping, which hurt America's feelings and kinda ruined how nice it was that England had finally stopped doing it.

In the middle of this madness, George Washington decided not to run for a third term in 1796. ("One last time... we'll teach them how to say goodbye..."). The unenviable task of following the Father of the Nation into office fell to John Adams with Thomas Jefferson as VP, which was tricky since they were from different political parties - Adams was a Federalist, and Jefferson, well... was *not*.

The Adams Tightrope

President John Adams wanted to patch things up with France without alienating England. He wasn't the towering figure Washington had been and often made decisions based on how he thought things *should* work instead of how they *did*.

Then again, Washington had struggled on this front as well. Before leaving office, he'd appointed Charles Pinckney as the U.S. "Minister to France." It wasn't a great match. Pinckney was a staunch Federalist from an essentially aristocratic background – the exact sort of person the French were gleefully beheading on a regular basis at the time. Adams hoped to do better.

Adams conferred with his VP, Jefferson, who suggested sending Madison – a Democratic-Republican with revolutionary street cred and who knew how to speak *liberté, égalité*, and *fraternité*. Instead, Adams chose the safer political path and selected more Federalists, the party who hated France to begin with and couldn't relate to them *at all*. They arrived in Paris disgusted with the people, the politics, and the culture in general – not the ideal foundation for diplomacy.

The French Foreign Minister, Charles-Maurice de Talleyrand-Périgord, initially refused to see them. Eventually he sent word through intermediaries that a meeting might be arranged if the Americans agreed in advance to pay off all claims made by American merchants against France, loan France a ton of money at rock-bottom interest rates, and offer Talleyrand a substantial bribe just to get things going.

In better dynamics, these might have served as a starting point for under-the-table negotiations. As things were, it merely offended and annoyed the American coterie. They wrote back to President Adams, who in turn informed Congress that things weren't going well and that maybe they should start preparing for the itsy-bitsy possibility of war. Not wanting to stir things up more than they already were, or risk the safety of his representatives in France, Adams substituted letters – W, X, Y, and Z – for the names of the French go-betweens.

The subsequent kerfuffle, then, could just as easily have become known as the ABC Affair, the WXYZ Conflict, or the Beta Epsilon Gamma Kappa Shenanigans. Adams also withheld numerous details of exactly what was going badly, informing Congress merely that the French were being uncooperative and things could get ugly. It didn't give Congress much to go on. Mostly it simply confirmed their suspicion that Adams was *not* George Washington.

Let Me Be Frank(ophile) With You

France had by this time closed its ports to ships from any nation not totally "Team France" and granted permission to French vessels to capture and search any ship they suspected of carrying British goodies – which could be any of them. Congress nevertheless insisted on knowing what the ever-loving heckity-darn was actually going on before taking further action. It passed resolutions and called Adams all sorts of bad names (although that last part wasn't exactly new). Eventually, Adams released the letters from his representatives in France, including the demands made by X, Y, and Z. ("W" had largely dropped out of the picture by this point.)

The Democratic-Republicans simply couldn't believe anything negative about their revolutionary brethren across the ocean. Surely Adams was lying, or the emissaries had misunderstood, or – and this one was a crowd favorite – Talleyrand's demands were a natural result of Adam's push for a military buildup, despite those two things having occurred in the opposite order, many months apart. (No sense letting a little thing like objective reality interfere with a good political barrage, then or now.)

American outrage was about what one would expect for a generation still drunk on the patriotic fervor of its own revolution. "Millions for defense but not one cent for tribute!" cried the masses. War was never officially declared, but this "Quasi-War" was definitely a few shoves and swear words past being "at peace."

À La Réflexion…

Talleyrand had by this point realized he'd miscalculated and that things weren't going the way he'd hoped. He began scrambling to reopen negotiations with the U.S. while navigating a revolution at home which was becoming increasingly unpredictable and bloody. Napoleon was rapidly gaining power as well, and while he loved a good scrap as much as anyone, the General was more interested in using France's claim on Louisiana Territory (which was technically owned by Spain at the time) to help finance his war in Europe.

President Adams sent new representatives to France, thus averting a real live shooting-and-killing war. They eventually reached a new agreement – the Convention of 1800. (It's also called the Treaty of Mortefontaine, but seriously – who even wants to try *saying* that, let alone *remembering* it?)

Hostilities ceased. France gave back America's boats and the U.S. agreed to reimburse owners for any losses incurred as a result. Perhaps most importantly, France and the U.S became trading besties again, although the U.S. was not required to quit seeing England in order to do so. This was to be something of an "open partnership." As long as the brides didn't have to share a bed or anything, they'd ignore one another and make it work.

Why It Matters

The XYZ Affair was the first major foreign policy dilemma faced by the young United States. It presented questions they'd face in various forms many times over the coming centuries: When is it better to compromise out of pragmatism than dig in over ideals? What does the U.S. owe to nations who've supported it in the past compared to those it might be nice to have around in the future? How much power should the president have over foreign affairs before Congress steps in and demands to know what's going on?

In terms of more tangible results, the U.S. slung enough testosterone during the conflict to bump up its status on the world stage. They weren't yet a "superpower," but they were becoming someone you didn't want to annoy if you could avoid it. The resulting treaties with England and France helped the young nation continue building its economy, which over time became an additional source of strength and influence – and remains so today.

Domestic disagreement over the event helped highlight key differences between the two parties beyond simply being pro-central government or pro-state autonomy. Each party came to represent a range of views about many different issues rather than simply arguing with one another over the same one repeatedly. Federalist frustration with growing Democratic-Republican moxie, as well as concerns over foreign influence, led to the passage of the Alien and Sedition Acts, which of course sparked all sorts of other shenanigans.

Not everyone loved the way the Federalists had handled the XYZ Affair, and even most of those who did had trouble embracing the Alien and Sedition Acts once their initial patriotic fervor began settling. This frustration probably contributed to the election of Thomas Jefferson in 1800 – the first peaceful transfer of power from one political party to another. We could argue that the whole XYZ kerfuffle was therefore responsible for the Louisiana Purchase and the founding of the University of Virginia, but that seems a bit of a stretch.

Making The Grade: What You're Most Likely To Be Asked

This one lends itself readily to multiple choice questions with "The XYZ Affair" as the correct answer (or one of the correct answers). They're often phrased in terms of "new challenges facing the young republic" or "issues which highlighted growing divisions between political parties." Other times they'll just keep it simple and see if you remember the colorful parts:

1. The slogan "Millions for defense; not one cent for tribute!" is most closely associated with...? (A) the XYZ Affair, (B) Jay's Treaty, (C) the Wilmot Proviso, or (D) Bacon's Rebellion.

2. What event sparked the XYZ Affair? (A) The new Congress raised taxes on whiskey. (B) The British navy boarded American ships and forced their crews into service. (C) The French foreign minister demanded a bribe before he would meet with American representatives. (D) Andrew Jackson chased runaway slaves into Spanish-controlled Florida.

It's possible you'll be asked about the XYZ Affair in the context of cause and effect – what prompted it to begin with (your response should include "Jay's Treaty"), or its connection to the Alien and Sedition Acts or Jefferson's election (and John Adams' loss). You should also remember the term "Quasi-War." While technically this *could* refer to any number of things, it almost always means *this* conflict.

It's unlikely you'll get an entire essay prompt over the XYZ Affair by itself, but it should certainly be part of your responses to all sorts of things from that time period.

3. What were some of the challenges confronting the new government under the Constitution?

4. Summarize the policy differences between Federalists and Democratic-Republicans in the late eighteenth and early nineteenth centuries.

5. How did the Federalists and Jeffersonian Republicans differ in their approach to foreign policy?

6. Identify the foreign policies of presidents Washington through Monroe.

APUSH or other advanced courses are likely to ask very similar questions in fancier ways. It may not always be immediately obvious that you know enough relevant material for a decent response… but you probably do:

7. Analyze the ways in which the United States sought to advance its interests in world affairs between 1789 and 1823.

8. How did the conflicts between France and Britain resulting from the French Revolution end up impacting the United States?

If you can keep track of 80% of the details and interwoven issues involved in the XYZ Affair, you're doing better than most. It's legitimately a tough topic to keep straight and knowing your basics is as impressive as you need to get.

**The term "Uncle Sam" didn't come along for a few more years, but you know exactly who I mean. Don't be difficult.

CHAPTER FIVE: THE VIRGINIA AND KENTUCKY RESOLUTIONS (1798-1799)
If At First You Don't Secede... (Part One)

Three Big Things

1. One of the fundamental questions running through all American history is "Who's in charge? And how much power do they (or should they) actually have?" One expression of this is found in the tension between states' rights and federal authority.

2. The Alien and Sedition Acts prompted Thomas Jefferson and James Madison to write the Virginia and Kentucky Resolutions, respectively, on behalf of their states. These resolutions claimed the right of individual states to ignore (or "nullify") acts of the federal government they considered unconstitutional.

3. The idea received little support from other states at the time, but the underlying reasoning would be utilized repeatedly in subsequent decades – most famously as justification for the secession of eleven southern states following the election of Abraham Lincoln.

The Alien & Sedition Acts

You probably remember these. Thanks to his resolution of the XYZ Affair, President John Adams experienced a brief surge of popular support he'd never had before (and would never manage again). And yet, the writing was on the wall. The Jeffersonians were playing the issue successfully in the public arena and Federalist support was rapidly slipping.

The Federalists still had their Congressional majority, however. They took the opportunity to strengthen their political position in the name of national security, the flag, apple pie, and baby eagles.

The Alien Acts erected new barriers to immigration and naturalization and gave the president the authority to kick out or imprison anyone from abroad who struck him as shady. Federalists also pushed through the Sedition Act, which essentially made it a crime to criticize elected officials or otherwise disparage the ruling party – which just happened to be them. (In retrospect, it was a blatant violation of the First Amendment, but the Supreme Court was controlled by Federalists at the time and hadn't yet begun asserting its authority over such things.)

The Jeffersonian Republicans won the next presidential election and made significant gains in Congress. The Alien and Sedition Acts which hadn't expired at the end of Adams' term were soon repealed. In the meantime, however, both Thomas Jefferson and James Madison (anonymously) composed arguments suggesting that because these laws constituted blatant overreach by the federal government, the states shouldn't have to follow them. In other words, Virginia and Kentucky called on their sister states to strike down these Acts within their borders – to nullify them as illegitimate.

This wasn't secession, but it relied on the same lines of reasoning. And the other states were having none of it.

The "Compact Theory" Of Government

To justify this rhetorical act of rebellion, Jefferson promoted what's often referred to as the "compact theory" of government:

> *Resolved, That the several states composing the United States of America are not united on the principle of unlimited submission to their general government; but that, by compact, under the style and title of a Constitution for the United States, and of amendments thereto, they constituted a general government for special purposes, delegated to that government certain definite powers, reserving, each state to itself, the residuary mass of right to their own self–government...*

In other words, the "compact theory" insists beyond all evidence and reason that the federal government is a creation of the states (by the states, and for the states). If true, states would naturally have the final say in cases involving federal overreach or other unconstitutional shenanigans.

The opposite of "compact theory" is sometimes called "contract theory" in reference to the Constitution as a binding contract between the people and the federal government. This would theoretically allow for a sufficient majority of individuals to change the terms – a provision built into the Constitution via Article V and the amendment process. Under "contract theory," the federal government has authority over the states unless otherwise specified by the Constitution.

After elaborating on this "compact theory" a bit, Jefferson turned to the issue of how awful the Alien and Sedition Acts truly were and called on other states to join Kentucky in its refusal to cooperate. It was time to show the federal government that he states weren't going to put up with such nonsense. "Reserving thereto the residuary mass, or death!"

The Virginia Resolution, penned by Madison, is shorter and less aggressive. Madison chose a "gosh we really hate that it's come to this (*scuffs-dirt-with-toe*)" approach. On behalf of his state, he carried on about how much Virginia loved being part of the Union, but gosh darn it, those Alien and Sedition Acts are just so... well, they're BAD, OK? Really, really BAD! We states gotta take a stand against this sort of thing!

> *That the good people of this commonwealth, having ever felt, and continuing to feel, the most sincere affection for their brethren of the other states; the truest anxiety for establishing and perpetuating the union of all; and the*

most scrupulous fidelity to that Constitution, which is the pledge of mutual friendship, and the instrument of mutual happiness,—the General Assembly doth solemnly appeal to the like dispositions in the other states, in confidence that they will concur with this commonwealth in declaring, as it does hereby declare, that the acts aforesaid are unconstitutional; and that the necessary and proper measures will be taken by each, for cooperating with this state, in maintaining unimpaired the authorities, rights, and liberties, reserved to the states respectively, or to the people.

It really just screams "straightforward, heartfelt conviction," doesn't it?

So Much For Revolutionary Spirit...

The "compact theory" espoused by Jefferson ran counter to the intentions and understanding of most of those involved in the creation of the actual Constitution (including Madison at the time). While they'd certainly designed the system so that states retained a degree of sovereignty in some areas, the Constitution itself had already anticipated the potential for conflict between the different levels of government – thus the inclusion of Article VI, Section 2 (quoted above), often referred to as simply the "Supremacy Clause."

In other words, the federal government is sorry you're upset, but you can't do that.

The remaining states didn't exactly rally around Kentucky and Virginia. Several ignored the request altogether. Georgia and Tennessee offered tepid support. Seven others replied with firm rejections not only of the request but of the ideology behind it. *Marbury v. Madison* (1803) was still several years away, but the concept of "judicial review" was clearly already assumed in the minds of numerous state legislatures:

[T]he General Assembly of the state of Vermont do highly disapprove of the resolutions of the General Assembly of Virginia, as being unconstitutional in their nature, and dangerous in their tendency. It belongs not to state legislatures to decide on the constitutionality of laws made by the general government; this power being exclusively vested in the judiciary courts of the Union.

[T]he legislature of New Hampshire unequivocally express a firm resolution to maintain and defend the Constitution of the United States... [T]he state legislatures are not the proper tribunals to determine the constitutionality of the laws of the general government; that the duty of such decision is properly and exclusively confided to the judicial department.

[I]n the opinion of this [Rhode Island] legislature, the second section of third article of the Constitution of the United States, in these words, to wit,—"The judicial power shall extend to all cases arising under the laws of the United States,"—vests in the federal courts, exclusively, and in the Supreme Court of the United States, ultimately, the authority of deciding on the constitutionality of any act or law of the Congress of the United States.

In short, the resolutions were a bust. It's unlikely we'd even keep bringing them up today if that were the last of it, but the question of nullification or secession by individual states wasn't going away anytime soon.

Why It Matters

The issue of who has the power and how much they should have is one of the ongoing essential questions in any American history course. It's relevant not only to secession and the Civil War, but to conflict during Reconstruction, Progressive reform movements in the early twentieth century, the New Deal during the Great Depression, the Civil Rights movement and desegregation efforts, all the way up to mask orders during a pandemic or right-wingers storming the Capital in an attempt to overturn the 2020 presidential elections.

The fact that it's come up repeatedly in so many different forms throughout our history doesn't make it an easy question to answer. It does, however, allow you to nod thoughtfully whenever the subject is broached and make all sorts of impressive comparisons when you respond – whatever your personal take on the specific issue of the moment might be.

Making the Grade: What You're Most Likely To Be Asked

You should at least have a working familiarity with the Alien and Sedition Acts (1798) as well as the Virginia and Kentucky Resolutions. Either or both make for good "identify and explain" type questions. You should also recognize the Virginia and Kentucky Resolutions as early examples of what's sometimes called the "doctrine of nullification," which is based on "compact theory" as explained above.

1. The argument that states had the right to declare "null and void" any laws they considered unconstitutional was a central element of...? (A) the Alien and Sedition Acts, (B) the Kentucky and Virginia Resolutions, (C) Washington's Farewell Address, or (D) the American System.

2. The Kentucky and Virginia Resolutions defined and defended which theory about constitutional government? (A) A strong federal government requires checks and balances between the branches. (B) The Supreme Court is the primary authority for resolving conflicts between state and federal governments. (C) Direct democracy must be balanced by indirect elements like the Electoral College and state appointment of Senators. (D) The federal government is a creation of the states, which can revoke the "compact" binding them together if that government oversteps its constitutional limits.

Many short answer or essay prompts will be of the "identify and explain" variety:

3. What were the Alien and Sedition Acts? Why were they passed? Who objected to them, and why?

4. Define and explain the Virginia and Kentucky resolutions. Why were they passed in their respective states? Discuss both the short-term reaction and

long-term impact of these resolutions.

There are a half-dozen variations of these same basic questions, but you get the idea.

If you're in APUSH or any other advanced class, you should be ready to compare "compact theory" with "contract theory" (summarized above). It's sometimes useful to note that the issue of nullification would come up again in the Hartford Convention (1814-1815), the Nullification Crisis (1831-1832), and of course the attempted secession of southern states (1860-1861) which sparked the Civil War.

Short answer or essay prompts may not nudge you with specific terms sparking your recollection of these events and issues, even when they clearly apply. Consider how the Alien and Sedition Acts, the Virginia and Kentucky Resolutions, or "compact theory" vs. "contract theory" might be used in response to questions like these:

5. How did the U.S. seek to achieve national security and political stability in the years following ratification of the Constitution?

6. Discuss ways in which different perspectives concerning constitutional, political, economic, and social issues contributed to debates over States' Rights. (Chances are the prompt will narrow this down to two or three categories for you to consider.)

7. Identify political conflicts in the early republic over issues such as the relationship between the national government and the states, economic policy, foreign policy, and the balance between liberty and order. (Again, in practice it would be unlikely to see all of these at once.)

There are other variations, but most center around the natural tension between liberty and order, state and federal, chocolate and peanut butter, etc. The Alien and Sedition Acts and the resulting Resolutions were certainly not the *only* appropriate examples of these larger ideas, but they were important ones. Use them.

CHAPTER SIX: EARLY POLITICAL PARTIES
You Gotta Fight For Your Rights Through Paaaaaarties...

Three Big Things

1. The earliest political parties grew out of a single debate – whether or not to ratify the Constitution (thus replacing the Articles of Confederation). The underlying debate over how much power the new federal government should actually have continued long after the document was approved.

2. The Federalists remained Federalists while the Anti-Federalists evolved into the Democratic-Republicans. Federalists liked a strong central government; Democratic-Republicans preferred something far more limited.

3. By the 1830s, the nation (and its issues) had evolved significantly. Two new major parties arose, initially divided by their support of or opposition to the policies of Andrew Jackson. The Democratic Party would be split by the Civil War but survive it; the Whigs would not.

Introduction

The earliest political parties in the United States weren't actually *parties* so much as two schools of thought over just how much power the federal government should have.

The decision to declare independence from Mother England involved a number of issues and was hardly unanimous across the colonies. Even those supporting revolution often differed in their motivations. Nevertheless, in the official declaration justifying this decision, one theme is very clear – the King was a tyrant. The colonies were being subjected to despotism. The government under which they operated was too strong, too abusive, and had far too much control over their local businesses, communities, and daily lives.

So, yeah... they were impelled to separation, friends. *Totally* impelled.

The first constitution governing the newly independent nation was the Articles of Confederation. Largely composed as a reaction against an oppressive central government, it went to the opposite extreme and created almost no central government whatsoever. IF the thirteen states agreed on something and IF they all did their part then stuff MIGHT sometimes happen on a national level – otherwise, it was pretty much every state for itself. This "firm league of friendship" was idealism built on a pinky promise and honestly lasted longer than it probably deserved.

Less than a decade into this decentralized adventure, delegates from most of the thirteen states met in Philadelphia to revise the Articles. As you no doubt already know, they instead went rogue and wrote a whole new constitution, one with three branches of government at the top holding it all together.

While the individual states would still largely manage their internal affairs, the central government would have far more functional authority in national matters. This system of "dual sovereignty" is called "federalism."

Uncle Sam & Aunty Federalism

Folks who liked the new constitution and its stronger central government became known as "Federalists." They argued that a stronger centralized government was necessary for the safety and prosperity of the nation. Folks who thought it undercut the whole point of the revolution to begin with were called "Anti-Federalists." They argued that the states had fought too hard to overthrow the oppressive central government of Great Britain to simply re-establish the same thing under a new name.

A series of essays were composed to explain and promote this new constitution to the nation at large – the "Federalist Papers." In response, those opposed published the less-successful "Whiny Loser Essays" (sometimes referred to as the "Anti-Federalist Papers.") Some historians point to this as the birth of political parties, but there were no candidates per se, nor organized structures, and only one real issue. Plus, the essays were written anonymously, making it difficult to get anyone's face on a t-shirt or capture sound bites for the evening news.

The Anti-Federalists lost, but they did manage to secure a substantial concession in the process. The new constitution would be almost immediately supplemented by ten amendments guaranteeing fundamental personal liberties. England's governing of the colonies had been too strong; the Articles of Confederation had created a central government which was too weak; the Constitution replaced it with a central government less oppressive than England's but more powerful than under the Articles; the Bill of Rights limited what that central government could just in case it ever started thinking it might look good with a crown and scepter.

So, while the Federalists and Anti-Federalists weren't political parties in the sense of being organized groups managing their own internal elections or promoting specific candidates across the nation, they *were* two clearly divided camps who had strong opinions about a specific set of issues and the ways in which important political decisions should be handled. For that, they at least deserve a place on the list.

Still, at this stage of things, one's stance on the new Constitution wasn't always determinative of other political positions or priorities. Geography, ethnicity, or even economic status were far more likely to shape one's social and political views at large.

The Jeffersons & the Hamiltons

After the new constitution was ratified, the focus shifted from *ratification* to *interpretation*. Thomas Jefferson and his followers insisted that any powers not explicitly granted to the federal government by the new Constitution were powers it *should* not and *did* not have. What the Constitution did not overtly permit, it forbade. This reading of the Constitution is known as "strict construction." Alexander Hamilton, on the other hand, had high hopes for the "stretchiness" of the document – particularly little bundles of potential like the Necessary and Proper Clause tucked away in Article I, Section 8. In his view, powers granted to the federal government were starting points, not limitations. What the Constitution did not clearly prohibit, it allowed – maybe even encouraged. This approach to the Constitution is known as "loose construction."

The Federalists kept their team name even as their ideology and influence expanded. Jefferson and fans of smaller government began referring to themselves as "Republicans" – a term which was technically descriptive of the new government while emphasizing the role of the people in choosing their leaders and the lack of a monarch at the top. It was often used interchangeably with "Democrats" (again highlighting their whole "power to the people" mindset) until eventually they became known as the "Democratic-Republicans." In order to better distinguish this group from the Democratic Party birthed in the 1830s or the Republican Party formed in the 1850s, history often refers to this group as the "Jeffersonian Republicans." (We're going to stick with "Democratic-Republicans" most of the time, although "the Jeffersonians" will no doubt creep in here and there.)

Most historians point to the 1790s as the official "birth" of American political parties. As Jefferson and Madison pushed back against Hamilton's rapid expansion of federal power via his influence with President Washington, their internal battles spilled into newspapers across the country, which in turn often aligned themselves openly with one camp or the other. Like weeds, weight gain, or reality TV, the fact that everyone agreed parties were *bad* didn't do much to prevent them from springing up – and then never, ever going away.

In very general terms, here were some of the main differences between Federalists and Democratic-Republicans:

Federalists (Hamilton, Adams, Marshall)	Dem-Reps (Jefferson, Madison, Monroe)
supported strong central government	supported states' rights
promoted manufacturing & commerce	promoted farming & agriculture
tended to sympathize with Great Britain	tended to support France
wealthy, educated men should lead the nation (proven ability, vested interest in its success)	slightly less-wealthy, somewhat educated men should also play a part in leading the nation
"loose construction" of Constitution	"strict construction" of Constitution
strong central bank, high tariffs, powerful navy	◀━━━ that stuff is totally boujee!

Despite this evolving sense of party identity, however, the views and passions of many citizens were still just as likely to be shaped by their region (north, south, etc.) as their party affiliation. Political parties wouldn't replace geography as the primary source of tribal organization until after the Civil War.

Demise of the Federalists

Nothing in history is every quite as simple as the numbered lists we love so much, but if you simply must cough up a list of reasons the Federalist Party collapsed, try this one.

#1: The Alien & Sedition Acts (1798). You remember these. What you may not remember is that they were a Federalist creation signed into law by a Federalist president, John Adams. In keeping with their "weak central government" philosophy, two iconic Jeffersonian Republicans – James Madison and Jefferson himself – wrote resolutions on behalf of their states claiming that the acts were unconstitutional nonsense and thus states did not have to obey them.

These early claims of a right of nullification on behalf of unhappy states didn't garner much support, but neither did the Alien and Sedition Acts themselves, what with them being horrid and self-serving and all. They made the Federalists look desperate and a bit insecure – not ideal characteristics when running a young nation.

#2: The War of 1812. The Jeffersonian Republicans took the White House in 1801 and held it until the election of Andrew Jackson in 1828. The War of 1812 which occurred halfway through that streak gave the Federalists a grand opportunity to reclaim some credibility, but they couldn't stop arguing with one another long enough to take advantage of it.

The U.S. Navy had been kept relatively small and weak by the Jeffersonian Republicans, making it rather tricky to combat the world's most renowned maritime superpower. Then, after the war, the U.S. struggled to pay its debts – largely due to "small government" types who'd refused to recharter the national bank. Despite America's unexpected victory over the British, it looked like this might be the last time anyone at home *or* abroad would loan the scrappy nation money.

The Federalists responded to this glorious opportunity at redemption by wandering off to hold secret meetings in Hartford, Connecticut, and discuss plans for seceding from the Union. At least, that's how it appeared to the rest of the nation – particularly once the Jeffersonians got hold of it.

#3: The Hartford Convention. Two dozen Federalist delegates, all from New England states, met in late December 1814 through the first week of January 1815 (when apparently nothing else was going on) to discuss their fears and frustrations with the Jeffersonian Republicans' control of, well… *everything*, it seemed. They complained that states' rights were being subsumed by federal control and that the controlling party wasn't equally concerned with the needs of every region, instead favoring some over others.

Given that these were the *Federalists*, it was not a good look. Clearly the party had lost its focus, if not its collective mind. At the very least they were having difficulty projecting a consistent message.

While there were apparently some calls for secession by the New England states at the Hartford Convention, there's no indication these were taking seriously by the majority of delegates. Such talk most likely reflected frustration and a sense of helplessness more than an actual move to separate from the Union. Still, the fact that it was discussed at all seriously undercut public perception of the Federalist Party. They were the original "it takes a strong central government to hold us all together" diehards, after all.

Whatever may have been discussed behind closed doors, the Hartford Convention concluded with nothing more than a few official resolutions calling for amendments to the U.S. Constitution whose practical effect would be to limit the political influence of the South – particularly Virginia. (Presumably this would strengthen Federalist influence in the North.) Right as they were wrapping up, however, news of the Treaty of Ghent hit the papers, officially ending the War of 1812 with the U.S. on top. The Federalists looked like short-sighted whiners at best and traitors at worst.

Like I said, not a good look. Within a few years, the Federalists were no longer a thing.

The Birth of the Democratic Party

In some ways, the success of the Democratic-Republicans led to their dissolution. Without serious challenge from another party for a generation or more, internal differences had room to grow and fester. These eventually contributed to the creation of two new parties – the Democrats and the Whigs. Unlike their predecessors in the "First Party System," this "Second Party System" transformed politics by stimulating more participation by a wider variety of citizens, inculcated stronger party loyalties by those participating, held the first formal political rallies, and prompted partisan newspapers supporting specific ideologies and candidates. It was also during this time that state party leaders began actively working to promote national candidates in exchange for later favors and political appointments.

For all practical purposes, the Democratic Party began with the election of Andrew Jackson to the White House in 1828. Martin Van Buren seized on his pal's popularity to host a national meeting of politicians from each state who supported Jackson and together they declared themselves the Democratic Party. They agreed to work together to promote several key policies, and suddenly the Andrew Jackson fan club was a real-life political party.

It's easy to consider the Democrats an evolutionary "next stage" of the Democratic-Republicans, but such a comparison is misleading. Like the Jeffersonians, Democrats were the "small government" party, but their focus was on the "common man" more than the states themselves. President Andrew Jackson was happy to wield veto power or call out the troops to secure state cooperation with federal laws – neither of which fit the Jeffersonian ideal of limited executive authority.

Still, the initial policies of the new Democratic Party were similar enough to those of its predecessor that for many it was a smooth transition. They favored agriculture over industry and insisted on economic policies which weakened the nation in favor of local autonomy. While not necessarily Francophiles, they didn't think much of the British. The policies of Jackson and others towards American Indians and other non-white groups reflect a passion for "the little guy" (well, the "little *white* guy") rather than a consistent hostility towards anyone else in particular.

Jackson's infamous war against the national bank helped spark the creation of the other new kid on the block, the Whig Party.

Whigging Out Over Jackson

The Whig's initial platform was a simple one – "Andrew Jackson must be stopped!"

That may not sound like much of a plan, but Jackson was enough of a polarizing figure that it was sufficient for a time. Whigs came from a relatively diverse variety of backgrounds, making them even less a descendent of the Federalists than the Democrats were of the Jeffersonians. They did, however, share the Federalists' belief in the need for a strong central government to coordinate the growth and prosperity of the nation – even if that sometimes annoyed individual states. The most recognizable policy of the Whigs was Henry Clay's "American System," a package of federal legislation supporting protective tariffs, infrastructure connecting all parts of the country, and a centralized economy – including that bank Jackson hated so much.

On the other hand, the Whigs weren't big fans of westward expansion, at least not when it led to never-ending conflicts with those already living there. They fought against expanding presidential power, although that sometimes had as much to do with who was in office as it did underlying principles. There would be a total of four Whig presidents, none of whom were particularly noteworthy or particularly horrible. (One is best remembered for the shortest time in office before his death, another for being the first Vice President to become President as a result of that death, and a third for his military victories prior to running for office. The fourth is honestly not remembered for anything at all. Presidents Tyler and Taylor didn't even support their own party's platform – that's rarely a good sign.)

In overly broad terms, the Whigs tended to garner support from New England and the middle states and from educated professionals and businessmen, particularly an evolving group which would eventually be thought of as the "middle class." They tended to appeal to members of the more conservative Protestant denominations. Democrats, on the other hand, were more popular in the South. They appealed to the less-dogmatic Protestant sects as well as Catholics and other social or theological outliers.

Neither party focused on the issue of slavery when they could avoid it. Although it was quickly becoming the single most divisive issue in the U.S., opinions were shaped by region far more than party and neither wanted to split their constituency if they could help it.

Whigs (Clay, Webster, Seward)	Democrats (Jackson, Van Buren, Polk)
supported strong, active central government	supported states' rights
promoted manufacturing & commerce (in theory, promoted every region equally)	promoted farming & agriculture (suspicious of industrial power)
supported national bank / tariffs / infrastructure	fought against unconstitutional overreach
the "American System"	Jacksonian Democracy / westward expansion
legislative branch should be dominant	executive branch should be dominant
focus on connecting regions and national self-sufficiency (gradual expansion)	support homesteading & expansion no matter who gets in the way
preferred not to talk about slavery	preferred not to talk about slavery

Evolution of the Democrats; Demise of the Whigs

The Democratic Party split in the decade leading up to the Civil War, but not fatally. They lost members to the Constitutional Union Party in the south and to the Free Soil Party in the north. The party nevertheless managed to survive the Civil War and found new life postbellum as the voice of the "Old South" – clinging to resentment over the war, white supremacy, and an inflated sense of nostalgia for the rest of the nineteenth century and well into the twentieth.

The Whigs, on the other hand, simply couldn't adapt to a nation increasingly split over the issue of slavery and largely divided by region. Third parties had been challenging the dominance of the major players since the 1840s. The Liberty Party was followed by the Free Soil Party, which in turn joined with northern Whigs and Democrats to form the new Republican Party (no relation to the Jeffersonian version). They ran a presidential candidate unsuccessfully in 1856 before scoring with Lincoln in 1860. They've been around ever since, although their platform has, er... *evolved* considerably over that time.

Southern Whigs split off to join the American Party (the "Know-Nothing" Party) or the Constitutional Union Party, neither of which had the numbers to sway major elections. Most ended up joining the Democrats after the war, where they could be found sitting on their porch shirtless, drinking off-brand beer, and longing for the "good ol' days" for another six or seven decades.

(OK, that's not entirely fair. Some wore tank tops.)

In short, the Whig Party didn't burn out so much as fade away. If pressed for a specific turning point, however, many historians point to the passage of the Kansas-Nebraska Act in 1854. The resulting hostilities drove voters into the arms of either the Democrats or the Republicans. The Whigs were simply left without a constituency.

Beginning with the controversial election of 1860, Republicans held the White House through the end of the nineteenth century with two minor exceptions – Andrew Johnson, who doesn't count, and Grover Cleveland, who won two non-consecutive terms as a Democrat near the end of the century, thus cementing his place in history as a trivia game answer no one knows anything else about. There have been numerous third parties in the 150 years since the Civil War, but to date the Democrats and Republicans have maintained the two top slots exclusively.

How Do I Remember This?

If for some sick, twisted reason you haven't watched the musical *Hamilton* a half-dozen times by now, you should probably get on that. The whole Federalists vs. Anti-Federalists (or Democratic-Republicans) debate is present throughout, particularly in the "cabinet battles" of the second act and pretty much anything the title character sings or says when he's not focused on having sex with every female in the cast.

The Whigs are easier to remember if you call up everything you know about Andrew Jackson (who was many things, but *never* boring). You've no doubt noticed how defensive he seemed, always lashing out at his many enemies, both real and perceived. *The real ones were usually the Whigs.* Whatever he was *for*, they were probably *against*, and vice versa. It was their defining characteristic. The other option is to simply equate the Whigs with the American System and extrapolate from there.

Making The Grade: What You're Most Likely To Be Asked

We've covered a pretty lengthy swath here. Rather than attempt to anticipate specific multiple choice questions, we'll stick to some general tips for the dedicated scholar:

* Federalists and Anti-Federalists are pretty much guaranteed to merit a question or two on any respectable quiz or state test.

* It's best if you remember the actual views of the Democratic-Republicans, but if you get stuck you can probably get away with thinking of them as Anti-Federalists doing the best they could with a constitution they didn't want ratified to begin with.

* For test review purposes, you can safely associate the Federalists with Alexander Hamilton, the first Democratic-Republicans with Thomas Jefferson, the Whigs with Henry Clay's "American System," the Democrats with Andrew Jackson (the "common man," states' rights, small government), and the Republicans with Abraham Lincoln (pro-business, pro-westward expansion, not crazy about slavery).

* Questions specifically about the Whigs themselves are uncommon, but you'll no doubt be asked about Henry Clay's American System, regional divisions, tariffs, evolving political parties, and especially Andrew Jackson. The Whigs are *essential* to any decent written response related to one (or more) of these.

* Prior to the 1850s, party affiliation certainly reflected a range of social and political views, but regional loyalties (north, south, west) often determined far more.

It's also a good idea to remember this general timeline:

1790s: Federalists vs. Anti-Federalists

1790s–1828: Federalists vs. Democratic Republicans (the "First Party System")

1828–1854: Whigs vs. Democrats (the "Second Party System")

1854–2016: Republicans vs. Democrats

2016-???: No one really knows what's happening now. *Hic sunt dracones*!

Here are a few of the most common types of prompts you may encounter for short answers or essays:

1. Compare and contrast key ideas debated between the Federalists and Anti-Federalists over ratification of the Constitution.

2. Compare and contrast the policies and beliefs of the Federalist and Democratic-Republican parties on (any two or three topics – foreign policy, the Alien and Sedition Acts, the National Bank, states' rights, etc.)

3. Evaluate the major policies and political developments of the presidencies of _____ (anyone from Washington through Polk) and their implications for the expansion of Federal power and foreign policy.

APUSH or other advanced classes may tackle the same ideas a little differently:

4. Explain how different regional interests affected debates about the role of the federal government in the early republic.

5. Explain the causes and effects of continuing policy debates about the role of the federal government from 1800 to 1848.

6. Compare and contrast the Jacksonian Democratic Party and the Whig Party of the 1830s and 1840s. (You'll likely either be given two or three topics of focus or a list from which to choose any two – social reform, the role of government in the economy, westward expansion, tariffs, federally funded internal improvements, etc.)

APUSH also loves asking about the American System and the development of political parties in the first half of the nineteenth century. This is also a favorite era for comparing political dynamics or priorities with those of some other designated time period, probably from the twentieth century.

Don't shoot the messenger here – I'm just trying to prepare you emotionally as well as intellectually. From what I can tell so far, you're doing just fine.

CHAPTER SEVEN: THE AMERICAN SYSTEM

Come Together. Right Now. Over Me.

Three Big Things:

1. Henry Clay's "American System" was the centerpiece of the Whigs' political platform and legislative agenda. It consisted of (a) protective tariffs, (b) national transportation infrastructure, and (c) a centralized economy.

2. Clay and the Whigs believed the American System would bring the different regions of the country together and make the nation largely self-reliant. Whatever it's other successes, it didn't.

3. The South particularly resented the protective tariffs, which raised prices on many common goods and undercut the South's primary source of wealth – exporting cash crops. South Carolina and other southern states resurrected the doctrine of "nullification" in response; it took federal troops to bring them back in line.

Introduction

One of the trickiest things about Henry Clay's "American System" is that in addition to how boring it sounds all by itself, making sense of it requires dragging through a number of constituent elements which are serious yawners all on their own. Nevertheless, it's well-worth knowing. The American System is genuinely significant in U.S. history and many of the issues involved weren't so different from those being butchered in vacuous political rhetoric today.

More importantly, it's almost certainly going to be on the test.

What Was It?

At its most basic, the American System was a program pushed by Henry Clay (arguably the most influential member of Congress in the first half of the nineteenth century and a historical icon sometimes referred to as the "Great Compromiser") and the Whigs (a short-lived political party in the 1830s – 1850s who primary platform consisted of yelling "Andrew Jackson Sucks!" as often as possible).

The goals of the American System were simple, if grand: strengthen the U.S. through government support of economic development and connect the disparate regions of the young nation so everyone could do business and play nicely with one another. Accomplishing this would require a strong central government along the lines of that envisioned by Alexander Hamilton, who we remember because *he* got his own musical. (Clay, to date, has not).

The two other names most often associated with Clay's American System were John Quincy Adams (a former Federalist who gradually evolved into a Democratic-Republican and whom history sometimes labels a Whig) and John C. Calhoun (also a Democratic-Republican who morphed into a Democrat once that was a thing someone could be, but whose true political party was "Southern-by-the-Grace-of-God, Huzzah!").

This was an era in which political parties, which had previously been somewhat informal, began to evolve and solidify simultaneously; issues and priorities were shifting even as party identification was becoming more overt (and at times, determinative). As the nation continued to expand, however, region still often trumped party in determining one's social and political convictions. When Calhoun was eventually forced to choose between the interests of the South and the interests of the nation as a whole (as represented by the American System), he didn't waiver. It took armed intervention by President Jackson just to keep the southern contingent on the team – something of a recurring theme during the first century or so of these "united" states.

More on that later.

The Trinity Of Prosperity

Clay's American System can be broken into three basic elements. You should remember them even if you're fuzzy on the details:

1) High protective tariffs to protect American manufacturing and generate revenue for the federal government. Additional income would be derived from the sales of public lands, primarily in the west. This tariff thing was essential for the rest of the plan to work; in addition to helping out American businesses, it was supposed to pay for the necessary infrastructure and such. Tariffs also turned out to be the most controversial part of Clay's American System – especially in the South.

2) National infrastructure (roads, canals, etc.). While the Constitution gives Congress the power to build roads for purposes of getting the mail delivered (Article I, Section 8), anything beyond this was iffy. The Whigs insisted improved transportation would be good for business of all kinds – manufacturing, agriculture, and whatever else – as well as helping to bind the nation together through commercial interaction. This last bit was perhaps a tad optimistic.

3) A more centralized economy. A national bank (which already existed) issuing national currency would facilitate interstate trade and help stabilize smaller banks across the nation. It already served as the bank of the United States for purposes of taxes, tariffs, and other federal transactions. This was the same National Bank famously opposed by Andrew Jackson, who hated the idea both on principal and in fact. (Two famous political cartoons resulted from this kerfuffle. In the first, Jackson fought a "many-headed monster," or hydra. That "monster" was the national bank. In the second, "King Andrew" held a VETO in his hand. One of his most famous vetoes was the rechartering of the National Bank.)

Clay's Idealism

The American System wasn't purely political. By all accounts, Henry Clay was genuinely sold on his legislative agenda. He insisted that each region would benefit from closer ties with one another and that the U.S. could be truly self-sufficient, providing all the raw materials, food, and finished goods it could ever need. No need to do business with anyone outside its red, white, and blue borders. U! S! A! U! S! A!

Making that happen, of course, required affordable, reliable transportation from every part of the country to every other part. It also meant severely restricting the importation of cheaper or better materials or goods from anywhere else. Americans would be happy to pay more for everything, Clay assured doubters, because... *patriotism*! Besides, the system would all soon fall into perfect balance and no one would ever be unhappy about anything ever again. The Era of Good Feelings would give way to the Era of *Great Everything*!

In Clay's defense, American commerce *had* been severely disrupted during the War of 1812. Before that, it was shaken by whatever Napoleon was doing in Europe. Eventually, there'd no doubt be some other conflict making it difficult to buy or sell overseas. Since the U.S would obviously never go to war against *itself*, the American System would eliminate this inconvenience permanently.

At least, that was the plan.

The Tariff Problem

Tariffs (as you no doubt already know) are taxes on imported goods. Depending on specific rates and terms, they can be used primarily as a source of revenue for the government or as a means of manipulating trade with foreign nations. There'd been some friction between the American colonies and British Parliament in the late eighteenth century over this very issue – something about taxation and repressed nations? (I forget the exact wording, but you can probably look it up.)

It turned out the South hadn't forgotten what it looked and felt like when a large, oppressive government claiming to be working in their best interest abused them via economic policies, whether internal or external. When Clay began pushing for higher protective tariffs, southern states had flashbacks to tea being dumped in harbors and a guy with a head wound playing the fife. It got so bad that John C. Calhoun pulled his support for the plan and began pushing nullification through his home state of South Carolina. President Jackson eventually had to call up 5,000 troops and a half-dozen ships before South Carolina and Calhoun backed down. (Given that Calhoun was Jackson's vice president at the time, this didn't bode well for their future together.)

What was it about Clay's tariffs that upset some southerners so much?

There's A New Tariff In Town

Imagine that you're a northern industry making some common item, like socks. Your socks sell for $4/pair. The problem is, there's a factory in Gutzenberg cranking out socks by the thousands. Even after the cost of shipping them to the United States, they're able to sell their socks for $2.50/pair. Maybe they're not quite as good, but socks are socks and many people, given the choice, buy the cheaper product.

Well, that's capitalism and the free market, right? Maybe. But if your sock company goes under, it doesn't just impact you. You have a dozen or so employees – most of them with families – who are now out of work. The café across the street where many of them had breakfast or lunch will have to close, meaning several cooks and waitresses lose their income as well. The local saloon, the neighborhood barber, the theater where you first discovered your love of musicals – they all downsize or call it quits altogether.

The ripple effect could be brutal, especially if you're not the only business going under due to foreign competition.

You call your congressman and demand that he *do* something, so he introduces a tariff bill which passes easily. Every pair of Gutzenberg socks will now be hit with a charge of $1/pair upon arrival in any American dock. They naturally pass that increase along to their customers, meaning you now have much more competitive socks. With a little advertising and a holiday sale or two, you have a fighting chance of selling your $4/pair socks over their $3.50/pair cheap imitations.

Your employees are happy to pay the difference because it means they still have jobs. The local saloon owners, waitresses, cooks, actors, and barbers can live with the cost increase because it keeps them in business as well. Everyone's happy, right?

Well, not everyone. See, the states south of you are mostly made up of farmer types. Let's put yourself in *their* shoes (although not in their cheap, worn-out foreign socks). They grow crops for a living, much of which they sell overseas. The nation of Gutzenberg has just informed them they've passed a substantial tariff on stuff imported from the United States, including corn, tobacco, and cotton, meaning suddenly the South is unable to sell their crops at a profit – if they can sell them at all. To make matters worse, the next time they head to the store to pick up some socks, the price has skyrocketed to nearly $4/pair!

Why? To protect northern businesses, of course – the important part of the country which the government *actually cares about.* These southerners, on the other hand, are completely and totally screwed. Henry Clay did his best to persuade them it would all work out for the best because *reasons* and *America* and *kumbaya.* All most agricultural types heard, though, was "Gosh, I love the North! Aren't they great up there in the North! I'll bet you wish YOU were in the North instead of here in this horrible place, the Not-North!"

This was the point at which Calhoun bailed on the Whig agenda and stood with the South in defying Clay's "Tariff of Abominations." It's also when Jackson threatened them with military force if they kept it up. (That's the "Nullification Crisis" discussed in the next chapter.) While the South eventually caved in the face of military force, the kerfuffle didn't do much for Clay's "it will bring us all together!" motif.

Infrastructure

Clay hoped the additional revenue from protective tariffs would make it easier to finance the building or extension of roads, canals, and bridges. He almost immediately ran into political opposition.

First was the question of whether the federal government should even *be* in the transportation business. Other than making sure the mail gets delivered, nothing in the Constitution specifically grants Congress the power to do that sort of thing.

Second, and often interwound with the first, was the fact that not everyone would see the exact same benefits all at the same time. Many roads and canals would start or connect to the northeast, where most manufacturing occurred. Bridges tend to connect two states at most, and often don't even do that – they begin and end within the same states' borders.

Third was Andrew Jackson. He didn't like the idea of federal spending on roads, and even more than that, he didn't like Henry Clay. It didn't help that at least one of the major projects took place entirely within the boundaries of Kentucky, Clay's home state. Whatever the intent, that sort of thing fed Jackson's perpetual suspicion that everyone except him was up to something, and he alone could stop it.

Despite this opposition, hundreds of miles of roads were built, canals were extended, and bridges were constructed. The Erie Canal was completed during this time, and it seems to have worked out pretty well. It became easier for western farmers to transport crops to the east and even southerners benefitted from the improvements. That didn't mean they were happy about it, however.

We're Getting The Bank Back Together

The First Bank of the United States was created in 1791 to bring some stability to national currency (which was exclusively in the form of "specie" – gold or silver coins – until the Civil War) and to give the government a mechanism for handling financial matters. (Those taxes and appropriations have to come and go from *somewhere*.) It had a twenty-year charter which expired in 1811 when Congress couldn't quite find enough votes to renew.

Presidents Jefferson and Madison had already managed to reduce the size of the military, roll back some of Hamilton's tariffs so that less money was coming into the national treasury, and put the responsibility for internal improvements back on the states, where they believed it constitutionally belonged. It looked like team Small Government might win the endgame after all.

Then the War of 1812 happened.

Wars are expensive, and when the shooting stopped a few years later, the nation found itself in substantial debt with no reliable way to climb out. The value of the American dollar began dropping rapidly and the government stopped exchanging real gold or silver for bank notes. As other countries began wondering if perhaps England had been right about these young upstarts all along, President James Madison and his supporters in Congress pushed through legislation establishing the Second Bank of the United States in 1817.

This sequel was given a brand-new twenty-year charter. It was bigger than the original and had regional branches scattered across the country. It was this version of the bank which President Andrew Jackson later tried so hard to shut down. Efforts to renew the charter early in 1832 led to a big kerfuffle, and Jackson vetoed renewal in 1836. (He instead began depositing U.S. funds into his "pet banks.") It was one of the major victories of the Jackson Administration and helped send the nation into an economic death spiral in 1837 – by which time it was President Martin Van Buren's problem to deal with.

Aftermath

The collapse of the Whig Party in the 1850s ended official efforts to complete the American System as envisioned. It certainly helped improve transportation across the nation, however, and the idea that the federal government has a role to play in highway and other infrastructure is widely assumed in modern times. The U.S. hasn't been without a national bank of some sort since the Civil War and the power of "the Fed" today dwarfs anything envisioned by Clay or even Hamilton. The federal government in general has played an increasingly dominant role in almost every facet of American life – economically, socially, and legally.

Tariff policy, on the other hand, continues to be a major source of conflict between parties and throughout the U.S. It's one of the few issues for which regional experiences may influence opinions as much (or more) than political affiliations. On a broader scale, the debate about the role of federal government in regulating or supporting businesses, labor, or economic activity in general continues to rage.

Making The Grade: What You're Most Likely To Be Asked

The American System will not always be asked about by name, but when it's not, the ideas behind it (as well as the ideas of those opposing it) almost certainly will be. It's a convenient correct answer for any number of multiple choice questions, which makes things easy. You should know its three main elements and always associate it with Henry Clay and the Whig Party.

1. Which of the following was NOT a key component of Henry Clay's American System? (A) protective tariffs for American businesses, (B) improvements to U.S. infrastructure, (C) a strong centralized economy (including a National Bank), or (D) increasing the exports of cash crops to Europe.

2. The Whig Party advocated an "American System," by which they meant...?

(A) a strong, permanent military to discourage European involvement in the Western Hemisphere, (B) <u>a system of high tariffs to keep out imported products,</u> (C) letting the states finance and manage their own roads, canals, and other infrastructure, or (D) an improved method of scientific assembly line management to increase efficiency and profits.

I should warn you that test-makers have a bizarre, possibly unhealthy obsession with the Erie Canal. You could be in the middle of an art history or calculus quiz and come across questions about it. Fortunately, they're usually pretty much all looking for the same things:

3. How did the completion of the Erie Canal (1825) impact the city of New York? (A) New York gained more political power due to an increase in migration from other states. (B) <u>New York became a major commercial center.</u> (C) New York increased its agricultural production and sales outside the state. (D) New York was able to absorb New Amsterdam and nearly doubled in size.

4. The opening of the Erie Canal in 1825 was important because...? (A) <u>it created a permanent and efficient route between the Great Lakes and the eastern seaboard,</u> (B) it established the role of the federal government in improving infrastructure, (C) it facilitated increased trade with Canada, or (D) it dispersed the commercial activity of New York across numerous other cities.

5. Which of the following was NOT true of the Erie Canal? (A) It provided a direct water route to the Midwest, triggering large scale emigration westward. (B) It transformed New York City into the commercial capital of the nation. (C) <u>It allowed the U.S. Navy to more easily patrol multiple borders.</u> (D) It allowed easier trade of consumer goods across the Midwest.

Basically, when it comes to standardized tests, you should assume the Erie Canal connected every part of the U.S. with every other part instantaneously – the water version of "transporters" on Star Trek. While not literally true, this will satisfy most test-makers' dysfunctional fawning over the thing. Keep in mind that just because they don't mention it by name, that doesn't mean they're not thinking of it just as lovingly:

6. Canal building was important to economic growth in the early nineteenth century because...? (A) canals could be used year-round, (B) canals allowed homesteaders to travel westward at no cost, (C) canals allowed faster transportation of crops and manufactured goods, or (D) <u>canals charged lower rates than the transcontinental railroad.</u>

For short answers or essay prompts, it's possible you'll get nice, straightforward prompts like "Explain the American System" or "What were some of the major differences between the Whigs and the Democratic-Republicans?" Just to be safe, however, you should be prepared variations like these:

7. Analyze the rise of capitalism and the economic problems and conflicts that accompanied it. (It's too early for labor unions or red scares, so think about conflicts over the National Bank, Jackson's specie circular, and the like. Whatever side Jackson was on, the Whigs and their American System were on

the other.)

8. Compare conflicting interpretations of state and federal authority as emphasized in the speeches and writings of statesmen such as Daniel Webster and John C. Calhoun. (Webster, of course, was a Whig. Calhoun was whatever seemed most southern at the moment.)

9. Identify the constitutional issues posed by the doctrine of nullification and secession and the earliest origins of that doctrine. (Don't forget to reference the Virginia and Kentucky Resolutions for this one. Duh.)

10. Discuss political, social, and economic differences between the North and the South. Include the impact of geography on each region and the differences between agrarians and industrialists.

If you're thinking that those last two sound like they belong with different topics, you're right – except that they belong with this one as well. Nullification, the American System, sectional tensions which led to civil war – it was all related and interwound and each part impacted all the rest for better or for worse. (History's wacky that way.)

APUSH or other advanced classes may get a bit more elaborate. (That is, after all, kind of their thing.) Notice how easy it is to ask about the American System, the Whigs vs. the Democratic Republicans, Clay vs. Jackson, etc., without even mentioning them by name:

11. Discuss the evolution of political parties in the first half of the nineteenth century, including debates over issues such as tariffs, the powers of the federal government, and relations with European powers.

12. Explain the impact of regional interests on how national concerns were perceived and addressed by political leaders. (This one can be tailored to anything from slavery to economic policy to reform movements to westward expansion.)

If your teacher is especially gung-ho, they might actually want examples of some of that "connecting the regions" mojo Clay was going for:

13. Discuss ways in which new transportation systems and technologies expanded manufacturing and agricultural production.

Or the "super-sized" version:

14. How did legislation and judicial decisions supporting the development of roads, canals, and railroads benefit each region – the North, the Midwest, and the South? Were these benefits equitably distributed? Explain your response.

The American System wasn't the only issue of note in the antebellum United States. It did, however, relate to a range of issues and personalities who will come up time and again and which are far more interesting than tariffs or infrastructure. A solid grasp on Clay, the Whigs, and the American System along with the *interesting* stuff from the same period – Jackson and "Jacksonian Democracy," the birth of the Democratic Party, the "Tariff of Abominations" and the resulting Nullification Crisis – will help you sound like you have a pretty firm grasp on the *entire era*.

And hey – maybe now, you do.

CHAPTER EIGHT: THE NULLIFICATION CRISIS

If At First You Don't Secede... (Part Two)

Three Big Things:

1. As political parties evolved throughout the first half of the nineteenth century, regional differences continued to shape the debate over many issues – particularly that of protective tariffs.

2. The old question of whether the Union was a creation of the American people or of the sovereign states continued to provoke strong emotions and heated debates. Could states reject federal legislation they considered unconstitutional?

3. When South Carolina attempted to nullify the "Tariff of Abominations" (and some even spoke of secession), President Andrew Jackson threatened to send federal troops to enforce federal law. South Carolina backed down... at least for the time being.

The Story So Far

The Alien and Sedition Acts passed by the Federalist Party at the end of the eighteenth century prompted Thomas Jefferson and James Madison – speaking through their respective states – to issue strongly-worded protests. The Virginia and Kentucky Resolutions not only criticized the acts themselves, they claimed the right of individual states to reject *any* act of Congress they deemed unconstitutional. In other words, if a law went beyond what was allowed by the Constitution, it wasn't really a law. States had an obligation to "nullify" such efforts within their own borders.

This "Compact Theory" of government ("compact" here referring to the U.S. as a creation of its component states rather than as an entirely sovereign, independent entity) didn't gain much support from other states, but neither would it ever quite go entirely away. It was the nineteenth century version of trying to delete your old social media posts or persuade Google Ads you no longer need THAT particular cream (and that you regret searching for information about it to begin with). It just kept popping back up.

The Hartford Convention (1814-1815)

In 1814-1815, Federalist delegates from several New England states met in Hartford, Connecticut, to discuss trade, foreign policy, and the general suckiness of the Democratic-Republican Party – especially the way they just kept getting elected to stuff. Several northeastern states had resisted President Madison's call for troops when the War of 1812 erupted, insisting that state militias should remain under state control. Madison had responded by threatening to institute a draft, starting with their youngest eligible males. It got kinda ugly.

Two-and-a-half years of war against the British and their Amerindian allies had highlighted the need for a stronger navy (which the Democratic-Republicans opposed) as well as a national bank (which the Democratic-Republicans had managed to kill). Federalists hoped this was their chance to make some serious changes in how things were being run, including restoring some of the states' rights which had (in their views) been trampled by federal government overreach. If they managed to shift the political balance of power back to themselves in the process, well... *bonus*.

And yet, the Hartford Convention instead became a national embarrassment when the U.S. (operating largely under Democratic-Republican leadership) unexpectedly *won the war*, leaving New England Federalists looking like traitors – or worse, whiners. Word began spreading that the delegates had proposed secession from the Union, using the same basic reasoning utilized in the Virginia and Kentucky Resolutions fifteen years before. There's no evidence the topic was seriously considered by the majority present, but it was at least a topic of discussion and may have gained some traction behind closed doors. Either way, the convention was hurriedly concluded with a handful of resolutions calling for amendments to the U.S. Constitution to better balance the nation's regional and political factions (i.e., to reduce the influence of the Democratic-Republicans). Delegates were then released to skulk home with false bravado.

A mere fifteen years later, secession (or at least nullification) was on the table again. This time, however, it was the South feeling all marginalized and misunderstood. At least *that* part of the equation was back to normal.

Whigs, Democrats, and "Old Hickory"

The 1830s saw the rise of the short-lived Whig Party, spearheaded by the "Great Compromiser," Henry Clay. Clay, you may recall, was one of the four candidates who ran for President in 1824. None received a majority of electoral votes, so the election was thrown to the House of Representatives. According to the Constitution, they could then choose from the top three candidates.

Andrew Jackson received a clear plurality of electoral votes, followed by John Quincy Adams, William Crawford, and Henry Clay. Clay threw his substantial Congressional influence behind Adams, who became president and appointed Clay as his Secretary of State. Jackson threw a fit and labeled the entire thing a "Corrupt Bargain," making this one of the most famous and troubling elections in American history, at least until recent times.

What's often overlooked when telling the story is that the Election of 1824 occurred during a time of substantial political readjustment. The Federalist Party was all but extinct and failed to offer a viable candidate in 1824. The

Democratic Party didn't exist yet, and since Jackson wasn't yet president, there could be no Whig Party living largely to oppose him. All four major candidates in 1824 were Democratic-Republicans, at least until after the election. It's just as well they made the most of it while they had the chance; four years later, the Democratic-Republicans would ride into the political sunset as well.

Crawford, the most forgettable of the lot, was the official candidate of the party, which rather than boosting his campaign seemed to work against him. The nation was in the birthing throes of what would later be called "Jacksonian Democracy," longing for outsiders and fresh leadership and bad grammar and such. Jackson certainly typified this (it's the number one thing for which he's remembered two centuries later), while Adams was the exact opposite – a former U.S. Senator, Ambassador, and two-term Secretary of State. Jackson won the most popular and electoral votes, but Adams became the sixth POTUS.

Four years later, in 1828, Jackson won the majority he needed, initiating not only two of the most influential presidential terms in American history (for better or worse) but a new party and a dramatically expanded approach to democracy in the process. And with the election of a personality like Andrew Jackson to the White House, an opposition part – the Whigs – almost *had* to be born as well.

The "American System" and the Tariff Problem

The Whigs envisioned a nation made stronger via implementation of what came to be known as the "American System" – a legislative agenda with three interrelated priorities:

1) A strong national bank to help centralize the national economy

2) Infrastructure programs across the nation to better connect all regions

3) Protective tariffs to promote American manufacturing

Clay and the Whigs believed America would be strongest if self-sufficient, requiring little or no foreign trade to survive. As a bonus, this would require the different regions to work together more closely, further strengthening the U.S. culturally as well as economically. The problem was that this "American System" seemed tilted to favor the northeastern region of the U.S. at the expense of the other two. The South had never been crazy about a national bank or overly centralized economy and the West had other priorities. Infrastructure had some potential, but most of it seemed chosen to promote easier distribution of goods manufactured in the North.

And those tariffs – those were the *worst*. They made everything more expensive except the crops on which the South relied for their livelihood. They annoyed foreign trading partners, who instituted tariffs of their own against American products – mostly those same cash crops grown in the South. For many of the lower states, it was the Townshend Acts all over again. Simply intolerable! There was no sugar-coating it – they had to stamp this out now, or there'd be trouble with a capital tea.

They saw themselves in the same situation as the original revolutionaries, is what I'm saying. If you remember how that turned out for King George and Parliament, you can understand why this was less than ideal.

Southern representatives proposed alternatives. They offered compromises. They even made a few threats about the results if they were unable to offer their constituents *something*. It was perhaps inevitable that nullification would eventually be mentioned. Once that happened, talk of even more extreme measures wasn't far behind.

The Webster–Hayne Debate

In the midst of this turmoil came a landmark exchange in the annals of the U.S. Senate. It began as a debate over land policy – how the federal government should manage the sales of public lands as the nation expanded westward and such. Disputes over tariffs and nullification and states' rights and Indian Removal and fiscal policy were ubiquitous at the time, so perhaps it wasn't particularly surprising that the question would evolve into yet another front in the larger ongoing conflict.

Senator Daniel Webster, a Whig from Massachusetts (who was already something of a political legend), argued for Whig stuff – westward expansion, internal improvements, and those protective tariffs which never failed to give the Whigs a little tingly feeling inside. The Union had been formed under the Constitution for the good of all people, Webster explained, specifically as a rejection of state sovereignty. It was a creation of the people and served the people – not the states. To frame the issue any other way was to invite civil war!

Senator Robert Hayne, a Democrat from – where else? – South Carolina, felt differently. The states had created the Union as an extension of their collective decision-making, and thus had the right and the authority to rein that Union in from time to time. That included the right of individual states to periodically nullify federal laws which they deemed unconstitutional. The Union was important, Hayne argued, but it wasn't designed to enslave the states to its will, no matter how distorted! Such thinking was a recipe for civil war!

So at least they agreed on that last part.

This was the loftiest version so far of the same old debate – the Virginia and Kentucky Resolutions, the Hartford Convention, and now Webster-Hayne. It's the same argument which would be made three decades later when eleven southern states duct taped a pretend border down the center of the country and demanded the north stay on their own side... or *else*.

From Toast to Toast

A few months later, President Jackson, Vice President Calhoun, and other notables attended a formal dinner honoring Thomas Jefferson (who'd died only a few years before). It was by that time an open secret that the author of the Declaration of Independence and the third President of the United States had authored the Kentucky Resolution on which so much of the current nullification talk was based; the temptation to reference the matter was no doubt irresistible for some.

Several officials toasted Jefferson in this capacity, some subtly praising nullification and others outright promoting it. Many assumed that Jackson – a southerner by nature and a states' rights advocate for his entire political career – would share their sentiments.

What happened next was super-dramatic and eternally memorable. You'll simply have to trust me on this, however, because it really doesn't translate well in the modern imagination. Nevertheless, at the time it was high drama... politically, personally, and rhetorically. (If this were an audio book, I'd be fading in the theme from *The Good, the Bad, and the Ugly* to emphasize the point.)

President Andrew Jackson rose to offer a toast. The crowd turned to him expectantly, drinks in hands. Jackson looked directly at John C. Calhoun and said, "Our federal Union: it must be preserved!" (*clink*) (*try-to-act-normal-while-wondering-what-everyone-else-is-thinking-because-OMG*) (*drink*)

Calhoun may have been a troublesome fellow and wrong about just about everything, but he was also a political veteran and didn't hesitate long before responding. As the tension in the room lingered, Calhoun stood with a toast of his own. Staring at Jackson calmly and courteously, he uttered, "The Union!" (*the-briefest-dramatic-pause*) "Next to our liberty, most dear!" (*clink*) (*oh-my-god-this-is-happening*) (*drink*) (*uncomfortable-smiles-and-shielded-glances-all-round*)

The precise phrasing is debatable, but it doesn't matter – if it had been a movie, that's the scene which would have guaranteed at least one Oscar. It would have been quoted and parodied endlessly alongside other dramatic classics like "You can't handle the truth!", "I coulda been a contender," and "Whassssuuuuuuuup?!"

It was a big deal, is what I'm saying.

The "Tariff of Abominations"

Despite the rhetoric, the emotion, and the South's many efforts to compromise, in 1832 Congress** passed what became almost immediately known as the "Tariff of Abominations." (You can probably guess why.) It was largely a repeat of the Tariff of 1828 against which the South had been fighting for four years, and thus perceived as a bit of a slap in the face.

The South reacted vociferously. South Carolina took things a step further than the rest and flatly refused to accept the results. Jackson's own Vice President, John C. Calhoun, resigned in order to head back to South Carolina, where he was immediately elected Senator and led the state's opposition to this per-

ceived federal overreach. Talk of nullification and secession once again pep-
pered emotional conversations and heated editorials.

Calhoun and his supporters argued that the Constitution gave Congress the
power to impose tariffs in order to raise revenue, but not to protect American businesses. As the true sovereigns in the political equation, the people
of each *state* retained the power and authority to nullify federal decisions
which they considered unconstitutional. Calhoun built on the ideas codified
in the Virginia and Kentucky Resolutions of 1798 which framed the union as
a "compact" between willing members. Those signing the original Constitution were joining a mutually beneficial confederacy of equals, not submitting
themselves to slavery in service of key northern states.

The "Ordinance of Nullification" passed by South Carolina required all state
officials to take an oath supporting nullification and threatened to secede if
the federal government attempted to push the issue. In short, it was a bright
red line warning the federal government not to push the issue any further.
"You can't make us!"

Jackson's Reaction

Jackson hated the national bank, and he wasn't a big fan of federal funding
of infrastructure projects. The original Democrats leaned heavily towards
states' rights and local control... sort of. "Old Hickory" was with the South in
principle on the whole tariff issue. He exerted pressure on Congress to gradually dial back the most egregious rates.

At the same time, while Jackson could be reactionary and stubborn, he was
also the President of the United States. He expected everyone to play within
the rules while he was the nation's chief law enforcement officer.

Jackson considered South Carolina's talk of nullification and secession to be a
direct threat to the Union. It didn't matter that he might have sympathized
with them regarding the underlying issue. A certain amount of blustering
and grandstanding was just politics as usual. But disloyalty? Defiance of the
constitutionally elected leadership of the nation? All this talk about nullification, or even... *secession*? Jackson took that kind of thing personally.

(To be fair, Jackson took EVERYTHING personally. But still...)

Jackson issued a "Proclamation to the People of South Carolina" in which he
reminded them of the Supremacy Clause and warned that what they were
attempting was treason. South Carolina's reasoning was faulty, and a slip-
pery slope towards complete dissolution of the Union. The state initially
attempted to call his bluff, but when they found themselves alone in their
efforts – without a single other state willing to join them – South Carolina
backed down.

Reflection and Considerations

What's often left out of the story is that Henry Clay (you remember, "the
Great Compromiser"?) was already working on a reduced tariff in hopes of

appeasing the nation's lower regions. South Carolina backed down in the face of Jackson's threat of sending in troops, but they also got at least *some* of what they asked for. It may not be the lesson we'd like to glean from history, but sometimes extreme measures get things rolling.

Despite this consolation prize, some historians argue that the Nullification Crisis left South Carolina particularly aware of their fragile position in the Union and their relative lack of influence in their own national government. It may have made it that much easier a generation later to officially attempt secession after the Election of 1860 only heightened that sense of marginalization.

On the other hand, maybe that's what they were looking to justify all along. In a personal letter written in 1830, Calhoun posited a clear correlation between tariff disputes and tensions over slavery:

> I consider the tariff act as the occasion, rather than the real cause of the present unhappy state of things. The truth can no longer be disguised, that the peculiar domestick institution of the Southern States [he means "slavery"] and the consequent direction which that and her soil have given to her industry, has placed them in regard to taxation and appropriations in opposite relation to the majority of the Union.

A few years later, Andrew Jackson wrote an unrelated personal letter in which he summarized the Nullification Crisis from his point of view:

> I have had a laborious task here – but nullification is dead, and its actors... will only be remembered... for their wicked designs to sever & destroy the only good government on the Globe, and that prosperity and happiness we enjoy over every other portion of the world...

> The tariff {issue}, it is now well known, was a mere pretext... and disunion & a southern confederacy the real object. The next pretext will be the negro, or slavery question...

Neither Calhoun nor Jackson would not live long enough to see themselves proven correct.

Making The Grade: What You're Most Likely To Be Asked

The Nullification Crisis can be asked about in a variety of contexts. The most common would include...

* the presidency of Andrew Jackson (major events, stuff showing what sort of president he was, etc.)

* events related to "sectionalism," states' rights, or early hints of civil war

* anything involving political parties in the nineteenth century

You may, of course, get one or two specific questions about the Hartford Convention, the Webster-Hayne Debate, or the "Tariff of Abominations":

1. One major impact of the Hartford Convention (1814-1815) was...? (A) <u>Federalist delegates were embarrassed, and some labeled them "traitors,"</u> (B) the

Federalist Party was strengthened by American victory in the War of 1812, (C) a resolution was passed supporting secession from the United States unless several amendments to the Constitution were put before the public, or (D) the British were formally expelled from disputed territories in the northeast.

2. The Webster-Hayne Debate of 1830 began as a dispute over distributing public lands in the west, but soon became an extended conflict over...? (A) the rechartering of the National Bank, (B) the extension of slavery into the territories, (C) the nullification of federal laws by the states, or (D) direct vs. indirect democracy.

3. The Tariff of Abominations was so labeled because...? (A) it excluded select industries from protective tariffs and duties, (B) it maintained extremely high tariff rates despite objections from the South, (C) it based tariff rates on the country of origin for most imported goods, or (D) it quietly re-charted the National Bank in order to manage revenue from import taxes.

Honors or APUSH courses love connecting the Nullification Crisis to the Whigs and their "American System" or to changing political party dynamics in general. It's also an easily overlooked element of any "change and continuity" essay involving the Virginia and Kentucky Resolutions, the Hartford Convention, and the eventual (attempted) secession of the south which sparked the American Civil War.

Prompts taking a broader approach will probably be similar whether formatted for multiple choice, short answer, or essay. Generally, if you're prepared to *write* about something, any multiple choice questions on the topic will take care of themselves. For example:

4a. Discuss major events or developments in the mid-nineteenth century which increased sectionalism and heightened the political tensions which would eventually lead to civil war.

4b. Which of the following events sparked increased sectionalism and heightened the political tensions which would eventually lead to civil war? (A) The Wilmot Proviso, (B) The Webster-Hayne Debate, (C) The Nullification Crisis, (D) The Dred Scott Decision, or (E) OMG ALL OF THE ABOVE AMIRIGHT?!?

5a. Analyze the impact of tariff policies on sections of the United States before the Civil War.

5b. Which of the following best describes the impact of protectionist tariff policies on different sections of the U.S. in the years before the Civil War? (A) Neither the north nor the south favored tariffs – no one likes paying taxes, (B) The north favored high tariffs, but the south felt extremely violated and threatened to take extreme measures in response, (C) The north discouraged high tariffs, but the south benefitted from increased prices for cash crops they shipped overseas, or (D) Both sides accepted reasonable tariffs as part of the "American System" which benefitted all sections equally.

6. Select three major compromises reached by Congress in the first half of the

nineteenth century which arguably delayed the onset of civil war. Discuss the events leading to each and the terms of each compromise.

This one can be made into a multiple-choice question as well, but I doubt most educators would include Henry Clay's "slightly lower tariffs" bill pushed through thanks to the Nullification Crisis as one of the possible answers. It's a GREAT unexpected choice for a short essay, however – especially since it's not entirely clear how much it *actually helped*. In fact, I propose a toast:

"Historical gray areas – they must be preserved!"

"Acknowledged complexity – next to my grade, most dear!"

**The Congress which passed the "Tariff of Abominations" did not technically have a Whig majority, since the party didn't officially exist yet. It was made up of "Jacksonians" (the majority), "Anti-Jacksonians" (the minority), and a small but significant number of what we'd today call "third-party" members. Historically, however, we tend to simplify things and simply transition from the "First Party System" (Federalists vs. Democratic-Republicans) to the "Second Party System" (Whigs vs. Democrats).

CHAPTER NINE: THE FALLON TREATIES

The Webster-Ashburton Treaty (1842), the Clayton-Bulwer Treaty (1850), and the Gadsden Purchase (1854)

Three Big Things:

1. The Webster-Ashburton Treaty (1842) between the U.S. and Great Britain settled boundary disputes between New England and Canada as well as a handful of other "play nicely together" logistics. Larger issues like the slave trade and Oregon Territory were left for another time.

2. The Clayton-Bulwer Treaty (1850) between the U.S. and Great Britain primarily consisted of promises by both sides not to bulk up their presence in Central America and mutual assurances neither would build a canal through Central America without consulting the other first.

3. The Gadsden Purchase (1854) added strips of land along southern Arizona and New Mexico to territory already taken from Mexico by the Treaty of Guadalupe-Hidalgo (1848). It was primarily motivated by the needs of the transcontinental railroad.

The "Fallon Treaties"?

Several years ago, talk show host Jimmy Fallon did a wonderful bit with planted audience members in which they argued about which historical treaties were the coolest. The humor was built on the relative obscurity and banality of the treaties being discussed contrasted with the passion shown by the faux audience members. In other words, it was engaging because the subject matter was presumed to be so boring that no one could possibly care about it that much – and yet, they did.

Sound familiar?

The Fallon video has since practically become required viewing in any American History class dealing with the first half of the nineteenth century. (If you're not familiar with it, try searching "Fallon Gadsden Purchase" on YouTube. I'll wait.)

The sketch references the Treaty of Guadalupe-Hidalgo (1848) which ended the Mexican-American War and granted the U.S. a big chunk of land known as the "Mexican Cession." This one should be well-known to any student of history, in school or otherwise. The Louisiana Purchase is mentioned in passing as well, but it, too, is pretty hard for anyone to have missed. That leaves the three agreements covered below.

And yes, they're worth knowing – even beyond what's covered in the sketch.

Contextualization

There are so few truly engaging treaties in U.S. history. They sometimes end interesting wars, like the Treaty of Paris (1783) which granted the colonies independence. They may come about as the result of a memorable surrender, like the Confederacy at Appomattox Court House (1865), Japan on the deck of the *USS Missouri* (1945), or Cheap Trick on *Heaven Tonight* (1978). But the treaties themselves? Not so much.

Treaties created to *prevent* wars are even less exciting, and yet remain stubbornly present in state standards and APUSH course descriptions. It's like they don't even *want* history to be fun.

Boring or not, treaties are an essential element of foreign policy and by their very nature suggest that a nation is grown-up enough to solve at least *some* of its problems with words rather than violence. They require two parties to acknowledge one another as sufficiently legitimate for a signed agreement to be both appropriate and reliable. For a relatively young nation like the U.S. in the mid-nineteenth century, the fact that nations like Great Britain and Mexico would negotiate small print with them proved that – if nothing else – they were practically a real country.

Understanding treaties you're *required* to know sometimes starts by exploring a few things you're *not* – so buckle up and let's see if we can hit enough essentials that you can (a) remember these boring-but-somewhat-important treaties, and (b) throw in enough details when asked that you'll sound like you know (and care) way more than you actually do.

The Webster-Ashburton Treaty (U.S. & U.K., 1842)

You mean the 1842 treaty that resolved minor boundary disputes between the U.S. and Canada? Negotiated by U.S. Secretary of State Daniel Webster? I LOVE the Webster-Ashburton Treaty! (Late Night w/ Jimmy Fallon)

The *Caroline* Affair

In 1837-1838, several British colonies in Canada began pushing back against what they perceived as oppressive rule and inadequate representation in their own government. (Who knows where people get these wacky ideas?) The result was a small-scale revolution which the British promptly put down, although the Motherland did subsequently attempt to address a few of their complaints.

A handful of unsatisfied Canadian rebels ended up on a little island in the Niagara River along with a smattering of Americans who were either sympathetic to their cause or just couldn't resist the chance for a good scrap. Canadian soldiers (still loyal to the British Empire at that point) intercepted a U.S. ship named the *Caroline* which the islanders had hired to bring them supplies, killing one of the crew in the struggle. The captured ship was then sent over Niagara Falls.

Sadly, no one thought to post the video.

The *Caroline* Affair, as it became known, was certainly unpleasant for those involved, but it didn't become an international incident until a guy named Alexander McLeod showed up in New York claiming to have been the guy who killed the crewmember and bragging about his role in seizing the *Caroline*. Whatever his motivations, this was totally uncool. New York arrested him, but England intervened, claiming McLeod could not be punished by criminal law for something he'd done as a member of the British military – even if he was being a jerk about it *now*. The U.S. agreed but lacked the authority to force New York to release him. (Obviously state-federal dynamics have evolved a bit since then.)

New York tried McLeod and acquitted him, thus saving face for themselves without actually incarcerating or executing a British soldier. Despite this diplomatic (and possibly predetermined) outcome, emotions remained raw all 'round.

The Aroostook War (aka, "Battle of the Maps")

Around the same time, in an otherwise unrelated incident, another contingent of British troops almost came to blows with the state of Maine.

The Treaty of Paris (1783) which ended the American Revolution failed to clearly define boundaries between the new United States and what later became Canada. The U.S. and England quibbled about sections of this border off and on for several decades, until someone finally realized they'd been overlooking the most obvious solution in the world. They asked the King of the Netherlands to decide everything.

Yes, seriously.

He did, but the U.S. didn't like his answer, so they stomped their national little feet and refused to accept it. The conflicts continued.

In the meantime, New England settlers had begun drifting into the disputed region – as had Canadian lumberjacks coming from the other direction. At first, the two groups settled for scowling at one another across the greens, but by the late 1830s, things were escalating. Violence became a very real possibility.

Canadians began arresting New Englanders as "trespassers." New Englanders in turn arrested Canadian "intruders." In 1839, the British sent in troops from Quebec. The state of Maine responded by sending in 10,000 state militia volunteers (who'd apparently missed the bit in the Constitution about how states can't go to war with foreign powers all by themselves). This is what's known in the history biz as "escalation."

President Martin Van Buren, who you probably thought never did *anything* cool, ordered General Winfield Scott and 50,000 federal troops into the area to calm things down, which seems counterintuitive until you remember that they were the only ones in the mix without a personal stake in the outcome (one of the many benefits of a "professional" army). It also didn't hurt that they substantially outnumbered everyone else.

A truce was reached, and the two nations agreed to finally get serious about resolving their boundary problems. Sadly, they'd have to do so without the help of the King of the Netherlands this time.

The *Creole* Revolt

In 1841, the U.S. experienced arguably the most successful slave uprising in American history, which is probably why we don't talk about it that much. (We tend to prefer all the times white people quickly took back control and killed everyone involved.)

A ship called the *Creole* was transporting 134 slaves from Virginia to New Orleans (an entirely legal venture at the time since it didn't involve bringing in newly enslaved chattel from abroad). The slaves revolted and managed to steer the *Creole* to Nassau in the Bahamas, knowing it was under British rule and believing British law would require they be set free.

They were right.

This wasn't the first time the British had freed American slaves who for whatever reason ended up in their hands, but it was certainly the largest group emancipated all at once. Americans could hardly contain their outrage – do the British have NO respect for property rights or personal freedoms? Who DOES that to other people?!?

We Need To Talk

Ongoing tensions between the U.S. and Great Britain finally led to the Webster-Ashburton Treaty of 1842. It was negotiated by Secretary of State Daniel Webster (by this time serving under President John "Yes, I'm A 'Real President'" Tyler) and did, in fact, settle those pesky boundary disputes between Maine and Canada. It established criminal extradition between the two nations and granted the U.S. navigation rights on the St. John River, which runs through Maine into Canada before emptying into the Atlantic Ocean via the Bay of Fundy – a name so cool it simply *had* to be Canadian.

The treaty also included some lofty language about working together to suppress the slave trade, but other than informal assurances, the issues at the heart of the *Creole* conflict were left unresolved. A year after the treaty was signed, Great Britain agreed to compensate the "owners" of the freed slaves for their loss – a pragmatic move, no doubt, but one which kinda took the moral shine off the whole affair.

The two nations deferred discussions of similar boundary disputes further west (perhaps hoping the Grand Duchy of Finland or the Governor of New Zealand could somehow be persuaded to get involved). This decision would later provide James K. Polk with one of the most memorable campaign lines of the mid-nineteenth century. If *he* were elected president, he assured the nation, there'd be no compromising with the British in Oregon Territory – "Fifty-four forty or fight!" Never had a line of latitude been loaded with so much patriotism or testosterone.

It worked, by the way. Contrary to all appearances, Oregon is today part of the United States.

Finally, the nations agreed that the next time either one of them decided to send an entire ship over a waterfall, they'd absolutely make sure the video was posted on YouTube. (Presumably this language was accidentally omitted from the final draft.)

The Clayton-Bulwer Treaty (U.S. & U.K., 1850)

The Treaty of Guadalupe-Hidalgo is nothing more than a poor man's Clayton-Bulwer Treaty. (Late Night w/ Jimmy Fallon)

Oh Man, This Plan... A Canal?

The Monroe Doctrine announced by the U.S. in the 1820s had never quite overcome the young nation's hesitance to openly challenge British influence in Central and South America. They'd been there longer, and despite several embarrassing defeats at the hands of the U.S. and its allies, were still very much the big kid on the block for most of the nineteenth century.

The British had for years flirted with the idea of building a canal right through Central America to allow their massive navy easier access from the Atlantic to the Pacific. Over time, the U.S. started thinking maybe that wasn't such a bad idea – although they, of course, assumed American merchants and military vessels would be the primary beneficiaries. Neither side was ready to push ahead with such an ambitious project, but each began worrying that the other *would* – perhaps cutting them out in the process.

In the meantime, they at least agreed on the most appropriate location of such a venture. The geography, the political dynamics, even the catchy name once completed:

The "Nicaragua Canal."

Half of the envisioned canal was already present in the form of natural waterways. Nicaragua had spent the previous few decades being tossed back and forth like the ugly kid in a divorce – first it was part of Mexico, then it was a semi-independent member of a Central American "league" to periods of independence, all while technically remaining part of a British "protectorate" in that section of the globe. ("Oh, great – you left your good sneakers at Mexico's house AGAIN?!")

In any case, there's no record of anyone in the U.S. or Great Britain consulting Nicaragua as to their thoughts on the matter.

The Actual Treaty

The Clayton-Bulwer Treaty was signed in 1850 while President Zachary Taylor was in office and the Whigs were still a thing... barely. It focused primarily on what each side promised NOT to do:

* Neither the U.S. nor the U.K. would establish new colonies in Central America.

* Neither the U.S. nor the U.K. would build up, arm, or fortify any existing interests near the proposed canal.

* Neither the U.S. nor the U.K. would attempt to build the canal without the cooperation and consent of the other.

* If a canal were eventually built, neither the U.S. nor the U.K. would take steps to maintain exclusive control of the canal or territories bordering the canal. It would be made available to everyone on some sort of neutral basis.

The young Democratic Party declared the treaty to be a violation of the Monroe Doctrine, an accusation which didn't change much but gained enough traction to help speed the Whigs' journey into political irrelevance. The treaty held off British influence in Central America and continued to strengthen the relationship between the U.S. and its ex-Motherland. It held for half a century until replaced by the Hay-Pauncefote Treaty (1901), by which time Panama had become the favored site for this long-desired canal. Great Britain was by that point happy to let the U.S. do the building and administrating, knowing they'd have all the access they needed without the expense or headaches of running the thing themselves.

The Gadsden Purchase

Why haven't you done any jokes about the Gadsden Purchase? Signed in 1854 by President Franklin Pierce? Granted the U.S. sovereignty over the southern tips of Arizona and New Mexico? See, uh... the terrain in the southernmost portion of the Mexican Cession (1848) was, uh... too rocky for the Transcontinental Railroad, so...

Well, if you love this thing so much, why would you want me to make a joke about it?

You gotta be able to laugh at the Gadsden Purchase. I mean... it's what life's all about.

(Late Night w/ Jimmy Fallon)

A Lone Star Is Born

You probably remember the highlights of Texas Independence from Mexico – empresarios like Stephen Austin curating settlements of mostly white folks from the north who never quite believed they weren't in the U.S. anymore, larger than life figures like William Travis, Sam Houston, David Crockett, Juan Seguín, Jim Bowie, and of course General Antonio López de Santa Anna and his two healthy, attached legs. You may even remember details like the "Come And Take It" flag, someone scraping a runway in Houston (I'd have to look up the details), and a scuffle involving an old mission called the Alamo.

Somehow out of all that craziness, Texas won.

After a decade or so of doing quite well for themselves as an independent republic (something they still won't shut up about, honestly), Texas was annexed by the United States in 1845 and became the twenty-eighth state. If Mexico had begun getting over the events of the previous decade, seeing

Texas in the arms of another stirred up old passions and resentments, many of which were now directed at new beau Uncle Sam.

As with any messy breakup, there were lingering disputes. In this case, the biggest issue involved the southwestern border of Texas. Mexico claimed the ceded territory ended at the Nueces River, while Texas – and now the U.S. - placed it at the Rio Grande. This wasn't a difference of a few miles or a dispute over where to park the camper on Labor Day weekend. The maps envisioned by Mexico and the U.S. differed by over half-a-million square miles, including most of what today is New Mexico and a significant chunk of Colorado as well.

The Mexican-American War (1846 – 1848)

President Polk sent Zachary Taylor into the disputed area to provoke Mexican troops repeatedly until someone finally fired back or hit them with a stick or something. At that point, Polk ran to Congress yelling that Mexico had "invaded" American territory and attacked U.S. forces for *no reason*! Here we were, trying to peacefully resolve things through diplomacy, but those darned Mexicans and their violent natures, etc.

The resulting war commenced in April of 1846 and lasted until the Treaty of Guadalupe-Hidalgo in February of 1848. The U.S. received the disputed territory (the "Mexican Cession") but agreed to pay Mexico several million dollars in return. The "Wilmot Proviso" was introduced in Congress, seeking to ban slavery in any territory acquired from Mexico. It didn't pass, but the resulting debates certainly helped speed the nation towards civil war.

Then again, you probably know all of this already. It's juicy stuff, even if it's not all particularly flattering to our forebears. Then came the dull bits...

What Life's All About

Boundary disputes lingered even after Guadalupe-Hidalgo was signed. There were other issues as well, but none merited renewed hostilities. What finally reopened negotiations between the U.S. and Mexico wasn't the specter of war, but Uncle Sam's commitment to trains and westward expansion.

The Whig dream of connecting the various regions of the nation hadn't faded, and visionaries of all political stripes coveted an infrastructure to support the nation's rapid expansion. As the Fallon sketch points out, however, the topography of southern plains suggested that the best route for laying railroad tracks dipped ever-so-slightly into Mexican territory – and that wouldn't go over well. President Pierce sent James Gadsden to Mexico to negotiate with whoever happened to be in charge that week.

Between the Texas Revolution and the Gadsden Purchase, leadership of Mexico changed hands approximately 873 times. About a third of these resulted in Uncle Sam's old friend Antonio López de Santa Anna running things for a season or two at a time, and that's who happened to be in the big chair when Gadsden arrived. Gadsden's timing was ideal; Santa Anna was distracted trying to squash internal rebellions (something of a theme for Mexico in those days) and in need of quick cash. Gadsden was authorized to offer him just that in exchange for what seemed a few negligible swaths of land way up north.

The treaty was signed and one more little chunk of glory was added to the United States. Several other minor issues between the two nations were addressed as well, but none quite as almost-interesting as the Gadsden Purchase.

Why The Fallon Treaties Matter

As previously mentioned, treaties are one indication that a nation is either all grown up or well on its way. As any middle school educator can tell you, the ability to resolve our differences using words is something that comes only with maturity and a sprinkling of hard-won wisdom.

After the War of 1812, the U.S. never again took up arms against Great Britain, whatever their disagreements. Some of this was simply pragmatic; the English still had one of the most powerful militaries in the world and there was no sense messing with them if it could be avoided. Plus, they'd become excellent trading partners. Just as importantly, however, the U.S. and Britain *understood* one another – and not just because they shared a common language. Culturally, religiously, economically, and politically, they were far more similar than different. Even when they argued, they wanted the same basic things and approached disputes in similar ways.

Not so the U.S. and Mexico (or any other Latin American country). Neither ever quite understood the other. The U.S. looked down on what appeared to be a backward people and their chaotic government, while Mexico had little use for smug Americans and their manifestly violent destinies. They could negotiate, perhaps even settle – but they could never truly come to peace with one another.

The tendency of the U.S. to get what it wanted from other nations by dangling bags of cash in front of them would continue (and still does today). It may not be particularly glorious or noble, but it's often more economically practical and morally defensible than going to war, whatever the cause.

The Webster-Ashburton Treaty was an important step in establishing a preference on both sides for negotiation over calls to arms whenever the U.S. and Great Britain were at odds. The Clayton-Bulwer Treaty eventually led to the Panama Canal (although there were several steps in between). The canal, in turn, was important for most of the twentieth century – from Teddy Roosevelt's first cartoon shovel all the way through President Carter's "giveaway" in the 1970s. And the Gadsden Purchase really did make it easier to run those railroad lines all the way across the continent, despite the project being delayed by a civil war before it could be completed.

Making The Grade: What You're Most Likely To Be Asked

Webster-Ashburton and Clayton-Bulwer are, sadly, more likely to show up as detractors ("wrong answers") for multiple-choice questions than as correct responses:

Which of the following attempted to prevent the expansion of slavery into territory acquired from Mexico? (A) The Webster-Ashburton Treaty, (B) The Clayton-Bulwer Treaty, (C) The Wilmot Proviso, or (D) The Ostend Manifesto.

Remember that both Webster-Ashburton and Clayton-Bulwer signed during the same general time period (1840-1850) and both were between the U.S. and Great Britain. While you may not be asked about these first two treaties by name, they're excellent details for short answer or essay responses related to foreign policy or political parties in the mid-nineteenth century. If you're really lucky, you'll be asked about accomplishments of the short-lived Whig Party. Obviously, you'll focus on stuff related to the American System (infrastructure, a strong centralized economy, etc.), but both Webster-Ashburton and Clayton-Bulwer were negotiated under Whig Presidents, so there! Look at you go, tiger.

Gadsden will come up slightly more often since it involved westward expansion and Texas (er... sort of). It's the only one of the three likely to manifest itself as part of a map question – "Identify the following territories" or "label these territories and the date each was added to the U.S." (Such maps will tend to show the Louisiana Purchase, the Mexican Cession, Oregon Country, etc., as well as the Gadsden Purchase.) Gadsden is right up there with "Fifty-four forty or fight!" in terms of being nearly name-brand history and only partially boring. It's essential to remember that it was largely motivated by the needs of the transcontinental railroad. You can rarely go wrong connecting details back to westward expansion or technological progress.

Now, go back and watch the video again. The faux obsessions of the various characters don't seem quite so out there anymore, do they?

OK, maybe still a little.

CHAPTER TEN: WHILE YOU WERE BUSY WITH THE CIVIL WAR...

Tariffs, Land Grants, and Transcontinental Choo-Choos

Three Big Things:

1. Tariffs have been the source of all sorts of difficulty throughout American history, partly because they impact different regions in such disparate ways and partly because it's impossible to separate their role as a revenue-generators from their ability to promote (or hurt) specific American industries. The Morrill Tariff of 1861 was a clumsy move by Lincoln and Congressional Republicans which alienated England at a critical time.

2. Federal involvement in education has been going on since at least 1862, when the Morrill Land Grant Act pushed states to incorporate agricultural training and the "mechanical arts" into existing college curriculums – or build new schools which would.

3. The Homestead Act (1862) and the Pacific Railway Act (1862) were efforts by the federal government to promote westward expansion by both companies and individuals. Both support the premise that one of government's primary functions is to "promote the general welfare" – even of the "little people."

Introduction

There are few events in American History which capture the imagination like the glories and horrors of the Civil War. The suffering, the sacrifice, the strategies, the stories within stories – it's still one of the most mythologized and misunderstood undertakings in all of American history. It especially fascinates those of us who've never taken part in such a thing, whether we're perversely drawn to it, repelled by it, or some combination of both.

Land grants and fiscal legislation, on the other hand, lack the same punch. They rarely produce the sorts of immortal rhetoric we've come to expect from wartime:

> *It is well that protective tariffs are so terrible, otherwise we should grow too fond of them.* (Not Robert E. Lee)

> *The object of homesteading is not to die for your plot of land but to make the bastard who was there before you die for theirs.* (Not George S. Patton)

> *I am tired of paper money. Our bills are paper. Our receipts are paper. Our checkbooks are paper. My ledger is all filled with paper. Hear me, my accountants – I am tired. My wallet is empty. From where the Department of the Treasury now stands, I will print no more forever.* (Not Chief Joseph)

Nevertheless, the legislation and maneuvering of Congress and the president during wartime – even in matters not directly related to killing people and breaking things – sometimes matter very much. In the case of the Civil War, legislation passed while the south was fighting for the freedom to deny others *their* freedom was unfettered by southern input or resistance. The values and priorities of a young Republican Party (and northern interests in general) could now be unleashed on a distracted nation.

These original Republicans believed one of the primary purposes of a constitutional government was to create conditions in which even the humblest citizens had every opportunity to succeed. That meant reliable infrastructure, support for education, and a realistic shot at land ownership and self-sufficiency.

Wartime Measures

Many of the steps taken by President Lincoln and his Republican Congress which *were* directly war-related would reverberate long after hostilities had ceased (or at least became less fatal). The first "national income tax" was passed several months after the war began and lasted until well into Reconstruction. The agency we'd later know as the Internal Revenue Service was created a year later to manage "indirect" taxation of individual incomes. The progressive tax rates and "sin taxes" we associate with the early twentieth century were also birthed during the war, a half-century before the Sixteenth Amendment made any of it undeniably constitutional.

(It wasn't long before the Confederacy instituted similar income taxes of its own, although it had even more trouble collecting than Union officials did.)

Another wartime measure with lasting consequences was the introduction of paper money issued by the national government. The history of scrip in the U.S. is a convoluted one, but in general paper money had been the purview of local banks or other large institutions. (States were constitutionally prohibited from issuing their own currency in *any* form.) Federal currency, when it existed, was in the form of specie – coins minted from actual gold or silver. Since there's only so much gold and silver laying around (which is, of course, part of what makes it so valuable), this was rather limiting in terms of total funds available.

But war is expensive, and Lincoln needed cash. Real financial institutions demanded outrageous interest rates when Uncle Sam asked for a loan (American businesses have always been naturally patriotic that way), so the president and Congress began producing something they called "Demand Notes" which could theoretically be taken to one of the handful of approved banks across the country and exchanged for specie.

Demand Notes were soon replaced by "Legal Tender" which wasn't nearly as easy to exchange for specie but still wasn't technically "money." Somewhere along the way, the distinctive green ink used in printing these various not-quite-currencies led to the nickname "Greenbacks," which stuck around even as the paper itself evolved. It wasn't long before Republicans dropped any pretense that Greenbacks were tied to anything more than one's trust in the long-term viability of the Union. There simply wasn't enough gold or silver on the planet to back up the amounts they were printing to finance this war.

(And yes, the rebelling south – which fundamentally opposed this sort of government overreach – resorted to very similar methods itself. Necessity does terrible things to even our loftiest ideals, it seems.)

While The South's Away...

Often overlooked, however, are the things Congress and President Lincoln did which were NOT directly related to their wartime endeavors. We're going to look at four-and-a-half of them. None established entirely new goals, but each redefined how those goals would be pursued. Each would impact how the government operated not only during the war, but for generations after.

I know, sounds kinda dramatic, doesn't it? Don't worry, it's not. These are all *quite* boring – I promise.

#4.5 – The Department of Agriculture (USDA)

Despite the popular vision of farmers, ranchers, homesteaders, and whatnot, as rugged individualists who neither required nor accepted government help, elected officials have often promoted and assisted the agricultural arts in America.

There's the obvious stuff – Indian Removal (to make room for white settlement and white farming), war with Mexico (again, more land for farming), the postbellum Indian Wars (protecting homesteaders on the Great Plains), the transcontinental railroad, and eventually the bulk of the Populist agenda – including government regulation of those same railroads and anything else related to the success of small farmers scattered across the nation (grain elevators, communication networks, etc.).

But it wasn't always about killing Amerindians and regulating infrastructure. Federal officials had been actively pursuing newer and better varieties of livestock and seeds since at least the turn of the century. In 1839, Congress added an agricultural division to the U.S. Patent Office (yes, you read that correctly) to gather agricultural statistics and promote "modern" growing methods as opportunities presented themselves. A decade later, the Patent Office was placed under the umbrella of the newly created Department of the Interior.

In 1862, President Lincoln made the Department of Agriculture an independent agency (although it would be 1889 before it was granted a seat on the Cabinet). The department's first commissioner was famed agriculturalist Isaac Newton. (No, not THAT Isaac Newton – but this guy was a fairly well-known figure in his day as well. Plus, he hadn't died 150 years earlier.)

Why does this matter? Because it's one more indication that the success of farms and farming across the United States was a high priority to the federal government. It's a nice symbolic reminder that Washington, D.C., was ready and willing to invest in research, education, and the sharing of agricultural information with any interested citizen and that doing so wasn't part of some post-New Deal socialist overthrow. It was simply part of "promot[ing] the general Welfare" – one of a constitutionally-established government's primary functions.

#4 – The Morrill Tariff (1861)

Tariff policies are arguably the most tedious of all American history essentials. If they're not the single *least* interesting element of any curriculum, they're right down there with labor unions and understanding the federal court system. And yet, it's difficult to find a decade prior to the twentieth century in which tariffs weren't front and center in the national conversation for some reason or another.

They involve money, of course – often substantial amounts of money. Tariffs also serve a dual purpose of raising revenue and protecting select American businesses. Until 1846, tariffs were assigned to specific products rather than as a simple percentage applying to all imported goods. That meant that Congress could (and did) quite literally choose winners and losers every time they tweaked the rules. Finally, tariffs impacted the various regions of the U.S. quite differently. As other nations adjusted their own policies in response to U.S. tariffs, exports of manufactured goods or cash crops were dramatically impacted – and rarely equally.

In short, tariffs were kind of a big deal. They still are, if you ask Canada, China, Mexico, the European Union, or anyone else still trading with the U.S.

Taxes Are Tarrrrr-ific!

Complaints over tariff policies go back to colonial times. While many of the taxes so offensive to colonists were technically "duties" or other variations, the basic sense of outrage and unfairness was the same. These debates resumed after independence, starting with Alexander Hamilton's conviction that some sort of protective tariff was necessary to protect American's "infant industries." Protective tariffs were foundational element of Henry Clay's "American System" in the 1820s and 1830s. This, in turn, led to the infamous "Tariff of Abominations" in 1828 and eventually sparked the Nullification Crisis of 1832-1833.

After President Jackson threatened to send in troops to enforce federal law, South Carolina backed down, temporarily ending (or at least pausing) the crisis. By way of a consolation prize, Congress agreed to a new schedule of gradually descending tariff rates via the Compromise of 1833. A few years later, however, the Panic of 1837 hit. Conventional wisdom blames Jackson's fiscal policies – moving funds out of the National Bank and into his infamous "pet banks," pushing through the Specie Circular, etc. Unfortunately for Martin Van Buren, the worst of the fallout occurred during his term and the public thus largely held him responsible.

The effects of the recession were still lingering in 1841 when John Tyler assumed the presidency upon the death of William Henry Harrison (who died after only a month in office). Not wanting to end up like Van Buren, and having enough other problems of his own to deal with, Tyler took a more aggressive approach and cancelled the remaining reductions in tariff rates scheduled by the Compromise of 1833. He pushed for a return to the rates of the early 1830s which had led to the Nullification Crisis to begin with. This "Black Tariff" predictably stirred up the south yet again and nearly led to Tyler's impeachment by his own Whig party.

Next came President Polk and his Democratic majority in Congress. They kept the pendulum swinging with yet another set of tariff reforms in 1846 – the "Walker Tariff". In addition to rate reductions, Polk's reforms took the sensible step of tying tariff rates to the *value* of the goods being imported rather than assigning various duties to *specific goods*. This reduced the "picking-and-choosing" that occurred every time Congress decided to tweak tax policy. Tariffs were still not universally popular, but at least they were arguably much more "fair."

Tariff rates were decreased again a decade later, but then the Panic of 1857 hit and folks got skittish as federal revenue plummeted once more.

The Morrill the Merrier

As tensions over slavery amped up, many feared civil war was becoming inevitable. Still, the economy was the economy, so Congress began working on legislation to once again increase tariffs.

The central figure in this effort was Representative Justin Morrill of Vermont. Nothing he proposed, however, overcame southern objections to the increases. He tried several different approaches and modified the logistics of the bill repeatedly without success. Then, in December of 1860, South Carolina declared they were seceding from the Union – thus eliminating their delegations in both houses of Congress. They were joined in January by Mississippi, Florida, Alabama, Georgia, and Louisiana; come February, Texas was gone as well.

While it was a shame about them leaving and all, it certainly did free up the majority party to live their best lives. The Morrill Tariff was passed and signed into law by President James Buchanan in early March of 1861.

The South hated the tariff, but they'd just left the Union. Their opinion no longer mattered. Of far greater concern was the reaction of Great Britain. Given their extensive trade with the U.S., many took it as something of a personal affront. However happy Republicans were to have pushed through their protectionist tariff, they'd managed to alienate one of their most powerful allies before shots were even fired. For the first two years of the Civil War, the Confederacy wooed England, hoping for logistical support against a better-equipped foe. Not until Lincoln issued the Emancipation Proclamation in late 1862 (confirming to the rest of the world that the war was, in fact, primarily about *slavery*) was it certain that England would stand by the North.

It was from the British press that the idea first developed that southern secession had, in fact, occurred primarily *because* of the Morrill Tariff. Not only is this incorrect, it would have been impossible in any universe bound by linear time. The tariff didn't pass until *after secession began*. It literally *couldn't* pass until southern delegates had left D.C. That hasn't stopped proponents of the so-called "Lost Cause" mythology from busting it out every time someone suggests the South was primarily motivated by their desire to protect slavery.

It would be World War I before trade would once again become as relatively free as it had been under the Walker Tariffs (1846 – 1861). And in case you're wondering, changing tariff rates didn't start *that* war, either.

#3 – The Morrill Land Grant Act (1862)

As far back as 1787, when the U.S. was still operating under the Articles of Confederation, the federal government (such as it was) had looked for ways to promote education. The Northwest Ordinance of 1787, which established guidelines for managing territories to the west of the original thirteen states, famously included this proclamation:

> *Religion, Morality and knowledge being necessary to good government and the happiness of mankind, Schools and the means of education shall forever be encouraged.*

Granted, this didn't exactly implement a national curriculum or fund any scholarships, but it was a bold statement given the very limited role expected of government at the time.

Nearly a century later, most formal education still focused on the liberal arts. Students recited in Greek and Latin and primarily studied rhetoric, history, and law or religion. A handful of schools had recently begun including science or engineering, but very few professions required a degree, so college was largely optional for most. By the 1850s, however, some hoped to steer higher education towards something more practical. Much of the U.S. was still largely agricultural, and despite our romanticized membrances, successfully working the land often required more than a cheap plow, a plucky attitude, and melodramatically wiping your brow from time to time.

In 1855, Michigan became the first state to establish its own agricultural college (today it's Michigan State University). Other states took note and began pressuring Congress to encourage similar endeavors pretty much *everywhere*. More productive farming and animal husbandry would be good for the entire nation, and while the Whigs were no longer a major political party, their ideal of a self-sufficient nation connected by reliable infrastructure hadn't exactly vanished. Besides, this was still the Age of Jackson; the "common man" was annoyingly vocal at all levels of government. If Americans wanted something more than lessons in reciting Latin from their educational institutions, their elected representatives in Washington, D.C., would look for ways to make that happen.

Fortasse Aliquid Utilius

Representative Justin Smith Morrill (whose name should sound oddly familiar) of Vermont began pushing a bill in Congress modeled after Michigan's efforts. The Morrill Act provided federal land grants to each state to be utilized in pursuit of colleges devoted to agriculture and "the mechanical arts" - hence the "A&M" still lingering in the names of a number of these institutions even today. The amount of land was based on the total number of representatives and senators each state had in Congress, indirectly tying it to population. Besides being practical (more people meant the need for more or bigger schools), this was politically pragmatic as well. While Morrill's bill was largely intended to benefit new states as the nation expanded west, this provision provided impetus for established states in the east to cooperate. After all, it benefited them even more than it did those unwashed newbies out west, right?

Land grant schools didn't have to be built on the provided land. States could sell their grants to finance the establishment of a new college focused on agriculture and the mechanical arts (think "vocational training," but fancier) or fund the expansion of an existing institution to include the relevant departments. If the federal government didn't own sufficient land in a particular state, it would grant them land in a neighboring state and let the two of them work it out.

When the Morrill Act was first presented to Congress, many southern states opposed it. The only thing worse than a bunch of ambitious, college-educated farmers competing with established southern growers in the seemingly unlimited lands to the west was the idea that their own government would use public resources to make it happen. When a version of the bill finally did make it through both houses, it was vetoed by President James Buchanan (a Democrat) in 1859.

By 1862, however, things had changed. Abraham Lincoln (a fellow Republican) was in the White House. The southern states had seceded (or attempted to secede, if you prefer), meaning they no longer had representation in the U.S. Congress. Representative Morrill reintroduced his bill, this time with a new provision adding military training to agriculture and the mechanical arts as a required element of these new schools. The Union had been woefully unprepared for war, at least in terms of training and leadership, and the war was *not* going well, so this last bit brought on board many who may not have been otherwise excited about agriculture other practicalities.

A follow-up to the Morrill Land Grant Act was passed in 1890. It required land-grant colleges to either prohibit racial discrimination in admission policies or to establish separate facilities and programs for people of color. This laid the groundwork for many of the schools we today think of as "Historically Black Colleges and Universities" (HBCUs).

#2 – The Homestead Act (1862)

Prior to the Civil War, government land sales were primarily intended to generate revenue. The system evolved from time to time, but generally the folks looking to leave everything behind and start a new life out west weren't the same folks who could afford to buy the land and necessary provisions to make it happen. There were certainly some hardy souls who boldly headed towards the frontier and figured it out as they went, but most of them died or found themselves repeatedly chased out of places and called hurtful names. One way or the other, moving was expensive – just like today.

Westward expansion, for all its struggles and glories, was rarely as individualistic or exciting as we often make it sound. It required planning, resources, and – more often than not – paperwork. Ideally, you'd travel in good-sized groups for safety and mutual support. Even then, you'd probably die – but at least your odds were substantially improved. And only rarely did the rest of your party decide they had to eat your corpse to survive.

So that was a plus.

Of course, life in the northeast wasn't always glorious, either. As cities grew more crowded, laboring for others became more brutal, and conditions became increasingly unbearable, many northerners began petitioning their government for easier egress from their grievances. And they weren't the only ones.

While true "bonanza farms" wouldn't be a thing until the late nineteenth century, there were enough large, wealthy plantations across the south by mid-century to eliminate smaller competitors. These displaced farmers needed a fresh start, preferably somewhere further away – like, say... out west. But fresh starts required affordable land, and plantation owners (who largely controlled the politics of the south) didn't want to make things any easier for their future competition. They also worried that the small or medium scale farming likely to be practiced in the west would discourage the expansion of slavery, and the last thing they needed were more "free" states sending delegates to Congress.

Southern leaders had an unlikely ally in this opposition. Northern factory owners opposed anything that made westward expansion easier as well. Part of what allowed them to keep wages so low and conditions so awful was the gross surplus of workers (especially immigrants) with no other options. If the laboring classes started believing they could start a new life for themselves out west, the dynamic would quickly change – and what fun would *that* be?

By the end of the Mexican-American War (1846-1848), momentum was shifting in favor or potential homesteaders. Continued immigration meant huge numbers of highly motivated individuals and families anxious to try their hand at self-sufficiency. The Whig passion for infrastructure meant more options for moving people, crops, or other goods around the country. Great Britain repealed its "corn laws" in 1846 (largely in response to the onset of the Irish Potato Famine), dramatically increasing export opportunities. It made more sense than ever to let as many people as possible farm their little hearts out – *wherever* they were able to make stuff grow.

The House of Representatives (whose membership was based on population, giving the north an advantage) passed several homesteading bills which would have made migration easier for those in need of a new start. Each time, they were stymied by the Senate (in which every state had two votes, giving the south a sort of 'veto' power). If you've read this far, however, you know what happened next.

The south left. Just as with the Morrill Tarriff and the Morrill Land Grant Act, their departure allowed the remaining legislators to push through the bill they'd been trying to pass for years. Thus, the Homestead Act of 1862.

Three Easy Steps

Nothing could make actual homesteading "easy," but the Homestead Act did what it could.

Any U.S. citizen (or resident on their way to becoming a citizen) could pay a small fee and do minimal paperwork to receive 160 acres of government land in the west. They were expected to live on and "improve" the land for at least five years, after which they became its legal owners.

The system was designed to encourage *settlement* while discouraging *speculation*. The goal was to put families on farms, not to allow wealthy investors or organizations to buy up huge tracts of land to sell at a profit later. While many found ways to game the system, the intent is what's important to remember. The federal government of the United States (which at the time was controlled almost entirely by the young Republican Party) believed it was perfectly appropriate to encourage and facilitate homesteading for the "little people" in the name of overall national prosperity.

The frontier itself could be brutal, but that's a whole other story and *not at all* boring to discuss. "Soddies," frozen cows, swarms of locusts, Sears catalogues, and eating radishes three meals a day, every day... that stuff is *fascinating* – and thus of no interest to us here.

Sorry, but you saw the title before you bought the book.

#1 – The Pacific Railway Act (1862)

In many ways, the Pacific Railway Act made a nice companion piece of legislation for the Homestead Act passed six months earlier. The act created two distinct companies – the Union Pacific and the Central Pacific. Their job was to connect the east with the west by laying tracks across the Great Plains. The Central Pacific would start from Sacramento, California (which had become an "American" city thanks to the Gold Rush) and build east. The Union Pacific would begin around Omaha, Nebraska, and build west. Eventually, they'd meet somewhere in the middle.

It took a bit longer than expected, thanks to the interruption of the Civil War, but eventually the tracks were completed and joined in Promontory, Utah, on May 10th, 1869.

The issues surrounding the Pacific Railway Act should be familiar ground by now. Should government be involved in "internal improvements" like transportation? How much should be left up to free markets or private enterprise, and when should the government step in and direct events from on high? Does every region benefit equally, or just the north (as usual)?

It's also worth noting that once again, the myth of private enterprise overcoming every challenge and meeting every need was thoroughly dispelled by the facts on the ground. Business played a hugely important role in the nation's progress, before, during, and after the nineteenth century. Individuals took huge risks and worked themselves to death (sometimes literally) to civilize the frontier and earn their role as landowners. Innovation, perseverance, and other thoroughly "human" characteristics are and always have been essential to whatever good America has accomplished over the centuries. But it's rarely been done entirely removed from the regulation, support, or other involvement of government – even at the federal level. As is so often the case with real history, we can speak in glittering generalities and push our preferred political platitudes all we like, but reality usually manages to be far more complicated.

No wonder it's ignored so often.

Making The Grade: What You're Most Likely To Be Asked

You're not going to be asked specifically about the USDA unless your teacher is particularly weird (and draws attention to it in class as well). It's far more likely you'll be expected to recognize or identify the Morrill Tariff and the Morrill Land Grant Act, at least in general terms. You'll probably get at least one or two questions related to the Pacific Railway Act or government support for railroads in general. Usually they'll be tied to westward expansion after the war.

1. States which sold the lands granted to them under the Morrill Land Grant Act (1862) were required to do what with the profits? (A) <u>Promote education in agriculture and the mechanical arts.</u> (B) Construct factories which supported the war effort. (C) Support homesteading efforts within their state. (D) Swear an oath of allegiance to the Union.

2. Which of the following was a major factor in the expansion of railroads across the U.S. after the Civil War? (A) Congress excluded railroads from antitrust legislation. (B) The stock of several major railroad companies was made public. (C) <u>The federal government provided vast amounts of free land to railroad companies in exchange for laying tracks.</u> (D) As railroads lowered their rates and improved customer service, more and more people took advantage of travel by train.

3. How did the growth of railroads in the postbellum nineteenth century MOST benefit farmers? (A) Railroad access raised the prices of cash crops both at home and abroad. (B) Trains brought in more settlers who in turn began working for bonanza farms. (C) Railroads had to feed large crews of workers

laying tracks or building stations. (D) <u>Trains gave farmers more affordable access to distant markets</u>.

You may see that last question with "ranchers" instead of "farmers." Either way, the answer is the same.

You'll absolutely see at least one question about the Homestead Act (1862). Most of the time it will be about the primary goal of the legislation or its three key provisions:

4. Which of the following was NOT one of the requirements of the Homestead Act? (A) Applicants had to be citizens or on their way to becoming citizens, (B) Applicants had to pay a small fee to cover the paperwork, (C) Applicants had to live on and "improve" the land for at least five years, or (D) <u>Applicants had to offer valid reasons why they wished to move west.</u>

5. Passage of the Homestead Act in 1862 encouraged settlement of the Great Plains by...? (A) <u>providing nearly-free land to farmers</u>, (B) removing barriers to Asian immigration, (C) supplying land to railroad companies in exchange for laying tracks westward, or (D) providing low-cost building supplies and starter seeds for farming.

6. Which of the following was a primary cause of increased settlement of the Great Plains after the Civil War? (A) Many of the Plains Tribes voluntarily moved further west to avoid further conflict. (B) The Specie Circular allowed speculators to buy up land cheaply and resell it later. (C) <u>Congress passed a law making it easy to claim public land and own it in a short time period by homesteading it</u>. (D) Freedman enjoyed greater rights and had more opportunities in the west.

When confronting short answer or essay prompts from this brief time period, you have an amazing opportunity to sound thoughtful and committed to historical excellence (whether you feel it or not). You can easily reference one or more of the 4.5 items covered above anytime you're asked about...

* Foreign policy during the Civil War, particularly in terms of perceived British support for one side or the other.

* The role of economic policies in heightening sectional tensions (or anything asking you to compare and contrast northern and southern interests or viewpoints).

* Factors promoting westward expansion (including the entire second half of the nineteenth century).

* The relationship between government and business (the railroads, in this case) or between businesses and the growth of cities or the expansion of white settlement.

* The expansion of higher education across the U.S.

If you're in APUSH or other advanced course, and have a particularly feisty instructor, you may encounter creative variations which seem rather intimidating until you break them down...

7. Discuss the factors which led to the development of better agricultural equipment and a focus on labor-saving technology in the late nineteenth century. (Smaller farms in the west didn't use slave labor, so there was new incentive to innovate. Agricultural and mechanical colleges promoted the idea that science and farming weren't mutually exclusive, both educating a new generation and changing mindsets about agriculture. Improved infrastructure and technology made it easier to share ideas and innovations over larger distances. You get the idea.)

8. What issues not directly related to slavery motivated the secession of the South? (Yeah, I don't love it either, but it comes up from time to time and is – in and of itself – a valid question.)

You can never go wrong referencing the economic tensions between the north and the south as a factor in bringing about the Civil War. Bring up the American System, Compact Theory, even strict vs. loose constructionism if you're up for it. The south *was* repeatedly subjected to financial policies which certainly seemed designed to favor the industries and economic interests of the north. They had representation, but not enough (it seemed) to ever quite turn the tide back. Their rallying cry could just as easily have been "no indirect taxation without better representation!"

In other words, yes – there were numerous factors leading to secession and civil war. As we've noted several times, history is complicated.

It's worth remembering, however, that when offering their own arguments as to why they were leaving the Union, southern states focused heavily on one issue alone. South Carolina's declaration of secession mentions "slaves" and "slavery" over a dozen times, and tariffs zero times. Georgia's references "slaves" and "slavery" nearly three dozen times; taxes and tariffs, nada. Mississippi's was shorter – it only mentions "slaves" and "slavery" seven times; taxes and tariffs, still zero. Texas referenced "slaves" and "slavery" around twenty times and tariffs – let's see... if we total that column and carry the three... zero. It mentions it *zero* times. The south may have been upset about economic policies and genuinely believed in states' rights, but they started the Civil War to protect slavery.

But that's getting off track a bit and into something genuinely *interesting*. We should move on.

CHAPTER ELEVEN: THE CRÉDIT MOBILIER SCANDAL

I Think I Scam... I Think I Scam... I Think I Scam...

Three Big Things:

1. After the Civil War, American businesses became increasingly large, wealthy, and complicated. With this growth came increased influence over all levels of government.

2. The Union Pacific was one of two railroads chartered by Congress specifically to complete a transcontinental railroad connecting east to west. They eventually completed the task, but along the way, Union Pacific management bilked taxpayers and investors for millions and millions of dollars (with the help of their allies in Congress and the Executive Branch).

3. Crédit Mobilier was only the first of numerous scandals during and after the Grant administration. Collectively, they left the general public feeling frustrated and helpless in the face of corrupt power. A general distrust of both big business and government lingered for decades afterward.

Prequel: The Phonic Menace

Crédit Mobilier might be the single most frustrating item still featured in every American History curriculum in the universe. It taunts us with its familiarity (we see it repeatedly) combined with its elusiveness (we can never quite remember whether or not we know what it is). As if that weren't enough, it feels like you're saying it wrong no matter how you pronounce it.

We feel foolish twice over, even if we're not. Stupid history.

Let's start with the pronunciation issue, then we'll see what we can do about the rest. First, ignore the accent mark over the 'e'. The term is entirely Americanized; crédit = credit, as in union, card, or give-me-a-little. Mobilier is pronounced as if with an exaggerated southern twang. "We'z headin' to Mo-BEEL, Alabammy." Then just add "yer." "CRED-it mo-BEEL-yer." Or, if you insist on trying to make it fancy, "CRED-it mo-BEEL-yay" works as well.

Honestly, if you simply say it with confidence, most folks will never know the difference. The important thing is to push through it so we can move on, yes?

Context and Background

Between the Civil War and the onset of the twentieth century, there were essentially three big themes driving most of American history:

1) The evolving rights of freedmen – America's former slaves. Was the United States finally going to live up to its whole "all men are... endowed by their Creator with certain unalienable rights" thing or not? (Spoiler Alert: we're still

working on that one.)

2) Westward expansion – homesteading, the postbellum "Indian Wars," the Transcontinental Railroad, and (my personal favorite) the development of barbed wire as the most revolutionary technology of the era.

3) The expansion and evolution of big business – the Second Industrial Revolution, "captains of industry" vs. "robber barons," the onset of the Gilded Age, and so forth.

Lost in the discussion of colorful characters like Andrew Carnegie, John D. Rockefeller, and Cornelius Vanderbilt is the fact that the very nature of big business and corporate structures and economic mechanisms catering to the interests of the rich and powerful were being dramatically re-imagined and reshaped throughout the latter half of the nineteenth century and well into the twentieth.

It wasn't all dishonest. Most of it wasn't even *illegal* – at least not yet. But creations like "holding companies" (designed to protect rich people from the consequences of exploitative business practices) and "trusts" (one of the most important means of ensuring that rich people's kids never have to mature, learn responsibility, or do anything useful) which are first-year business school stuff today were brand new back then. America's elite were giddy as they cranked up the nation's income inequality, all the while congratulating one another on their service to the greater good.

It's possible I'm not accurately reflecting the positives here. I'm sure there were some.

You've no doubt encountered ideas like vertical integration, horizontal integration, and Frederick Winslow Taylor's "scientific management" approach to labor. It was during this same era that businesses (starting with the railroads) began thinking of their internal structure in terms of "departments." Rather than a simple pyramid of authority, it became common to have managers in charge of different sorts of tasks. One might run scheduling while another was in charge of maintenance and equipment and a third handled personnel and training, for example. This allowed a new type of "specialization" while still requiring internal coordination – a manager over the managers, as it were.

Corporate structures and financing were undergoing similar innovation and experimentation. Many of the procedures and mechanisms created in the late eighteenth century are still utilized today. Others were eventually outlawed, once Congress (or their constituents) understood how they worked. The primary reason we don't often discuss the legal and financial technicalities in class or on social media is obvious – most of us can't make heads or tails of them. If we did, we'd be *exploiting* the ignorant masses for personal gain ourselves instead of working so hard to make them slightly-less-ignorant.

In short, the late nineteenth century was at time in which economic policies and the legalities of big business were being hotly debated, both in terms of specifics and the larger question of whether the government should be regulating business or the economy to begin with. The industrial workforce expanded and became more diverse as a result of both domestic and international migration. Workers and management argued about wages and conditions and the first labor unions began popping up here and there, unsure of their actual power or potential. While many promoted a "New South" with a diversified economy – particularly in terms of increased manufacturing – the lower states remained largely agricultural, with sharecropping and tenant farming replacing slavery so neatly it was at times difficult to tell the difference.

It Is Not From Benevolence...

Capitalism at its most basic is founded on a simple idea: *let the market decide*. If there's a natural demand for something, someone will produce it. Price will be shaped by that demand vs. the available supply. Quality will be controlled by the same mechanism – if people aren't happy with the product, they'll quit buying it, or find another source. The "Invisible Hand" will ensure that everything works out just right, thanks to the sheer volume of enlightened consumers making rational choices about what they will or won't buy, just like they do about who they will or won't elect.

I'll give you a moment to dab at that single patriotic tear slowly working its way down your cheek.

In reality, unfortunately, things don't always work out as planned. People find ways to subvert the assumptions and mechanisms of system and to exploit the good intentions or natural ignorance of others for personal gain. It can be especially frustrating whenever politicians or bureaucracy are involved. Government adds a messy, illogical element to the equation; it's a major player with the power to regulate, participate, or otherwise interfere, but with nothing personally at stake. Any gains, they keep (or at least take credit for); any losses, they simply recoup from taxpayers.

"It is not from the benevolence of the butcher, the brewer, or the baker that we expect our dinner, but from their regard to their own interest." What Adam Smith didn't allow for as he wrote these words was the possibility that those same self-interests might lead many industries to seek the patronage of Congress rather than do the more tedious and challenging work of producing better beef, beer, or biscuits.

Such an approach probably didn't *begin* during the Civil War, but we have to start somewhere – so let's talk military contracts.

Do You Have These In Blue?

As it became clear the war would not, in fact, be settled in ninety days (as both sides had initially anticipated), the Union government began ordering uniforms for its soldiers. The contractors supplying those uniforms quickly figured out that while they could certainly make a reasonable profit by providing decent woolen shirts and pants, they could make far *more* by using what were essentially scraps – used, worn out wool. By the time the material began falling apart, it was being worn by soldiers in the field, and who cared what happened to them?

This cheap, deceptive material was known as "shoddy." The word quickly entered the general lexicon as meaning something cheap but presented as far better than it actually is – the same basic meaning it holds today. This was only one example of businesses exploiting ignorance, need, or both, in pursuit of undeserved profits. Like most good corruption, success in such a scheme required the cooperation of someone with a little political power – perhaps several someones.

The Crédit Mobilier scandal was one of these shoddy deals – maybe the shoddiest of its era. And that was a high bar.

Who's Keeping Track(s)?

In 1862, Congress passed the Pacific Railroad Act which created two railroad companies – the Union Pacific and the Central Pacific. It would be another decade or two before railroads would effectively become public utilities, subject to extensive government regulation in the name of the larger good, but the boundaries between railroads as a private industry and railroads as an extension of the federal government were already a bit fuzzy.

The Pacific Railroad Act established a specific, new relationship between Uncle Sam and these sorta-kinda-private companies. The railroads would lay tracks and establish routes as directed by Congress, and in return receive payments in the form of extensive land grants along the new routes, as well as plenty of nice, shiny thirty-year government bonds. Once completed, the railroads would maintain and operate the routes just like any other company – as long as they stayed open and available to support westward expansion and interstate commerce and the like. The project would be financed by tax dollars supplemented by private funding. Few investments seemed quite so reliable in the mid-nineteenth century as railroads.

The primary assignment of these freshly chartered companies was to build a transcontinental railroad. The Union Pacific folks would begin around Omaha, Nebraska (which was a brand new baby city at the time) and head west. The Central Pacific would start from Sacramento, California (which had become an "American" city thanks to the Gold Rush), and build east. Hopefully, they'd meet somewhere along the way. (They did. The famous "Golden Spike" was driven into the final railroad tie at Promontory, Utah, in 1869.)

By now, however, many in the choo-choo business had figured out that the real money was in *laying* the tracks rather than *running* the actual routes once built. That wasn't always the case; established routes through major cities, hauling people and freight, were still big money-makers. It was worth an initial investment to secure an ongoing, long-term payoff. But this "transcontinental railroad" project wasn't going through major cities or likely to carry much freight right away. It was aspirational. Long-term.

Americans don't do well with "long-term." It's too... *long-term.*

Owners didn't mind the brutal labor required to actually build it; that's what the Irish, Chinese, Mormons, and freedmen were for. Nor were they risking their own money along the way. It's just that the results wouldn't be all that profitable once completed. All they'd get out of the deal was the usual income and an extensive route which had cost them nothing to build but which they could operate as they saw fit until the end of time. This was unacceptable!

A few of the uppermost uppity-ups decided to modify their business model a bit.

An Anfractuous Econo-Legal Labyrinth

Thomas Durant was vice president of the Union Pacific Railroad. His primary confidant in these shenanigans was George Francis Train (his real name), an eccentric but successful figure who preferred to be known simply as "Citizen Train." (Seriously, I *wish* I were kidding.)

Train's story alone deserves more ink than we can justify here. He wasn't that "important" in the grand scheme of things and his life was definitely *not* boring, however, so for now we'll just note that while his involvement in Crédit Mobilier was very, very naughty, he did all sorts of interesting and generally positive things as well – including legal advocacy on behalf of radical feminists and a global journey which likely inspired Jules Verne to write *Around the World in 80 Days.*

Their first step was to create Crédit Mobilier of America, a company owned and operated by Durant and associates but which appeared on paper to be an entirely separate enterprise. Union Pacific "hired" Crédit Mobilier to lay tracks and provide other services, then paid them with government funds and investor dollars after taking a nice cut for themselves. Crédit Mobilier, in turn, hired actual crews to do the real work – at far less than what they were receiving from Union Pacific for the job.

Since the same men ran both organizations, they could bid on work at inflated prices, accepted their own bids, then pay themselves (twice) for satisfactory completion as judged only by themselves. On the surface, it appeared a respected railroad company was bidding out work to a subcontractor who only got paid if the railroad were happy with the results. In reality, it was fortunate the tracks were laid at all.

Durant also took advantage of recent changes in business law. Traditionally, investors were liable for business losses or internal fraud up to the full amount of their personal worth. At the dawn of this new age of big business, however, the concept of "limited liability" was born. The maximum any investor could lose was whatever they'd put into a business, dramatically reducing risk and thus encouraging increased investment.

Durant and his partners would later argue that nothing they'd done was technically *illegal*, and they may have been mostly right. Erring on the side of caution, however, they wrapped up their transactions in multiple transfers between different corporate entities and (seemingly) unrelated accounts, creating the sort of paperwork pretzel most of us only encounter in John Grisham novels and spy movies.

Still, there was always the chance Congress might start poking around and asking too many questions, so Durant and his trusted confederates began offering bargain shares of stock in the company to key Representatives and Senators, most of whom were more than happy to play along – especially when guaranteed annual returns of 300% or more. Eventually, nearly two dozen members of Congress, as well as Vice President Shuyler Colfax, owned stock in Union Pacific.

No Chill Among Thieves

One of the problems with corruption and greed, of course, is that the corrupt and greedy are rarely satisfied with their share for long, no matter what its size. The scheme had been running smoothly for over three years when an internal power struggle nearly ruined things for everyone.

Oakes Ames was a Republican Congressman from Massachusetts. While there were many influential Republicans (and one Democrat) deep in Crédit Mobilier's muck, Ames was in deeper than most. His brother, Oliver Ames, was also an investor, and in 1867 they made a power play for the presidency of Union Pacific – replacing Durant with Oliver. A vengeful Durant filed an injunction to halt construction based on some legal reason or other and began plotting his return to power. In response, the Ames brothers had him booted off the board altogether. He said *this*, they argued *that*, and there was *drama*. Lots of it.

Generally, when you're doing shady stuff, you avoid drawing unnecessary attention to yourself or your organization. Any Congressmen who grew curious, however, were either brought into the scheme or otherwise encouraged to look the other way. The occasional reporter was largely dissuaded by the sheer complexity of the legal and economic webs which had been so carefully woven from the start. They may have suspected shenanigans, but you can't prove something you don't understand to begin with. So, despite the shenanigans, no one could prove anything was awry.

It wasn't until 1872, as President Grant was running for re-election, that bits and pieces began coming to light, largely due to the efforts of the *New York Sun*. The *Sun* opposed Grant's re-election and gleefully laid full blame for the scandal at his feet. Even then, most folks weren't clear on what, exactly, had been exposed – let alone which parts broke what laws. Several of the big names first associated with the scandal turned out to be largely innocent while others escaped without serious examination. Some elected officials gladly answered questions, secure in the conviction they'd done nothing wrong. Others dumped their shares in hopes of avoiding further scrutiny, sacrificing future profits for continued political power.

In short, it was a confusing mess. What *was* clear to most of the public was that they'd somehow been shafted while those already in power were getting even richer at their expense. That part, everyone could clearly understand.

Impact and Aftermath

Only Oakes Ames and James Brooks (the only Democrat in the mix) received an official congressional censure. No criminal charges were filed, and the rest of those involved were free to keep doing whatever they were doing. The public was outraged, but they'd been outraged before and probably would be again. Besides, you can weather a LOT of public rumbling when you're pulling in 500% or more on your insider investments paid for by taxes *you* control for work *your own legislation* mandates.

The specific crisis would pass, but a general distrust of the federal government and Congress in particular would linger until the twentieth century when the requisite patriotism of two world wars would temporarily wash away anything not reeking of patriotism and faith in Uncle Sam. Railroads continued to exploit their favored status with Congress, taking in millions from taxpayers while establishing themselves as one of the dominant powers in the nation for the rest of the century. Money ran so freely through the informal partnerships between Congress and big business that historians often refer to this era as "the Great Barbecue" (with taxpayers as the main course).

More immediately, Crédit Mobilier reinforced the growing perception that the entire Grant Administration was corrupt. This was unfortunate, since by all accounts Grant himself had no idea what was going on. Then again, that was sorta the whole problem with Grant as president – he *rarely* had much idea what was going on.

Sorry, Ulysses – nothing personal.

Other Major Scandals of the Grant Administration

One of the most common reasons cited for the premature end of Reconstruction is the perceived incompetence and corruption of federal government during that time. While many historians argue this perception wasn't entirely fair, the Grant Administration was associated with at least two other major scandals you should probably know - "Black Friday" and the "Whiskey Ring." Don't worry – they were a big deal at the time, but both are pretty dry reading all these years later.

Jay Gould was another railroad guy who didn't mind bending the rules a bit (and who ended up one of the richest men of his century as a result). He was one of the essential players in Crédit Mobilier, but it was an unrelated scheme which secured his name in the index of high school history textbooks forevermore.

In 1869, Gould and fellow schemer James Fisk attempted to corner the gold market, thus driving up the price of gold and weakening the U.S. dollar. This would increase foreign demand for American wheat by lowering the relative cost, which in turn would mean increased shipments of that wheat to various ports via the railroads owned in part or full by Gould and Fisk. The plan required Grant's brother-in-law to schmooze with the president in order to glean insider information and influence policy – once again making Grant look the fool. The resulting "Black Friday" crash of the gold market in September of that year sent the U.S. economy into a spiral for months. Gould and Fisk, however, weathered the storm and came out far wealthier as a result.

The Whiskey Ring was an organization of whiskey distillers who in the early 1870s began bribing I.R.S. agents and other government officials in order to avoid paying their taxes. A percentage of the profits was set aside to aide Grant and other Republican candidates in the Election of 1872; the rest went into the pockets of those involved. The scheme wasn't exposed until 1875, when over 300 suspected ring members were arrested. As the investigation progressed, it began to look like the only person in the White House *not* directly involved was President Grant himself.

Making The Grade: What You're Likely To Be Asked

In terms of multiple choice, the most likely question you'll encounter is some variation of these:

1. Which presidential administration was hampered by scandals like Crédit Mobilier and the Whiskey Ring? (A) Zachary Taylor, (B) <u>Ulysses S. Grant</u>, (C) Rutherford B. Hayes, or (D) Andrew Johnson.

2. Although he was elected to two terms, Grant's presidency was largely considered unsuccessful due to...? (A) his refusal to support Radical Republican policies, (B) his lenient policies towards the South, (C) <u>repeated scandals during his time in office</u>, or (D) revelations about his military leadership during the Civil War.

Beyond that, this one can be a bit tricky to predict. You may encounter Crédit Mobilier or the other scandals in relation to public mistrust of government and/or big business throughout the late nineteenth century, or as part of the perceived incompetence or corruption that doomed Reconstruction. You should be able to cough up the basics of "Black Friday" and the Whiskey Ring as well as Crédit Mobilier itself (since they'll often come up together). Remember Jay Gould in association with Crédit Mobilier and Black Friday, especially the part about the controlling the gold market. (Durant and Train don't seem to come up by name. Like, ever. Kinda sad, really.)

For short answers or essays, it's unlikely you'll be asked to write in great detail about Crédit Mobilier itself, or even about Grant's presidency in isolation. On the other hand, teachers (and exam-makers) LOVE variations of this one:

3. "Were business leaders during the late nineteenth and early twentieth centuries better described as 'captains of industry' or 'robber barons'? Justify your response with specific examples."

As with so many of these sorts of prompts, it doesn't really matter which position you take so long as you back it up with relevant details. Avoid answers that go to either extreme: if you argue business leaders deserved the title "robber barons," give some acknowledgement to their roles as "captains of industry"; if you take the opposite approach, give token credit to the label "robber barons." Choose one or the other, however – don't try to go 50/50 or you'll sound wishy-washy. (That's a technical term we learned in teacher school. Hope I didn't sound all lofty busting it out here.)

In APUSH or other advanced course, expect broader prompts which expect you to figure out appropriate specifics all on your own:

4. Discuss the growing power and influence of big business on politics and the economy in the late nineteenth century. How did Americans respond to these changes?

5. Railroads expanded substantially in the postbellum nineteenth century. Compare the impact of this expansion on the northeast, the New South, and the west. (This one may include a map or primary sources.)

One of my favorites goes something like this:

6. Which of the following marked the true "starting point" of the Second Industrial Revolution in the United States – the Market Revolution, the Civil War, the period from 1877–1890, or the early twentieth century? Justify your response.

Again, it's not about identifying the "right" answer so much as justifying whatever you pick with specific historical examples and decent reasoning.

One final note: the Crédit Mobilier scandal overlaps several different "units" or "eras" commonly used to categorize history into manageable chunks. It happened during Reconstruction but wasn't directly related to freedmen or readmitting southern states into the Union. It was part of westward expansion after the war, but didn't involve homesteaders, soddies, Buffalo Soldiers, or the Plains Amerindians. Crédit Mobilier also played an early, but important, role in the gradual redefinition of the Republican Party – from the party of "free soil, free speech, free labor, and free men" into the party of big business and big profits by any means necessary.

If given the choice where to "place" it, Crédit Mobilier works best chronologically and thematically as a sort of "Grand Opening" for the Gilded Age. Mark Twain coined the term in 1873 while the scandal was still in the headlines, and the moniker is generally applied until at least the turn of the twentieth century. It's still fair game for prompts referencing any of these "eras," however, if you believe it relates to whatever's being asked. You'll look even more informed and insightful than usual if you work it in unexpectedly (but appropriately) than if you wait for an invitation.

CHAPTER TWELVE: BARBED WIRE
Westward Expansion... With An Unexpected Twist

Three Big Things:

1. Barbed wire became the fencing of choice in the west after the Civil War. It was relatively cheap, withstood a wide range of conditions, and held back even the biggest, most stubborn livestock.

2. Barbed wire favored homesteaders moving west, who tended to be small farmers. It threatened, and eventually helped subsume, cowboy culture and the mythical "open range."

3. Barbed wire is rarely asked about specifically in history standards, but it's central to a wide variety of stuff that *is*.

Introduction

There are barbed wire museums in nearly a dozen different states. That's right – museums devoted exclusively (or at least primarily) to the origins and impact of pokey wires in all its many varieties. The Oklahoma Cowboy Museum boasts over 8,000 varieties of prickly steel yarn. The Devil's Rope Museum in McLean, Texas, promises "everything you want to know about barbed wire and fencing tools." The Kansas Barbed Wire Museum in La Crosse has a half-dozen separate displays devoted to the subject, not to mention a gift shop packed with books, t-shirts, and other memorabilia. There are several collections in and around DeKalb, Illinois, the birthplace of barbed wire, and major displays scattered from the Murray County Museum in Georgia to the Paso Robles Pioneer Museum in California.

But... why? It's fencing. Made of wire. What's the big deal?

Expansion, Technology, and Conflict

American history is largely a tale of expansion. Many of our most noteworthy conflicts have resulted (at least in part) from our eternal drive to expand and renovate. As "Schoolhouse Rock" waxed so rhapsodically:

> *Elbow room, elbow room, got to, got to get us some elbow room. It's the west or bust; in God we trust – there's a new land out there... There were plenty of fights to win land rights, but the West was meant to be; it was our Manifest Destiny!*

Prior to the Civil War, westward expansion was resisted – if not noticeably hindered – by both northeastern businessmen (who didn't want their cheap immigrant labor to have other options) and southern plantation owners (who didn't want competition from new farmers). During the Civil War, however, businesses were distracted by wartime production and the southern states lost their political influence (having "left the Union" and started a war and everything). Lincoln's Republicans were able to push through the famed Homestead Act of 1862, and it was on.

The Homestead Act wasn't the first offering of its sort, but it was arguably the most important. Almost anyone could get a chunk of land out west at minimal cost as long as they were willing to go live on it and improve it. After the war, Americans cranked up their expansion mojo and the country began (or rather, resumed) sprawling westward.

In the meantime, demand for beef was rising. Soldiers needed to eat, and all that meat had to come from somewhere. Then, after the war, a prosperous and victorious North wanted steak for dinner. Creative cross-breeding eventually produced a fairly hearty steer which was nevertheless edible – the Texas Longhorn. Railroads connecting the west to markets in the northeast didn't quite reach Texas, so the age of the great cattle drives was born as cattlemen drove their steer from wherever they were raised to the nearest railroad – often several states away. Despite its eternal popularity in TV and movie westerns, the era of "git along little doggie" was only about two decades long – from the 1850s to mid-1870s.** After that, the major railroads reached pretty much everywhere, and cattle drives were no longer necessary or practical.

The culture of cattle ranching required easy access to grazing and water. In both law and custom, cowboys could drive their herds pretty much *anywhere* as long as they used a little basic courtesy. This wasn't just "how they did things" – it was an entrenched ethical and legal reality on par with any other "natural right." Life, liberty, and free use of the open range were as self-evident as they were God-given.

The settlers who began showing up to partake of all that nifty government land had slightly different unalienable truths lodged in their hearts and minds. They'd been marinating since birth in the sacramental wine of private property rights and the obligation of every good American to defend those rights – preferably against savages, but against cowboys as well if necessary. It didn't take long for these disparate American ideals to begin chafing against one another in the most unpleasant ways.

Offensive Fences

Farmers knew in the core of their being that they had every right to their 160 acres, wherever it happened to be; ranchers were just as certain that limiting others' access to water or grazing was both tyrannical and tacky. Either way, farming homesteaders needed better fences if they were going to survive.

This was problematic, given the realities of flora on the Great Plains. There's a reason it's not called the "Great Forest," the "Big Ol' Woods," or "Trees-a-Palooza." Even when settlers could find wood, it was windy on the Plains. It sometimes rained or snowed heavily. Pretty much every season was brutal on wooden fences in one way or another. Some settlers tried rocks, but the difficulty with that system was self-evident. Others built boundaries out of the same sod they used for their homes, only to have them washed or blown away by the elements. Just to really rub it in, the creatures fences were primarily intended to keep out weren't particularly intimidated by wooden posts or nailed boards. Humans could kick them down or pull them up with a little effort; cattle knocked them over and went about their business like they hadn't even noticed.

Barbed wire changed all of that. There are competing accounts of just who deserves the primary credit, but the first versions were patented in 1867 and being mass produced less than a decade later. There were dozens (and eventually hundreds, then thousands) of varieties, but most came down to thin, sturdy steel wire with intermittent "barbs" – ridges, spikes, or other pointy metal shapes – firmly embedded along the entire length. Barbed wire was relatively inexpensive and easy to put up. Wind had zero impact on the thin steel wires; rain and snow had even less. Animals, on the other hand, quickly learned not to test this new "devil's rope." The barbs were painful enough to discourage pushing through or knocking over this new anathema, but unlikely to do real damage to most livestock.

This nasty little innovation shifted the balance of power in the west considerably. Pretty much anyone could now easily stake out and claim any section of land they wished, whether they legally owned it or not. Sure, you could sneak in and cut the wires (and hope you weren't shot), but unlike wooden fences they could be repaired and replaced just as quickly. You could try to go over, under, or through, but the wire discouraged this. No matter how tough or clever you were, that stuff *hurt*.

Just to complicate matters further, some rogue souls began raising sheep instead of cattle. Sheep provided meat, milk, and wool, and proved an economically viable alternative in areas already saturated with moo-cows. Sheep grazed like crazy, however, which required even more fencing to be erected – thus proving doubly-problematic for old school cowboys still trying to get their lil' doggies along. In Arizona, Texas, Wyoming, and Colorado, the "Sheep Wars" were a big – if often overlooked – deal.

Barbed wire wasn't the only reason homesteaders and private property took over the west, but it was arguably the deciding factor. As to cattle drives, it would be unfair to pin their demise entirely on this one innovation. The railroads finally reached Texas. There were a few brutal winters in the 1880s which killed tons of livestock (literally). And of course there were all those annoying sheep. But there's no denying the impact of wave after wave of desperate settlers now armed with the ability to slice the frontier into private little homesteads defended by cheap, durable, pokey wire.

How Do I Remember This?

If you've endured any version of the musical *Oklahoma!*, you probably remember the hootenanny in which the ensemble sings that "the farmer and the cowman should be frieeeends!" Imagine this particular number concluding with the "farmer" contingency busting out a large role of barbed wire (with wooden posts already attached every few feet) and wrapping up the cowmen en masse, who then remain cut off from the festivities until they die. (The rest of the ensemble, of course, continues singing "territory folks should stick together; territory folks should all be pals!", seemingly oblivious to the plight of the filthy, outdated cowpokes rapidly losing both relevance and consciousness just off stage.)

If you're not familiar with it, that's what YouTube is for. It's an annoying little number, making it all the more likely the memory will stick. You know, like barbed wire.

Making The Grade: What You're Most Likely To Be Asked

It's unlikely you'll be asked about barbed wire *specifically*, or at least not in isolation. Typically, it comes up in conjunction with the settling of the West in the latter half of the 19th century, the end of the "cattle drive era," or the end of "open-range ranching" (the dates of which vary from source to source).

1. Open-range cattle ranching dramatically declined in the late nineteenth century due to...? (A) the rise of barbed wire fencing across the Great Plains, (B) declining beef prices due to overproduction, (C) backlash from the Plains Amerindian tribes against homesteaders and ranchers, or (D) the segmentation of the plains by railroads.

2. Which new technology proved a substantial advantage to homesteaders over open-range ranchers on the plains? (A) steel plows, (B) rifled barrels, (C) the windmill, or (D) barbed wire.

If presented with a more open-ended prompt, you'll want to include other factors in the demise of cattle drives and/or open range ranching (note that these are not the same thing even though they have much in common).

3. What led to the end of the great cattle-drive era of the late nineteenth century? (railroads reached Texas, several brutal winters 1885-1887, falling beef prices)

4. What led to the end of open-range ranching in the late nineteenth century? (overgrazing, those same brutal winters 1885-1887, homesteaders with barbed wire, and to a lesser extent those darned sheep; it wouldn't hurt to bring up the Homestead Act, Morrill Land Grant Act, and/or Pacific Railway act as well)

APUSH or other advanced courses like to ask the same basic things with bigger words:

5. Explain how technological advances, large-scale production methods, and the opening of new markets encouraged the rise of industrial capitalism in the United States. (This prompt is more obviously concerned with the Second Industrial Revolution, but you'll sound totes academic if you work in something relevent from further west – like barbed wire and the expansion of the

railroads.)

Don't be surprised if you get a map of migration during this time period showing westward movement of some sort and a prompt asking about the "migrations that accompanied industrialization" and how they "transformed both urban and rural areas of the United States and caused dramatic social and cultural change." (This particular phrasing is from the APUSH Key Concept Outline, but the same ideas appear in other fancy curriculums as well.)

6. Between 1865 – 1900, large numbers of migrants moved to the West in search of land and economic opportunity, frequently provoking competition and violent conflict. Explain one federal government action supporting this migration, one source of competition and conflict, and one long-term impact of these shifts.

Just TRY to tell me you're not giddy with the possibilities of THAT one!

In short, barbed wire is an excellent detail to work into almost any short answer or essay related to westward expansion after the war, particularly if the prompt involves conflicts between homesteaders and the Plains Indians or between homesteaders (largely farmers) and cattlemen. It's also a powerful example of technology changing how and where people live, impacting the environment as well as the economy – literally reshaping everything else that was possible (or not) wherever it was utilized.

And despite its relative simplicity, barbed wire was (and is) a *technology*. Like many other examples of technological progress, it helped some and annoyed others, but impacted almost everyone in one way or another.

Hang on – this is where it gets deep:

You can resist technological change, or even fight against it, but just as the winds and rains pass right on through that barbed wire without measurable impact, technological progress does what it's going to do, with or without our cooperation. We can seize it and utilize it to our own ends or let it pass us by... but pushing back against it usually just leaves us cut up and wincing a bit from the results.

I'll give you a moment to find some tissue before we move on.

**OK, technically there were still cattle drives until the early twentieth century, but they were far less common. Just because your grandma still has a rotary dial phone doesn't mean cell phones didn't take over how we make calls a generation ago. You want to celebrate the handful of cattle drives taking place in 1907 or whatever? Live it up, pardner.

CHAPTER THIRTEEN: THE BESSEMER PROCESS
Steel Your Heart Away

Three Big Things:

1. The Bessemer Process made better steel more quickly and more cheaply.

2. Better, affordable steel played a significant part in the Second Industrial Revolution. It may have been its primary cause; it was at least a major catalyst.

3. Bessemer steel made it possible to build skyscrapers, massive bridges, and reliable railroad tracks, as well as lots of other cool stuff. It's dangerously close to being more interesting than it sounds.

Context and Background

Prehistoric man used a number of elements he discovered in nature. Stones of various sorts were made into weapons or used to grind food. Lead was shaped into vessels for storing or transporting liquids. Copper was used to create some of humanity's earliest tools, until eventually a few clever types figured out how to combine it with tin to make something even cooler – bronze.

Bronze was king for a while until iron became practical enough to take over. Its earliest uses were in jewelry or ceremonial items using iron from meteorites which had fallen to earth – a gift from the gods, as it were. Over time, people figured out that Earth actually had plenty of iron already; they just had to mine it and refine it and make it usable. (Seems like there's a metaphor in there somewhere.) The iron used to make weapons or farming implements was the same substance you ingest in order to grow up big and strong, albeit it in a different form. In its swords-n-plows form, however, iron can be brittle. It corrodes easily when exposed to moisture, limiting its usefulness.

Still, iron was a big enough deal that human pre-history is typically divided into three general eras – the Stone Age, the Bronze Age, and... well, you get the idea.

Eventually, somewhere around 1000 BCE, iron was alloyed with carbon to make a new metal – steel. Steel was (and is) super-nifty and comes in several varieties, depending on the exact mix. Steel is ridiculously strong but can still be shaped into useful items once heated sufficiently. As of 2021, something like 95% of all metal used in the world is some form of steel.

It's kind of a big deal, is the point.

Before the Bessemer Process, however, steel was laborious to produce and quality could be inconsistent. It was a very popular metal for certain small items – expensive cutlery, sophisticated springs, etc. – but in practical terms, it was a limited resource.

What IS The Bessemer Process?

The technical details aren't important to understand its historical significance. The short version is that the Bessemer Process forces cool air through molten iron to remove impurities. It's named for its supposed inventor in the 1850s, a British fellow named Sir Henry Bessemer, although an American chap known as William Kelly may have stumbled across the same idea at roughly the same time. (You're welcome to be super-patriotic and refer to it as the "Kelly Process," but then even *fewer* people will have any idea what you're talking about.)

It took a few decades of refining and improving, but by the late 1800s it was possible – thanks to the Bessemer Process – to produce vast quantities of high-quality steel far more cheaply than before.

Honestly, this statement alone should be sufficient to excite anyone. Over the generations, however, we've allowed silly things like electricity and child labor laws to somehow overshadow just what all this nifty steel meant for the nation.

Why It Matters

Bessemer steel became feasible just as the nation was heading into the Second Industrial Revolution, leading many to argue that the Bessemer process itself was largely responsible for the era. Those railroad tracks that began connecting the nation after the Civil War? They lasted far longer and could handle heavier loads and more severe environments once the Bessemer Process was involved. Factories and manufacturing? Sure, they existed before Bessemer steel – but machinery became more affordable, more accurate, and more durable thanks to the process. High pressure boilers made from Bessemer steel meant better steam engines. Over time, it allowed the evolution of larger and safer ships, automobiles, and airplanes.

And that's not even the best part. Steel girders meant that man could finally build structures taller than a few stories. Skyscrapers became a thing in America's wealthiest cities – twenty stories, thirty stories, and eventually a hundred or more. Safe, affordable, strong, and available – steel was (and is) pretty much *magical* when it comes to building stuff.

Taller buildings meant more people, more business, and more overall activity, all with less urban sprawl. The country could pack its population, services, workplaces, shopping, and whatever else it might desire into relatively few square miles by going *up* instead of always having to extend *out*. Those same steel girders combined with fancy steel cables allowed some seriously heavy-duty bridges to be constructed over major bodies of water so that the people and commerce could move back and forth far more quickly and easily. That sucked for ferryboat owners, but for everyone else? Whooo-Doggies!

Eventually, technology found an even *better* way to produce high quality steel efficiently and affordably. By the late 1960s, the Bessemer Process had become the "old way," replaced by more modern methods which you don't need to know about because there was way too much else going on in the 1960s for you to worry about Blast Furnaces or the Electric Arc Method. Today the U.S. only makes about 4% of the steel produced in the world. China produces over half; no other nation accounts for more than 6% or so.

How Do I Remember This?

Imagine life before the microchip (no computers, at least in the modern sense of the term), or before the internet. Imagine your world before automobiles or cell phones. The introduction of each of these technologies sparked massive changes far beyond what the items themselves actually *did*. That's what Bessemer steel did for construction, industry, business, infrastructure, and the rest of the Second Industrial Revolution.

And don't forget those trains. Just picture Uncle Sam's face on the front of history's choo-choo wearing a steel mortarboard hat – "I think I can... I think I can..."

If that's too weird, there's a famous photo from the Great Depression of eleven men sitting on a steel beam having lunch, way up in the sky. (Google "Lunch Atop A Skyscraper" if you're not familiar with the visual.) Imagine these men are all wearing shirts (sorry ladies) with large, fraternity-style letters on the front. Eleven men means eleven characters, so... "G-O-B-E-S-S-E-M-E-R-!"

I supposed you could add two more guys in your mental image and go with "B-E-S-S-E-M-E-R-S-T-E-E-L," or seven more guys to spell out "T-H-E-B-E-S-S-E-M-E-R-P-R-O-C-E-S-S." But come on – there's really not that much room on the beam to begin with. (You want someone to fall off just so you get a better grade or sound a bit smarter trash-talking on social media? Selfish, much?)

Making The Grade: What You're Most Likely To Be Asked

Unless your teacher is particularly weird, you're unlikely to be asked to elaborate on the technicalities of the Bessemer Process itself. As long as you know the "better, cheaper steel" part and you can rattle off some of the things it made possible in its day, you should be in decent shape.

The most common appearance of Bessemer in multiple choice questions is as one of your options on a "which of the following?" type question:

1. Which of the following most directly contributed to the massive increase in manufacturing, the expansion of railroads, and the first skyscrapers in the late nineteenth century? (A) the Bessemer Process, (B) the Compromise of 1877, (C) Crédit Mobilier, or (D) steam engines.

Less common are questions asking about the Bessemer Process specifically:

2. The Bessemer Process contributed to the Second Industrial Revolution by... (A) allowing electricity to travel greater distances, (B) making assembly line procedures more efficient, (C) producing higher quality steel more cheaply

and easily, or (D) using offsetting diagonal cables to stabilize large bridges or towers.

It's with short answer or essay prompts that the Bessemer Process really gives you chance to shine – particularly since it will rarely be mentioned by name in the prompts themselves. One of the most popular prompts for the Second Industrial Revolution is the "good/bad" question which works for so *many* different things:

3. Explain two positive impacts and two negative impacts of the Second Industrial Revolution economically and/or socially. (Bessemer gives you some options for positives; you're on your own for the negatives.)

Or, if you wanted to get all fancy about it:

4. In the half-century following the Civil War, the United States was transformed from an agrarian to an increasingly industrial and urbanized society. Although this transformation created new economic opportunities, it also created societal problems which were addressed by a variety of reform efforts. Identify and briefly explain (some narrowed down element of this).

5. New technologies and economic models created rapid industrial growth and transformed the United States in the latter half of the nineteenth century. Select one of these new technologies and discuss its impact in terms of two of the following: industrialization, energy sources, natural resources, transportation, communication.

There are endless variations. These are phrased rather broadly; most of the time, teachers or exam makers will narrow the focus of the prompt for you a bit up front. Generally speaking, however, if it involves the Second Industrial Revolution, technology, innovation, economic systems, industrialization, the Gilded Age, or anything else related to the span between Reconstruction and World War I, there's a good chance the Bessemer Process was somehow involved.

CHAPTER FOURTEEN: THE INTERSTATE COMMERCE ACT (1887) & THE ICC
Stop Them On Their Tracks

Three Big Things:

1. After several states struggled to regulate railroads and grain storage facilities on behalf of farmers and other citizens, Congress passed the Interstate Commerce Act (1887). This established the Interstate Commerce Commission (ICC) to regulate railroads, including shipping rates and route choices.

2. The ICC was the first federal regulatory agency; it's "success" spawned hundreds of others in subsequent decades. Ideally, regulatory agencies attempt to balance the good of society and the general public with the rights of companies to make reasonable profits from providing useful goods and services. They oversee "public services" – things considered essential for most citizens but which don't easily lend themselves to a competitive marketplace due to the infrastructure required or the necessary scale of the service.

3. When you hear people complain about "big government," these sorts of agencies are often what they mean. At the same time, they remind us that economic systems are not natural rights; they're practical mechanisms designed to serve the largest number of people in the most efficient ways possible – at least in theory. Regulatory agencies attempt to make sure that's what actually happens.

Context

The second half of the nineteenth century was one of America's greatest (and most controversial) eras of expansion. Rugged, individualistic homesteaders navigated bureaucracy and accepted a degree of government oversight to secure their own plots of government-sponsored land in the west, where the government was hard at work clearing out the local populace on their behalf. Railroads, arguably the most poignant symbol of progress in all of Americana, were bravely and capitalistically accepting massive government land grants in exchange for laying their tracks across the Great Plains in order to connect the east coast with the west. Along the way they manipulated local townships into catering to their every fiscal whim, lest they alter course and instead bestow their blessings on communities more willing to kiss their caboose.

For railroads, more miles of track, continued national expansion, and the vast quantities of crops farmers were shipping further and further from where they were grown meant increased profits and political influence. For farmers, more land, technological advances, and increased production meant lower prices, endless struggles, and increased debt just to stay in the game. Eventually, farmers began setting aside their individualistic natures in order to form collectives – the Grange, the Farmers' Alliance, etc. Together, they pressured their state and local governments to balance the scales a bit. They weren't looking for handouts, just some restraints on what they saw as unchecked corporate power and greed. As it turned out, other segments of society had been thinking the same thing.

Regulating For The Public Good

In *Munn v. Illinois* (1877), the Supreme Court determined that it was perfectly constitutional for a state to regulate industries within its borders, including capping the amounts grain elevators and storage warehouses were allowed to charge for their services. As the Court explained,

> When one becomes a member of society, he necessarily parts with some rights or privileges which, as an individual not affected by his relations to others, he might retain. "A body politic," as aptly defined in the preamble of the Constitution of Massachusetts, "is a social compact by which the whole people covenants with each citizen, and each citizen with the whole people, that all shall be governed by certain laws for the common good."
>
> This does not confer power upon the whole people to control rights which are purely and exclusively private... but it does authorize the establishment of laws requiring each citizen to so conduct himself, and so use his own property, as not unnecessarily to injure another. This is the very essence of government.

In other words, capitalism is all very fine and well, and the individual's (or even the corporation's) right to property and profit is important – but only because this economic approach presumably serves a larger good. The U.S. doesn't practice a form of free market economics because it's holy and just to do so – it's a pragmatic decision based on the perceived shortcomings of alternative economic systems in comparison. (To paraphrase Winston Churchill, "Capitalism is the *worst* economic system except for all those *other* forms that have been tried from time to time.")

Munn made it clear that governments can and should regulate industries deemed essential to the general welfare. At the time, this largely involved services related to farming and the distribution of crops, such as grain storage and railroad rates. As the nation and its technology evolved, the same principle came to encompass a variety of public "utilities" (electricity, water, gas, etc.) as well as some transportation systems, television and radio broadcasting, and even trash pickup.

Many would argue that as society and technology continue to evolve, the same sorts of regulation should apply to internet access, cell phone plans, and even health care and other medical services. While it's usually pretty easy to find a new burger joint if the one you've been going to starts skimping on fries or changes their menu, it's harder to change gas companies. The local sewer service rarely competes for your business, and only a small percentage of American homeowners get to actually *choose* who provides their electricity

– let alone at what rate. Anytime laissez-faire capitalism would result in an "essential" service being reserved to the elite few, government steps in and makes everyone play nice. Companies providing valuable services deserve to make a reasonable profit, but not at the cost of the larger social good – or so the reasoning goes.

The Commerce Clause Wins Again

Not quite a decade after *Munn*, the Court revised its opinion while pretending it was simply picking up where it left off. *Wabash, St. Louis and Pacific Railway Company v. Illinois* (1886) clarified that while states had the right to regulate industries within their borders, that power didn't extend beyond state lines. Just because a railroad route began in Chicago, that didn't mean the Illinois legislature could dictate shipping rates or other policies as it choo-choo-ed through Iowa or Missouri. This was "interstate commerce" in the truest sense of the term, making it the exclusive province of Congress – whether they chose to act on it or not.

Congress finally took the hint and created the very first federal "regulatory agency" – the Interstate Commerce Commission – in 1887. The ICC was charged with overseeing railroads and shipping of all sorts, and set strict guidelines for how the railroads could do business. Rates had to be the same for short trips as for long, and for all customers, however much or little they shipped. Railroads couldn't even offer special packages for "preferred destinations."

The specific rules aren't the historically important part, however. These were modified or eliminated as technology, transportation, and society evolved. The thing to notice is the way the nation was beginning to embrace the idea that government *could* and *should* set limits on important industries for the good of society. In practice, this usually meant the *federal* government. It's nearly impossible today to find a good or service functioning purely "intrastate." States can sometimes add to regulations while the good or service is withing their purview, but not beyond.

Over the next century, hundreds of federal agencies were created in the image of the ICC. While Congress still established guidelines and priorities, agency directors and bureaucrats were left with the detail work – writing the actual rules and at times even managing enforcement. When you hear people complain about the unending nightmare of red tape, small print, and regulatory burdens on pretty much everything, this is the sort of thing they usually mean. The positive side is that the meat you bought at the store today is probably not rotten and your kids' clothes probably won't burst into flames anytime the sun is too bright. The negative side is that unchecked bureaucracy tends to grow like the demonic kudzu and has proven nearly impossible to restrain, let alone prune back. As of the first quarter of the twenty-first century, no one can even agree on how many federal regulatory agencies there *are*, let alone which ones are necessary or what at each of them is actually in charge of.

The ICC was dissolved in 1995 after most of its regulatory power had been reduced or stripped away. Its few remaining functions were transferred to yet another agency – the "Surface Transportation Board" (as opposed to all those other sorts of transportation) which operates under the "U.S. Department of Transportation." The Secretary of Transportation, in turn, reports directly to the President.

How Do I Remember This? (And Why It Matters)

Much of American history can be viewed as an ongoing struggle between freedom and security – nationally, locally, legally, socially, and – as in this case – economically. Just like in school, the workplace, or raising your kids at home, too little freedom stifles innovation and productivity; too much freedom leads to chaos, abuse, and a breakdown of the system.

The Interstate Commerce Act and ICC were the federal government's first major effort to restrict what big business could and couldn't do in an effort to ensure the results served *everyone*, not just those already at the top of the economic ladder. The resulting arguments sound surprisingly familiar nearly a century-and-a-half later. Is it better to let big business run free or rein it in from time to time? Is government better or worse than raw capitalism at meeting the needs of the people as a whole over time? Do the basic rights guaranteed to American citizens as individuals apply to corporations as well?

If the answer to any of these questions seems obvious or easy, you're doing it wrong.

The ICC, while no longer with us, remains the granddaddy of all federal bureaucracy and regulation. From the "alphabet agencies" of the New Deal to the half-dozen different departments which today dictate the minutia of salmon treatment, processing, costs, transportation, and preparation long before you squeeze lemon on it at your local chain restaurant, it can all be traced back to the Interstate Commerce Commission – for better or worse.

Making The Grade: What You're Most Likely To Be Asked

It's unlikely you'll be asked to recognize or analyze the language of the Interstate Commerce Act itself (it's not that readable). Instead, make sure you understand its connection to pretty much everything else going on at the time.

Congress's authority to regulate interstate commerce is found in Article I, Section 8 of the U.S. Constitution. As a practical matter, this means that Congress can regulate almost anything by tying it in some way to interstate commerce – a power confirmed by the Supreme Court a half-century before in *Gibbons v. Ogden* (1824). Combined with the "Necessary and Proper Clause" (also in Article I, Section 8; unleashed by *McCulloch v. Maryland,* 1819), Congress and its regulatory power eventually became virtually unchallengeable when it came to regulating stuff. The use of and acceptance of this power changed over time, but the underlying questions involving constitutionality, federalism, capitalism, and all that other good stuff can be traced across a century or more of American history anchored midway by the creation of the ICC.

The Interstate Commerce Act is also a nice precursor to discussing populism (the late nineteenth century version) or even the Progressive movements of the early twentieth century. These were all about using government to balance the power of big business against the needs of the "common man." You may see fit to utilize it in response to prompts primarily concerned with related topics such as these. (It didn't go anywhere.)

It's possible you'll encounter one or two multiple choice questions related to the ICC or the cases which led to its creation. If so, they'll most likely be of the "recognize or identify" variety:

1. The Supreme Court cases of *Munn v. Illinois* (1877) and *Wabash, St. Louis and Pacific Railway Company v. Illinois* (1886) established which of the following constitutional principles? (A) <u>Congress can regulate industries in the name of public good</u>. (B) The Commerce Clause prohibits railroads from charging different rates to different customers. (C) Congress cannot overrule state regulation of businesses within their borders. (D) Railroads which accept public funding must abide by federal regulations in all aspects of their business.

2. What was the primary purpose of the Interstate Commerce Act? (A) To regulate trade between the states by establishing offices along major state borders. (B) To promote roads, railways, and other infrastructure in order to facilitate trade across the U.S. (C) <u>To regulate industries which provide "public services" but don't lend themselves to normal free-market competition</u>. (D) To standardize prices and shipping rates across industries and across different regions of the country. (NOTE: The same basic question could be asked about the purpose of the ICC itself.)

3. One way the federal government responded to the problems of the Gilded Age was... (A) implementing the silver standard for currency, (B) creating a federal jobs program for the unemployed, (C) lowering tariffs to increase market competition, or (D) <u>passing the Interstate Commerce Act</u>.

Think of the ICC any time railroads or the expansion of big business during this era is mentioned. You may also find it helpful when discussing the influence of farmers across the nation during this era, even before the glory years of the Populist Party.

4. Which of the following would have been considered a victory for farmers in the latter half of the nineteenth century? (A) the passage of the Interstate Commerce Act, (B) the Supreme Court's decisions in *Munn v. Illinois* (1877) and *Wabash v. Illinois* (1886), (C) the regulation of railroad rates and grain storage prices by the ICC, or (D) <u>All of the Above</u>.

In APUSH or other advanced courses, consider the possible impact of the ICC and related court cases any time you face a prompt from the latter half of the nineteenth century related to business, the economy, the role of the federal government, railroads, farming or populism, or anything else which might connect. For example...

5. Discuss arguments both for and against government intervention in (or regulation of) free market capitalism.

6. How did new systems of production and transportation prompt American farmers to form local and regional cooperatives? What were some of the primary goals or demands of these cooperatives, and how successful were they in accomplishing those goals?

7. Discuss the role of the Supreme Court in strengthening the power of the federal government over the states (or over private industries) in the decades after the Civil War.

Finally, avoid taking easy positions on the "good" or "bad" of railroads, regulation, farmers' demands, or even the ICC itself. Always reference specifics while acknowledging the inherent complexity and the valid claims of both (or all) sides – freedom, competition, and capitalism on one side and a reasonable opportunity for individuals to succeed (or at least survive) on the other. That's what makes it interesting – the lack of easy answers.

CHAPTER FIFTEEN: THE SHERMAN ANTI-TRUST ACT

Uncle Sam Has Trust Issues

Three Big Things:

1. The Sherman Anti-Trust Act of 1890 was the first federal legislation prohibiting not only outright monopolies, but any trusts or other collaborations "in restraint of trade or commerce."

2. The Sherman Anti-Trust Act was used by President Theodore Roosevelt in his "trust-busting" efforts during the Progressive Era in the early twentieth century.

3. The Clayton Anti-Trust Act (1914) fixed many of the problems of the Sherman Anti-Trust Act, strengthening and clarifying its language.

The Many Definitions of "Trust"

Whatever else this book is, it is definitely NOT a legal dictionary, nor would I rely on it for business advice or estate planning. (If you purchased it for any of those reasons... what's *wrong* with you?) Besides, the many varieties of "trusts" operating quite legally in the twenty-first century defy any single definition or casual categorization. We're not going to even *try* making sense of the term in modern usage.

The original "trusts" in the late nineteenth and early twentieth centuries, however, were simple but innovative business structures which allowed companies to circumvent laws against forming a monopoly. In a monopoly, one entity or organization controls all of something – all of the sugar in the western hemisphere, all of the operating systems on personal computers, all of the electricity available for residential consumption in Hoboken, etc. Monopolies are generally illegal because they discourage competition and allow businesses to exploit consumers without fear of competition, which is rendered impractical by the nature or scale of the business or by the dominance asserted by the monopolizer.

Trusts were a way to get around that little wrinkle.

In Brew We Trust

Imagine a mid-sized city called "Brewsville" which is home to four competing restaurants. Each considers itself an upscale burgers-and-beer place, generously abusing terms like "pub," "craft," and "artisanal" at every opportunity.

If the service is slow at Big Jake's Taphouse & Sports Pub, you can take your business to House of Hops. If prices there are too high, you can move on to Volstead's Craftworks. If Volstead's food is OK, but the place smells like grandma's bathroom, then it's off to the Pub-lishing House. You get the idea.

When there's healthy competition, chances are good that one or two of the existing restaurants will improve in order to stay in business. Motivation is strong for each one to offer better food and better service at a reasonable price in pleasant surroundings. It's the only way for them to make a profit... when customers have other options.

If they could *reduce* your options, on the other hand, that would make their lives much easier – and probably increase profits as well.

So, let's imagine Big Jake *buys* the House of Hops, Volstead's, and the Pub House. He either closes them down or turns them into new Big Jake's locations. Either way, he now has a *monopoly*. If you want burgers and beer, you have to live with whatever Big Jake is offering – or stay home.

Unfortunately for Big Jake, monopolies are illegal in Brewsville – even for burgers-and-beer establishments. Darn those godless socialistic big-government types! So he goes to Plan B.

Instead of buying out the other three pubs, Jake calls for a meeting with the other three owners. They invite their mutual friend Geezer (a vegetarian who doesn't even drink beer) and designate him their collective "trustee." The owners turn over management of each of their pubs to Geezer, who runs them more or less like a single entity. Everyone's prices are now the same. Menus are similar. Service will be just as bad no matter which pub you visit. They even spread that weird smell from Volstead's to the other three. The owners split their costs and profits (which are now higher for everyone) and take turns hosting get-togethers where they celebrate their collective brilliance.

Now wait just one fermented minute, you may say. They can't do that! Monopolies are *illegal* in Brewsville, and this sounds like a MONOPOLY!

Only it's not. The various restaurants are still owned by different people. They have separate bank accounts and none of them share employees or facilities. They may buy supplies in bulk together or get their menus printed at the same place, but legally they are *distinct entities*... who just happen to be working together as a single unit to control the pub and brewery market in your area. No one owner is in charge of the others – they all answer to Geezer, who doesn't own a pub. He bases his decisions on what works best for the entire group.

This was what was known as a "trust." Now expand the idea to entire industries like steel, oil, railroads, and the like. The men at the top of these trusts were the richest and most powerful men in the world at the time, and they were happy to use that money and power to maintain that status.

All's Laissez Faire When Business Is War

The Second Industrial Revolution and the many genuine advances which accompanied it are often celebrated as the natural result of unrestrained free-market capitalism. This was the era of "laissez faire" economics and Social Darwinism, and while few were arguing that such approaches were *kind*, many were convinced they were *necessary* – and perhaps even healthy, in the long run.

You no doubt remember horizontal and vertical integration. John D. Rockefeller perfected the former by buying up his competition until he was for all practical purposes the only oil game in town. Andrew Carnegie epitomized the latter by gradually taking control of his supplies, transportation, distribution, and the like, until his name became synonymous with "steel" in the U.S. These strategies weren't quite the same thing as "trusts," but they were products of the same mindset and practiced by the same moguls. As with monopolies, this level of market dominance allowed those in control to dictate prices, destroy competition, and practically own many elected officials.

All of which, it should be noted, were bad for capitalism, worse for consumers, and anathema to democracy.

The Sherman Anti-Trust Act (1890)

The Interstate Commerce Act (1887) was the first major effort by the federal government to restrict what big business was allowed to do in the name of Adam Smith and (cheap, mass-produced) apple pie. It created the Interstate Commerce Commission whose powers grew over time and eventually spawned an unmanageable universe of regulatory agencies.

The creation of the ICC was followed a few years later by the Sherman Anti-Trust Act (1890). This was the first federal legislation prohibiting not only outright monopolies, but trusts, cartels, conspiracies, or even those necklaces with the medallion broken down the middle promising to be "BFFs for LIFE."

There were exceptions, of course, and the language of the bill made it difficult to enforce until the passage of the Clayton Anti-Trust Act (1914) nearly a quarter-of-a-century later. It also didn't help that the Supreme Court wasn't in a particularly trust-busting mood in the closing years of the nineteenth century; any time federal authorities attempted to actually apply Sherman in order to dismantle a trust, the Court found a way to side with big business.

But the importance of the Sherman Anti-Trust Act isn't due to its effectiveness (or lack thereof). It matters because of the *principle* asserted – that the federal government has both the authority and the constitutional obligation to protect the ideals of the free market: effective competition, quality products, customer choice, and the like.

Plus, it gave Teddy Roosevelt something to do when he wasn't walking softly and carrying a big stick.

"Do What You Can, With What You Have…"

President Theodore Roosevelt, as you may recall, had a reputation as something of a reformer. He in many ways epitomized the Progressive Era, muckraking and trust-busting and regulating like crazy. He also had a unique look and a colorful personality, making him a favorite subject for political cartoonists everywhere (as opposed to, say, McKinley or Harding, who most of us can't even visualize without Googling them). The Sherman Anti-Trust Act gave Roosevelt leverage in dismantling (or at least diminishing) excessive concentrations of wealth and power.

The most famous of these was the Northern Securities Case (1904). The specifics get a bit tedious, even for this book, but basically several railroad guys partnered with J.P. Morgan and John D. Rockefeller to buy stock in competing railroads and control them via their role as majority shareholders. They created a "holding trust" called "Northern Securities" and used their combined resources to exercise a monopoly-like dominion over rates, routes, conditions, and so on. Roosevelt ordered his Justice Department to dismantle this arrangement as an illegal restraint of trade. Northern Securities naturally resisted, and the case ended up before the Supreme Court, who finally decided in favor of the federal government on this one.

The same vagueness for which the Sherman Act is often criticized gave Roosevelt and his officers a degree of flexibility with how it was applied. Trusts which controlled an industry or marketplace while offering good service and fair prices (as if they were still competing for business) were generally left alone. Those acting only in their own best interests were pressured or prosecuted. In a creative, if cynical, twist, some companies and their allies in law enforcement used the language of the act to shut down strikes or other forms of protest by labor groups, labeling them a form of "trusts" designed to hinder free competition for workers.

So that was ironic.

The rest of Roosevelt's "trust-busting" fervor was part of the "3 C's" of his "Square Deal" – Conservation of natural resources, Consumer protection, and Control (or at least regulation) of corporations – a topic far too entertaining to be covered in depth here. It's worth noting, however, that when Roosevelt ran in 1912 as a third-party (the "Progressive Party," better remembered as the "Bull Moose" Party) candidate, it was largely in hope of continuing the sorts of reforms he'd undertaken during his time in office as a Republican (1901-1909).

There was more to the Progressives than "trust-busting," and they never won the White House, but in the best tradition of third parties throughout history, they *did* get manage to get folk's attention and have an impact. Woodrow Wilson (a Democrat) won the election of 1912 on a platform which shied away from excessive regulation or other government oversight, instead pushing incentives for small businesses in order to encourage competition and consumer choice. Two years later, however, Wilson signed legislation to strengthen and improve Sherman's antitrust efforts.

The Clayton Anti-Trust Act (1914)

Just as any discussion of corrupt trusts pretty much has to include Teddy

Roosevelt, any reference to the Sherman Anti-Trust Act must include its 1914 sequel, the Clayton Anti-Trust Act. If Sherman was the *Star Wars: A New Hope* of the Progressive Era – breaking through and redefining the genre of federal oversight for the next century – then Clayton was *The Empire Strikes Back* – building on and dramatically improving the substance of this new approach. (Don't give me that look. Those movies are as classic as anything Shakespeare or the Greeks ever produced. Shut up.)

The Clayton Act was longer and more detailed than Sherman and sought to ban whatever variations of near-monopoly the elite could come up with, whether or not they actually existed at the time the law was passed. Like Sherman, it was more concerned with the *impact* of specific business practices than the structural technicalities themselves. Clayton also clarified that labor unions and farmers coops were *not* what anti-trust legislation had in mind, so stop the anti-labor nonsense, please. Congress created the Federal Trade Commission (FTC) shortly thereafter, primarily to enforce Clayton and related anti-trust legislation and to promote honest, competitive business practices (at least in theory).

Many Progressives had hoped Clayton would go much further in its efforts to reduce the power of big business, but such is the nature of political compromise. The Supreme Court was also in what's remembered as the "Lochner Era" and wasn't particularly sympathetic to efforts to regulate or restrain corporate omnipotence. All things considered, Clayton likely did all that was realistically possible at the time.

Whatever their shortcomings, Sherman and Clayton established beyond question that Congress can and should regulate big business in the interest of healthy competition and consumer protection. How often it *works* is a whole other story.

Making The Grade: What You're Most Likely To Be Asked

The most common multiple-choice questions related to the Sherman Anti-Trust Act look something like this:

1. The Clayton Anti-Trust Act was designed to strengthen and improve which previous legislation? (A) the Sherman Act of 1890, (B) the Morrill Act of 1890, (C) the Teller Amendment of 1898, or (D) the Hepburn Act of 1906.

Sometimes they're phrased in reverse:

2. The Sherman Anti-Trust Act was strengthened and improved by which subsequent legislation? (A) The Curtis Act of 1898, (B) the Tillman Act of 1907, (C) the Clayton Act of 1914, or (D) the Keating-Owen Act of 1916.

Other popular multiple-choice topics include defining the concept of "trusts" or recognizing them as one of the methods business leaders used in the late nineteenth or early twentieth centuries to increase profits and concentrate their wealth and power. It also helps if you can remember the general idea of how they worked (see the burgers-and-beer example above).

3. Many business trusts formed in the late nineteenth or early twentieth centuries were declared illegal because they...? (A) violated campaign finance laws by donating huge amounts to favored political candidates, (B) <u>hindered competition by creating virtual monopolies</u>, (C) allowed children and women to work in unsafe conditions, or (D) used horizontal and vertical integration to control the marketplace.

4. Major industries formed trusts in the late 1800s as a way to...? (A) push back against cheaper imports, (B) more effectively lobby with Congress, (C) reduce the influence of labor unions, or (D) <u>limit competition in order to increase profits.</u>

5. Both the Interstate Commerce Act (1887) and the Sherman Antitrust Act (1890) were intended to...? (A) <u>maintain fair business practices and healthy competition,</u> (B) increase the money supply by adding silver to the existing gold supply, (C) improve working conditions for women and children, or (D) promote American businesses with protective tariffs and federal infrastructure projects.

APUSH or other advanced courses may bust out multiple choice questions with a little more detail – expecting you to recognize the Northern Securities case or remember that the FTC was created largely to enforce anti-trust legislation (mostly Clayton), for example.

It's unlikely you'll be presented a short answer or essay prompt about Sherman itself, although it's an essential detail to include in response to broader questions about efforts to regulate big business in the latter half of the nineteenth century. Any question about major legislation or accomplishments of the Progressive Era could involve both Sherman and Clayton. (If the prompt specifically delineates the era to exclude Sherman – by specifying the Progressive Era as 1897 – 1920, for example – you can still use them both by listing Clayton as an improved version of the Sherman Act.)

Finally, any time you see a cartoon with Teddy Roosevelt in it, chances are good the prompt involves something reform-related, and trust-busting was one of his favorite reforms. There's also a famous political cartoon from *Puck* magazine in 1889 titled "The Bosses in the Senate" (you can Google it if the title doesn't ring any bells). It shows a bunch of fat wealthy men surrounding little Senators, presumably in Washington, D.C., indicating their control of the lawmakers working beneath them. The fat guys are labeled as various trusts - "Steel Trust," "Copper Trust," "Oil Trust," etc. This was published one year before Sherman was passed and is thus indicative of the very problems Sherman sought to address.

CHAPTER SIXTEEN: THE POPULIST PARTY (AKA "PEOPLE'S PARTY" C. 1900)

If Ever He Had A Chosen People...

Three Big Things:

1. "Populism" is a political approach which seeks (or at least claims) to empower ordinary people who feel that their concerns are being ignored or overridden by the rich and powerful.

2. The People's Party (aka "Populist Party") was formed in the late nineteenth century largely as an extension of various farmers' organizations. They sought more government regulation or control of powerful industries and pushed economic policies which favored the working man rather than catering to the elite.

3. The most iconic figure of the People's Party was William Jennings Bryan – the most famous presidential candidate in history who never actually won. His "Cross of Gold" speech is one of the finest rhetorical works in American history (which is rarely actually read).

Context

Farmers in the late 19th century were frustrated.

As the west filled up with homesteaders, choice farmland was increasingly rare. The U.S. Government had run out of people to remove, and even at their most Manifestly Destined could find no justification for another war with Mexico.

In a few more years, the 1890 Census would declare the frontier "closed" (i.e., settled and civilized to the point that it was no longer really a "frontier") to the chagrin of men like Frederick Jackson Turner who believed the westward struggle against nature and subsequent bouts of deprivation both defined and strengthened American character. Things were so desperate that homesteaders had already begun looking lustfully towards Oklahoma – the same "Indian Territory" (I.T.) to which the bulk of surviving Amerindians had been forcibly removed because it was *inconceivable* that any respectable white American would ever settle there by *choice*. By 1889, they were competing in vicious "land runs" to claim their slice of that same ugly before last call.

In the meantime, farmers across the Great Plains – even those in slightly more cooperative climes than Oklahoma's – were enduring hard times. This was not unprecedented, but it did seem to be unusually persistent this time around. And, thanks to advances in both literacy and communication, struggling farmers were aware that things seemed to be rolling along just fine for much of the *rest* of the country.

The Farmers' Dilemma

It wasn't a lack of production. Most farmers across the Plains were quite successful – at least in the traditional sense. They were growing more goodies than ever before – sorghum, turnips, wheat, more turnips, corn, even more turnips, cotton, and dear lord please *no-more-turnips*. Some were even raising chickens (who ate whatever scraps were left over) and cows (who ate grass, or, when times were hard, turnips), but as the twentieth century approached, most were focused on larger and larger-scale crop production.

The problem was Economics 101: supply and demand. The more farmers produced, the lower the selling price. Being individualists by nature, their initial solutions were individualistic. They already worked 365 days a year, sun-up to sun-down – including Sundays, birthdays, Christmas, and while ill. They labored in the earth and cared for their animals, enduring drought and deluge, heat waves and freezes, in hopes of coaxing forth sustenance for themselves and their world. They couldn't add hours to the day, so they rolled their dice on innovation, technology, and volume instead.

There were new varieties of crops to try, irrigation strategies to implement, evolving methods of planting, fertilizing, and harvesting, and new technologies and equipment – all of which required time, energy, and (most of all) *money* if one wished to remain competitive. Farmers took out loans to purchase new equipment and supplies and bought more land to increase production. Ideally, they'd be able to repay the loans when they sold their newer, better, more abundant crops. In reality, the more they grew, the greater their debt.

Most could see few alternatives. If one or two farmers dialed back production, another hundred would still grow and sell all they could and prices would crash just the same; the rebels would simply have fewer crops to sell along the way. More importantly, agriculture was rooted in a type of patience and faith few white collar types can fathom. If you do the parts you can do – whatever the struggle, whatever the cost – the proverbial (and literal) rainfall simply *has* to follow the plow. It's how things work. It's how they've *always* worked. It's how they *have to* work.

Except it wasn't working.

Banks, Business, and Bitterness

Looking east, farmers saw a world of bankers and businessmen, numbers and percentages, stock markets and manipulation. They didn't understand it, but it seemed to be thriving – at least for the guys in suits clocking what had already become known as "bankers' hours" (5 days a week minus holidays, done by mid-afternoon, next to the stove when it was cold and an open window when it was hot). These men didn't actually grow anything, or produce stuff your kids could eat or wear. Their labor resulted in nothing you could smoke, drink, or otherwise enjoy. Instead, they scribbled in little books, mysterious ciphers wrapped in obscure terms, and this somehow meant they got to keep part of your money anytime it passed through their hands.

You needed them – they held the power of loans, financing, equipment, and seeds. They could say yes or no to your very survival during the patience-and-faith years. And yet, you couldn't for the life of you explain exactly *what* they did or *how* they held this power. It was the opposite of everything the Great Plains believed or valued.

It wasn't just the banks, of course. Farmers felt taken advantage of by railroad owners, operators of grain elevators and silos, and pretty much anyone with money or influence in a system they instinctively understood to be warped in favor of the Ebenezers. They may have lacked the time or inclination to fully decipher that world, but they were increasingly certain it bore them malice – often with the support of their own federal government.

Some states attempted to rein in the powers of big business and its methods – efforts partly validated by the Supreme Court in *Munn v. Illinois* (1877). Less than a decade later, however, that same Court struck down the rights of states to regulate interstate industries (which even then was pretty much *all* of them) in *Wabash, St. Louis & Pacific Railway Company v. Illinois* (1886). Congress took the hint and created the Interstate Commerce Commission, but it wasn't yet clear whether this consolation prize would actually accomplish anything meaningful.

It all seemed so... *un-American.*

For the first time in western history, it appeared, a large demographic was doing everything right – they were honest, hard-working, productive, and responsible – and they were *failing.* Individuals had of course failed before, but individual failure can be attributed to fate, or sin, or some personal shortcoming hidden in the mix.

But these were the most revered and idealized of all American Dreamers – Jefferson's "chosen people of God." And they weren't just struggling – they were facing *bankruptcy.* Their kids were starving. They were losing their land. Either the system was broken, or malicious players were somehow gaming the results.

Farmers began to collaborate in search of solutions. The Grange was formed, then the Farmers Alliance and related local organizations. It soon became clear, however, that there was really only one entity powerful enough to tackle corruption on such a grand scale. The very group whose lifestyles had defined "individualism" since the nation's founding began joining together to petition their government for a redress of grievances.

The People's Party (aka "Populist Party") was born.

The Populist Paradox

The Populists demanded greater government control over railroads, grain storage, even telegraphs. It wasn't about making things "easier"; it was about keeping the system "fair" (although most railroads and other industries disagreed with their definition of the term). The status quo wasn't merely inconvenient for them; it violated their understanding of America's founding ideals. This was not a nation established to be of the rich, by the powerful, and for the well-connected. It was about everyone having some sort of shot, to win or lose on their own merits – not because the system was rigged.

Or so the Populists believed.

The People's Party reached its zenith in the 1890's. Although party candidates won scattered state and local elections, their only real shots at the Presidency came in 1896 and 1900. Both times they nominated William Jennings Bryan, and both times the Democratic Party joined them in the nomination.

Both times they were defeated by Republican William McKinley. So, that must have sucked.

Still, Bryan did leave behind one of the most memorable speeches in all of American history – especially the big finish:

> *"[W]e shall answer their demands for a gold standard by saying to them, you shall not press down upon the brow of labor this crown of thorns. You shall not crucify mankind upon a cross of gold!"*

Theatrics aside, the Populists fought for reforms not unlike those pushed by the Progressives a generation later or even the New Deal a generation after that. Depending on your point of view, they were either an important lurch towards a more equitable American experience or one of the earliest warning signs the U.S. was becoming a nation of whiners who needed the government to solve all of their problems for them.

The People's Party Platform

Specifics sometimes varied by locale and election year, but in general the Populists demanded practical policy changes they hoped would level the proverbial playing field a bit.

First, government regulation (or ownership) of railroads, telegraphs, banks, etc. – anything so ubiquitous as to essentially qualify as a public utility. In the same way government today regulates gas, water, or electricity, the Populists considered certain services too essential to be left to the whims and biases of the free market.

Second, they wanted a progressive income tax. Under a flat tax, everyone pays the same percentage of their income. You made $10,000 this year? Pay ten percent. You made $50,000? Ten percent. $250,000? Ten percent. Those making the least paid the least; those making the most paid the most.

The Populists argued for a weighted (or "progressive") system. If you make $10,000 in a year, you'd pay little, or nothing. You make $50,000? Maybe fifteen percent. $250,000? Twenty-five percent. $1,000,000? Forty percent. Those making the most were still left with more than everyone else, and those making the least were freed from the burden of paying at all.

The Populists called this equitable. Those higher up the economic ladder complained they were being punished for staying in school or working harder than everyone else. This basic argument continued for the next million years.

Third, and maybe biggest on the list, the Populists wanted to dramatically increase the money supply. They wanted more coins minted, and they wanted paper money to be backed up by silver in the national treasury as well as gold. The Sherman Silver Purchase Act (1890) had temporarily nudged the country this direction, but it was compromise legislation that stopped short of fully embracing bimetallism. President Grover Cleveland signed its repeal after only three years.

Singing "Bi... Bi... For Our Money Supply..."

The Populists called for currency based on a "bimetallic standard" – "bi," of course, meaning "two."

If you're a *bi*-cycle, you have two wheels. If you're *bi*-lingual, you speak two languages. If you're *bi*-polar, you have two emotional extremes. If you're *bi*-pedal, you walk upright on two feet. If you're *bi*...

Huh. I can't think of any other examples. But hopefully you get the idea.

Today, U.S. currency is backed up by the "full faith and credit of the federal government" – making us all feel much, *much* better about things. Not so in the 19th century. Back then it was actual specie. Precious metals.

Silver is valuable and not at all common, but it's far more plentiful than gold. The change in the money supply would be dramatic. More money in circulation would lower the value of each dollar – counterintuitively helping those with less money, and especially those in debt. It would also stimulate inflation, which isn't always a good thing. In this situation, however, higher crop prices would mean a much higher income for farmers, who would in turn invest in even more land, equipment, and innovation, and pay down more of their existing debt. At least, that was the theory.

Economic Pizza

Imagine a student – we'll call him Jacobie – showing up to class one day with pizza. It's nearly lunchtime and the food quickly draws attention. Maximillian offers him a dollar for one of the slices. Jacobie accepts. Oliana buys another two slices at a dollar each. The supply dwindles as more and hungry students express interest – thus increasing demand. Jacobie raises his price to two dollars a slice. One slice even goes for three (although he had to throw in the last packet of parmesan with that one).

As he's about to auction off the final slice, Leena approaches him, head down and eyes coyly up. She tells Jacobie that she has no money – but, if he'll "loan" her his last slice of pizza (because she's sooo hungry), she'll repay him *double* tomorrow.

Two hundred percent. In 24 hours. Also, pouty lips. Jacobie relents. The pizza is gone.

The next day, Vic shows up in class with a towering stack of saucy goodness – twelve full-size pizzas of various toppings. He starts the bidding at $2.00 per slice. He sells most of the first box, but things quickly slow. Lowering the price to $1.00 helps a little, but it still looks like he'll be stuck with 9 or 10 pizzas. With ten minutes to go, he panics and drops to 50 cents a slice… then a quarter…

Just before the bell, Leena slides up and hands him two quarters. She takes two slices of pizza in a napkin, glides sweetly over to Jacobie, and presents them to him with an appreciative smile. "Here you go – we're even," she states.

Has Jacobie made a profit?

On the one hand, he loaned *one* piece of pizza and was repaid with *two*. That's doubling his investment by any definition, surely? On the other hand, he loaned out $3.00 worth of pizza, and was repaid with 50 cents worth of the same pizza. Framed in those terms, he lost over 80% of what he put in.

So it is with paper money.

When there's not very much of it, it's worth more. This benefits those few who have the money (Jacobie and his limited supply of pizza). It makes things hard for everyone else, but the haves sometimes offer loans to the have-nots to get them through the day… for a reasonable return, of course.

Increase the supply, and the value of each individual dollar (or slice) goes down. This benefits the masses but hurts the people holding multiple pizza boxes. It particularly chafes creditors. They may receive promised payments, but they're being repaid in dollars which are now worth less than when they loaned them. The *numbers* say they're making more, but the *value* says they're losing – sometimes severely.

The Populist tended to have less money, and to owe more to banks and other creditors. The idea of "freeing up" the money supply was quite appealing to them – ironic, in a way, given how much of their distress was rooted in the overproduction of something to begin with.

Impact and Aftermath

The People's (Populist) Party peaked at the end of the nineteenth Century. While they'd secured several congressional seats and numerous state offices, the national party soon faded. Most of their platform, however, eventually became law – at least in part.

The omnipresent government regulations considered so radical at the time are more or less the norm in the twenty-first century, despite periodic efforts to reverse the trend. Our income tax rates are technically progressive (although the web of deductions and exemptions written in over the years largely eliminates any advantages this gives the non-opulent in practice). As to paper money, well… it's not backed up by gold, silver, or anything else. It's all a guessing game built around trust and mass delusion.

Nineteenth century populism serves as a reminder that our particular form of government exists to protect and support the *whole* people – societies as much or more than individuals. The Preamble to the U.S. Constitution lays out six primarily *collective* purposes for the nation. Decisions made within that framework – a capitalist system, government support of industry, defending individual rights – are shaped by the belief they'll serve the larger good. When they don't, something might have to be adjusted. While the People's Party fell short of many of its goals, the federal involvement and oversight it demanded gradually became the norm in almost every realm of American life – for better or worse.

Making The Grade: What You're Most Likely To Be Asked

Most multiple-choice questions over Populism are fairly basic, but it's difficult to anticipate which details they might zero in on or expect you to recognize. At their core, however, most boil down to the same two or three general topics:

1. Although the Populist Party attempted to draw in a variety of voters, its primary membership was made up of...? (A) immigrants, (B) <u>farmers</u>, (C) socialists, or (D) factory workers.

2. The roots of the Populist Party can most closely be traced back to...? (A) Union soldiers, (B) Eastern European immigrants, (C) <u>the Grangers and the Farmers' Alliance</u>, or (D) labor unions.

3. Which of the following BEST describes the goals of the Populist Party? (A) They demanded access to the same technology and innovations as wealthy bonanza farms. (B) They wanted more state and local control and less federal regulation. (C) They pushed the federal government to reduce tariffs and promote the export of cash crops. (D) <u>They sought more government regulation of powerful businesses who controlled essential public services</u>.

4. Which of the following was NOT a major goal of the Populist Party? (A) <u>federal support for public education and agricultural colleges</u>, (B) a bimetallic standard for American currency which would put more money in circulation, (C) more government regulation of railroads, grain storage, and other public services, or (D) a progressive income tax in which the wealthier paid a higher percentage.

5. Farmers in the Populist Party pushed for free and unlimited coinage of silver largely because they hoped this would lead to...? (A) increased westward migration, (B) <u>higher prices for farm products</u>, (C) lower railroad and grain storage rates, or (D) increased exports of cash crops.

6. Which of the following was an important impact of the Populist Party? (A) They elected one president and dozens of national senators and representatives. (B) The party united the interests of farmers, labor, and freedmen. (C) <u>The third-party successes of the Populists helped liberalize the Democratic Party and laid the groundwork for many Progressive reforms</u>. (D) Populist efforts dramatically reduced the power of big business and the moneyed elite in the U.S.

You may occasionally see a curve ball:

7. After booming in the 1870s and 1880s, agriculture in the west...? (A) changed little until the 1920s, (B) <u>faced decades of lower crop prices and economic struggles</u>, (C) was largely dominated by "bonanza farms," or (D) was transformed by the introduction of crop rotation.

8. Which Populist icon is best remembered for this quote: "You shall not press down upon the brown of labor this crown of thorns! You shall not crucify mankind upon a cross of gold!" (A) Grover Cleveland, (B) Mary Elizabeth Lease, (C) Frederick Jackson Turner, or (D) <u>William Jennings Bryan</u>.

Essays or short answer prompts will most likely be variations on the same topics. In APUSH or other advanced courses, this is a favorite topic to cover with primary sources, charts and graphs, maps, and the like. You'll still need to know the basics, but the rest will come down to your ability to process documents and visuals. It would be unusual to see a prompt asking more of you than the basics (What led to the Populist Party? What did they want? What was their long-term impact? How did they compare to this or that other social-political-economic movement?) without these sources or visuals to reference.

Excerpt from William Jennings Bryan's "Cross Of Gold" Speech (1896)

Whatever you end up thinking of the Populists or their goals, Bryan's "Cross of Gold" speech is objectively one of the finest in all of American history and worth reading in full, whatever your economic druthers. At the very least, you should recognize these bits:

[It has been said that this debate is] a struggle between the idle holders of idle capital and the struggling masses who produce the wealth and pay the taxes of the country; and my friends, it is simply a question that we shall decide upon which side shall the Democratic Party fight. Upon the side of the idle holders of idle capital, or upon the side of the struggling masses? That is the question that the party must answer first; and then it must be answered by each individual hereafter. The sympathies of the Democratic Party, as described by the platform, are on the side of the struggling masses, who have ever been the foundation of the Democratic Party.

There are two ideas of government. There are those who believe that if you just legislate to make the well-to-do prosperous, that their prosperity will leak through on those below. The Democratic idea has been that if you legislate to make the masses prosperous their prosperity will find its way up and through every class that rests upon it. You come to us and tell us that the great cities are in favor of the gold standard. I tell you that the great cities rest upon these broad and fertile prairies. Burn down your cities and leave our farms, and your cities will spring up again as if by magic. But destroy our farms and the grass will grow in the streets of every city in the country...

If they dare to come out in the open field and defend the gold standard as a good thing, we shall fight them to the uttermost, having behind us the producing masses of the nation and the world. Having behind us the commercial interests and the laboring interests and all the toiling masses, we shall answer their demands for a gold standard by saying to them, you shall not press down upon the brow of labor this crown of thorns. You shall not crucify mankind upon a cross of gold!

CHAPTER SEVENTEEN: WILSON'S FOURTEEN POINTS (1918) AND THE TREATY OF VERSAILLES (1919)

When War Hands You Lemons, Make Hitler

Three Big Things:

1. President Woodrow Wilson's Fourteen Points proposed a bold new "besties 4-evah" approach to international relations after World War I, including the formation of a "League of Nations." Other world leaders were not impressed and refused to sign on.

2. The Treaty of Versailles officially concluded World War I and placed full blame and financial responsibility on Germany, with ongoing humiliation thrown in as a bonus. It's commonly considered the number one cause of Hitler's rise to power and the eruption of World War II a generation later.

3. Wilson's thinking, while largely rejected at the time, previewed a shift in America's mindset towards the rest of the world – financial support and "guidance" as a more practical, less expensive alternative to war.

Introduction

Wilson's Fourteen Points and the Treaty of Versailles are forever bound to our cloudy recollections of World War I – a war we know *must* have happened at some point because we're almost certain there was a World War II. The memories we *do* have of WWI tend to center around trenches, mustard gas, and that thing where an archduke (there are *archdukes*?!) from... a country of some sort, probably... was assassinated by... *very bad people* who wanted, er... to kill him for what *must* have seemed like pretty good reasons. As a result, the entire world had to go to war with one another.

Also, don't drive with the top down... or *Hitler* shows up a few decades later.

None of this is entirely wrong (well, maybe the convertible thing), but we do tend to sell WWI a bit short when it comes to historical coverage. Nevertheless, whatever else wars may be – hell, justified, over-if-you-want-it – they are rarely *boring*. The treaties and other paperwork ending them, however... those are a different matter.

The Fourteen Points is a perfectly valid document (which was actually a speech) to study as part of "real" history, but it's also something of a "What If?" Given how often it shows up in state standards and course outlines, it's easy to forget that it was a complete and total bust. No one besides President Wilson even wanted to *try* it for a bit, see how it handled tight turns and check the gas mileage before deciding whether or not to buy it for the kids.

Nevertheless, Wilson's Fourteen Points remains strangely relevant... not to mention eternally popular on multiple choice exams and in mid-semester essay prompts.

The thing that actually *was* signed and approved (at least by most of the participants) – the Treaty of Versailles – we hardly recognize without some prodding or guiding context. (To be fair, half the treaties in the history of mankind are called the "Treaty of Versailles." It was a pretty important place and lots of big meetings were held there over the years.)

Let's see if we can unborify the thing that passed as well as the one that didn't, along with why each mattered (and matters).

Context

By the end of 1918, it was clear that the "War to End All Wars" (what we now call "WWI") was pretty much over and that the Central Powers (Germany and its cohorts) had lost. U.S. President Woodrow Wilson, who was hardly a role model for neo-Enlightenment values, had a rather ambitious remodel in mind for the world moving forward. Prior to the war, peace had been maintained (at least in theory) by an international "balance of power" and a complex series of treaties guaranteeing that the smallest conflict would almost immediately set off an apocalyptic chain-reaction ending all life on the planet. At the time, this was thought to be a pretty good system.

Turns out it wasn't.

The Fourteen Points

Wilson's "Fourteen Points" outlined his vision for a new world order, but not the scary kind right-wing vlogs and podcasts obsess over. He proposed a "League of Nations" (similar to what would later become the United Nations), free use of the oceans, unrestricted trade across the globe, dramatic arms reductions worldwide, several logistical compromises (X moves its troops out of Y as long as Z promises not to do that one thing), and no more secret treaties or slumber parties where they didn't invite the weird girl.

OK, maybe it *was* the sort of new world order the right-wing finds so terrifying. But that wasn't the *goal* at the time.

The key phrase to remember in association with all of this is "peace without victory" – a tad poetic, with just enough room for intentional misunderstanding to keep Wilson's detractors all worked up (not that it took much). It's easy enough to look up all fourteen points if you really care, but... you *are* reading *this* book, so that seems unlikely.

Wilson presented his "Fourteen Points" to Congress in January of 1918, and they were thoroughly unimpressed. The rest of the Allies didn't muster much enthusiasm either, leaving Wilson alone in the policy wilderness – which was especially unfortunate given that many Germans thought this was the deal they'd been promised in exchange for laying down their pointy helmets and ending the war in the first place. Oops. T

The Treaty of Versailles

Instead, the Allies (the "good guys") had their own plan – the Treaty of Versailles (pronounced "verse-EYE"). This one better received than the Fourteen Points and approved by enough involved parties to officially end the war (although the U.S. Senate refused to ratify it). The treaty took a very old-school approach to discipline: Germany had been very, very naughty, and they deserved whatever humiliation and subjugation the rest of the world chose. England and the U.S. tried to work a little "restorative justice" into the mix, but the rest of the Allies had skipped that workshop and weren't buying it. Plus, they didn't really try all that hard.

The Treaty of Versailles took away territory, placed all sorts of future limitations on Germany, and – this was a biggie – required extensive, seemingly eternal "war reparations." In other words, it demanded that a nation which had just bankrupted itself losing a world war should pay for everyone else's expenses as well, all while wearing the equivalent of hand-scrawled "shame signs" like those dogs on Tumblr and Facebook.

The next part you probably know. The humiliation and perceived degradation provoked an unpleasant mix of resentment, shame, and outrage in Germany, creating fertile ground for Hitler to come along and promise to make Germany great again. The terms of the treaty weren't even realistically attainable in Germany's collective mind. As any educator can tell you, once someone believes they can't possibly satisfy a set of expectations, they tend to say "screw it" and stop trying, whether they're openly defiant or not. In the 1930s, Germany became that kid.

Wilson did at least get his League of Nations, a consolation prize that would have been far more comforting if the U.S. had agreed to join. Instead, the Senate – for the first time in American history – rejected a peace treaty negotiated by a sitting president. Why? It kinda depends on who you ask.

Some argued it sacrificed too much U.S. sovereignty for a place at the world table. Others worried it would draw the nation into foreign wars even when U.S. interests weren't clearly at stake. It didn't help mid-term elections had shifted the Senate majority from Democrats (Wilson's party) to Republicans (*not* Wilson's party). Making matters worse was Wilson's refusal to include a few token senators in the negotiations and his love of announcing decisions made in those negotiations before discussing any of them with Congress.

There was some name-calling and fit-throwing as well, but it all gets a bit reality TV for our purposes.

Why It Matters

Wilson's Fourteen Points are often seen as foreshadowing foreign policies to come. The United Nations was established (after the *next* world war) in 1945 and most nations today at least *attempt* negotiations and diplomacy before calling on their militaries to resolve whatever's on their minds.

When discussing the Treaty of Versailles, the whole "pretty much guaranteed World War II" issue is obviously the biggie you can't overlook. It's usually the number one thing teachers and state tests want you to remember about the end of WWI. Long-term, however, the treaty and its eventual (unintended) consequences dramatically altered the way civilized nations view defeated enemies. Eventually the approach would be used with *potential* problem groups as well.

If oppression and hopelessness fuel greater hostility and end up costing more lives and resources down the road, maybe it's more practical to "nation build" or offer "foreign aid" before things reach that point. After World War II, the Allies didn't double down on punishing Germany – they helped to rebuild it, albeit under close supervision. Sure, results were mixed, but less than a century later, we had Angela Merkel and really good beer instead of World War III (at least so far). Japan had barely admitted defeat before the U.S. swooped in with financial aid and a new constitution for them to embrace freely under no duress at all (or else). Again, maybe not the perfect system, but way better than how things went after the previous war.

Foreign policy today is largely an effort to navigate this same dichotomy. Ideally, the U.S. maintains enough strength to seem threatening, but simultaneously seeks trade relationships or offers financial aid (LOTS of it) and other forms of assistance. The goal is to *increase* the odds of new allies and expanded markets down the road and *decrease* the likelihood of expensive, messy wars. It doesn't always work, and motives aren't always quite that pure, but it's way closer to what Wilson's Fourteen Points envisioned than what the Treaty of Versailles demanded.

How Do I Remember This?

Every adult authority figure goes through this same basic decision-making dilemma multiple times each day. Should I discipline or try to redirect? Arrest or recommend wraparound services? Dismiss or train better? Police forces around the country are being pressured to take part in "de-escalation" workshops and use fewer chokeholds. School districts are exploring "restorative justice" in place of suspensions. And parents who spank their children have learned to use hardback copies of *Love and Logic* because they leave fewer bruises and look better lying around if company drops by unexpectedly.

So it was with Wilson's Fourteen Points (the "kumbayah" approach) vs. the Treaty of Versailles (the "beat them down" method). It doesn't mean one approach is always right or the other always wrong, but you'll sound way smarter if you point out that the underlying dilemma is both ongoing and universal.

Making The Grade: What You're Most Likely To Be Asked

Remember first and foremost that the Wilson's Fourteen Points were rejected by everyone who mattered, including Congress. The Treaty of Versailles was accepted by everyone who mattered, *except* Uncle Sam. In retrospect, however, Wilson's approach has proven the more pragmatic (and possibly the more civil) while the Treaty of Versailles is the definitive example of how *not* to prevent future problems.

There's probably an inspirational metaphor in there somewhere.

Once you've locked into that, and remembered to associate both with the end of World War I, most multiple-choice appearances should be pretty straightforward:

1. One major goal of President Wilson's Fourteen Points (1918) was to...? (A) maintain U.S. naval superiority, (B) punish Germany for starting World War I, (C) create a League of Nations to prevent future wars, or (D) strengthen international trade in a way that favored American businesses.

2. Wilson's Fourteen Points reflected his belief that...? (A) travel among nations should be managed by a neutral international organization, (B) intervention in the internal affairs of other nations was never justified, (C) spending on national defense must be proportional to each nation's population, or (D) cooperation among international leaders was the key to maintaining world peace.

You may encounter questions about ways in which the Fourteen Points attempted to address the underlying causes of the war. You probably remember the MAIN pneumonic – Militarism, Alliances, Imperialism, and Nationalism – so watch for these to show up in reference to Wilson's proposals. A small but statistically significant number of questions related to the Fourteen Points ask specifically about Point Thirteen – Poland becoming an independent nation. It's an odd thing to come up so often in U.S. history courses, but it does, so you should probably try to keep it in mind.

3. Why did many senators refused to ratify the Treaty of Versailles (1919)? (A) It failed to sufficiently punish Germany for starting World War I. (B) It compromised U.S. sovereignty and threatened to draw the nation into future wars. (C) It lacked provisions for rebuilding territories controlled by America's allies in Europe. (D) They believed it was impossible to enforce without maintaining a substantial presence in Germany long-term.

4. The refusal of the U.S. Senate to ratify the Treaty of Versailles (1919) was also a rejection of...? (A) the concept of war reparations, (B) treaty commitments requiring each nation to aid the other in case of attack, (C) non-white immigration to the United States, or (D) U.S. membership in the League of Nations.

5. One of the primary goals of the war reparations required by the Treaty of Versailles (1919) was...? (A) keeping Germany weakened on the international stage, (B) funding the establishment of democratic government in post-war Germany, (C) building and maintaining a League of Nations headquartered in Europe, or (D) financing a "victims' fund" for survivors of the war in Europe.

Short answer or essay prompts will most likely seek a regurgitation of the same information for either the Fourteen Points or the Treaty of Versailles (as opposed to an in depth analysis of some sort). Once you get to World War II, expect at least one question about causes of *that* war. There were others, of course, but the Treaty of Versailles was certainly a biggie.

APUSH or other advanced courses may add questions about American isolationism vs. involvement in the world at large. They love asking about the emergence of the U.S. as a world power – a development traditionally tied to the Spanish-American War (1898) but which certainly continued to evolve throughout the early twentieth century and its two world wars:

6. Evaluate the extent to which World War I marked a turning point in the role of the United States in world affairs.

7. Evaluate the major debates in the U.S. over the nation's role in the world in the years 1918 – 1941.

8. Discuss dissenting schools of thought regarding U.S. security and perceptions of American interests in the world in the years 1890 - ??? (pick your favorite cut-off point.)

You may also be asked to evaluate the relative long-term "success" of Wilson's Fourteen Points despite their rejection at the time or explain ways in which the U.S. influenced (or influences) other nations around the world that don't involve military action or the threat of war. Even discussions of imperialism are arguably related to the issues addressed in the Fourteen Points or the Treaty of Versailles. It can get a bit out of control once you start thinking it all through.

I prefer to simply stick to the basics and move on. Otherwise, things could get interesting.

CHAPTER EIGHTEEN: FINANCIAL POLICIES OF THE 1920S
Cavalier, Renegade, and Steer Clear...

Three Big Things

1. The dominant ideology of the 1920s was succinctly captured by President Calvin Coolidge when he declared that "the business of America *is* business." While society was "roaring," politics were focused almost exclusively on supporting corporate leadership (in the belief this would somehow solve everything else).

2. Tariffs rose while government oversight and consumer protections were minimized, all in the name of capitalism and prosperity.

3. While the Stock Market Crash of October 29th, 1929, certainly *triggered* the Great Depression, the underlying *causes* had been in place for years. The economic policies of the 1920s practically guaranteed disaster, both individually and nationally.

Context

The 1920s was a funny little decade wedged between World War I and the Great Depression. It's easy to remember it merely as a caricature of itself – flappers, jazz, and prohibition, with a few shiny black automobiles and those long cigarette holders used by women wearing too much makeup. The image isn't entirely wrong. They were good times for many, and the entertainment produced during the "Roaring Twenties" laid the foundation for the music and movies we enjoyed for the next century. As is so often the case, however, there was a little bit more to it than that.

In many ways, the 1920s were a preview of the 1950s – an ambitious bit of foreshadowing, if you will. It's an imperfect analogy, of course, but useful for remembering the less glamorous stuff. Besides, there's something to that whole "history repeats itself" motif:

1920s	1950s
growth of the suburbs	explosive, paradigm-shifting growth of suburbs
growth of interstate highways	Federal Highway Act / massive expansion of interstate highways
the first "red scare"	the second, scarier "red scare"
technological conveniences in the home	way more and way cooler technological conveniences in the home
"Great Migration" of Black Americans out of the south and towards industrial jobs	"Great Migration" of Black Americans out of the south and towards industrial jobs
post-war debates about America's role in the world	post-war debates about America's role in the world
concern about public and personal morality based on the sorts of books, music, and movies the nation was embracing	*(OK, to be fair this one really didn't show up again full force until the 1960s, but it seemed a shame to leave it off the chart altogether.)*

There are, on the other hand, at least two important contrasts worth mentioning. First, financial decisions made in the 1920s helped bring about the Great Depression of the 1930s, while cultural norms pushed in the 1950s provoked much of the chaos of the 1960s. The former was primarily economic with a healthy side dish of political; the latter was largely cultural with politics for dessert. Second, after World War II, demand for pretty much everything *increased* across the United States. The federal government kept spending and investing in prosperity, and the economy boomed. After World War I, on the other hand... it *didn't*.

That's what we're going to focus on here – the economy of the 1920s and why it mattered.

The Business Of America Is...?

From 1921 to 1933, the Oval Office was occupied by consecutive Republican presidents who were in many ways interchangeable – Warren Harding, Calving Coolidge, and Herbert Hoover. Their administrations nevertheless provide a convenient way to break the decade into chunks.

President Harding (1921-1923)

Harding promised the nation a "return to normalcy," a slogan which sounded universally appealing without actually *meaning* anything. During his brief time in office, Harding cut taxes on the wealthy, raised tariffs to protect American businesses, and made it harder to immigrate to the United States. On a slightly more encouraging note, he oversaw the creation of the General Accounting Office which runs the numbers on government programs or proposals and tries to bring a touch of sanity to what counts as "math" in Washington, D.C.

Shortly after Harding died in office of heart trouble, stories began emerging about the various scandals and innovative corruption which had taken place on his watch – much of which were still rolling merrily along. In less than a single term, Harding managed to make Ulysses Grant look like Ida Tarbell. The most memorable of these (and the one most likely to show up in history texts a century later) was the Teapot Dome Scandal in which Harding's Secretary of the Interior accepted bribes from oil companies for the rights to drill on federal land. Suffice it to say that the primary business of the Harding Administration was *corruption*.

The Fordney-McCumber Tariff (1922)

Tariff policy had been tweaked periodically since the Morrill Tariff was passed during the Civil War, but generally they'd remained high (at "protectionist" levels). President Wilson had managed to lower tariff rates before the U.S. entered World War I, but the business-first dogma of Republicans in the 1920s dictated another reversal less than a decade later. The Fordney-McCumber Tariff (1922) set rates higher than they'd been in over a century and gave the president broad new powers to raise or lower future tariffs as he saw fit.

The results were predictable. Trade with other nations fell dramatically, making it all but impossible for many European nations to pay off their war debts. Prices across the U.S. rose rapidly as major industries once forced to compete with imports now monopolized entire marketplaces. Farmers suffered as other nations raised their own tariff rates in response and crop exports plummeted. On the other hand, the entrenched wealthy became even wealthier, so by at least *one* measure the tariff was an undeniable success.

Calving Coolidge (1923-1929)

Coolidge, as far as we can tell, wasn't the least bit corrupt, although with his devout commitment to limited government and low taxes (whatever the consequences) it was sometimes hard to tell the difference. "Silent Cal" didn't always have much to say, but when he famously told reporters in 1925 that "the business of America *is* business," he perfectly encapsulated both the sentiment and practical priorities of his Republican Party throughout the decade.

Given that the GOP controlled the White House and both houses of Congress the entire time, these were the only sentiments and priorities which mattered.

Progressive reforms weren't *discarded* in the 1920s so much as relegated to the world of bureaucracy and lip service. Republicans celebrated laissez-faire capitalism and Social Darwinism less vocally than they had a few decades before, instead appointing free market disciples to oversee regulatory agencies and fill federal benches. Consumer protections were enforced half-heartedly, if at all, and the "general welfare" was understood to begin and end with profit margins and market capitalization. In their defense, many political leaders seemed to genuinely believe that corporate profits and corporate profits alone could elevate the nation socially and spiritually as well as economically – that there were no problems so great they couldn't be solved by the "invisible hand" of capitalism.

Faith can be a strange and dangerous animal sometimes.

On a lighter note, Coolidge essentially invented the "presidential press conference." For someone so famously reticent, he cultivated a surprisingly good relationship with the press while offering few opinions about anything he didn't specifically wish to discuss. In an era known for prohibition, the resurgence of the KKK, the Scopes Trial, etc., we have very little extemporaneous commentary from the President of the United States. He didn't obfuscate and bloviate to cover up his true thoughts or pretend he knew more than he did; he simply refused to jump in. In retrospect, the approach seems oddly refreshing.

Herbert Hoover (1929-1933)

Hoover took office just as the nation was plunging into the Great Depression. While he couldn't rationally be held responsible for events in motion long before his inauguration, the public nevertheless largely blamed him for the whole mess, because... *America*. Despite popular mythology, Hoover did not remain completely inactive during the crisis; he spent several hours a day frowning with concern and even supported several legislative efforts to stimulate the economy. Unfortunately, their impact was minimal. Hoover and his Republican allies in Congress simply couldn't overcome their own convictions about limited government enough to effectively combat such an unprecedented crisis. They did what most of us do in the face of the inconceivable – they asserted their own assumptions and doubled down on their entrenched beliefs in defiance of all reason until the bitter end.

The Smoot-Hawley Tariff (1922)

Perhaps the most glaring example of these stubborn GOP ideals was the passage of the Smoot-Hawley Tariff (or Hawley-Smoot, if you prefer) in 1930. You probably learned about this one from *Ferris Bueller's Day Off*:

> *In 1930, the Republican-controlled House of Representatives, in an effort to alleviate the effects of the... Anyone? Anyone?... the Great Depression, passed the... Anyone? Anyone? The tariff bill? The Hawley-Smoot Tariff Act? Which, anyone? Raised or lowered?... raised tariffs, in an effort to collect more revenue for the federal government.*

Keep in mind that at the time this legislation was first being written, the Stock Market hadn't yet collapsed. The economy looked like it was going great in terms of employment and consumer activity, and the nation had collectively agreed to ignore what we now consider the warning signs of impending doom (much like we do today).

But farmers were struggling. The end of the first world war meant substantially reduced demand for foodstuffs, and as Europe began recovering, so did their own farmers. Before long, European growers were not only supplying their own nations with food but exporting to the United States as well. American agriculture asked Congress to do for them what they did for other major industries and throw up some protective tariffs.

This being Washington, D.C., of course, nothing could be that straightforward. Other industries quickly jumped in and began demanding they be included as well. Because each state had different priorities, a simple majority became impossible without raising tariffs on pretty much every conceivable product coming into the nation – which Congress soon did.

By that time, the Depression *had* begun. Economists warned that a massive tariff increase would naturally make things worse, not only for consumers, but for the farmers and businesses the tariffs were intended to protect. This was nearly a century ago, however, and political leaders didn't set aside the passions of the moment and instead prioritize the facts and reality of each situation before taking action the way we insist they do today.

Did it work? Anyone? Anyone know the effects? It did not work, and the
United States sank deeper into the Great Depression.

The tariffs did what tariffs always do – raised prices for everyone while annoying allies overseas, two things the nation really didn't need during a major economic downturn. International trade all but vanished just as the country needed it most.

In short, Washington spent the 1920s and first few years of the 1930s trusting big business to do whatever it wanted and the believing the free market would work out any wrinkles for the best – except when they had to step in and protect those same businesses themselves from actual competition (apparently the "invisible hand" was only good economics when it was the "little people" suffering as a result). Instead, most of the globe was sent into crippling depression. Ending it required growing the federal government beyond anything it had originally been designed to do and then joining a world war already in progress halfway across the globe.

Your Foot Bone Connected To Your Heel Bone...

It's easy to think of the "Roaring Twenties" as somehow distinct and separate from the events which followed. With the chunking we do to keep history manageable, we've created an implied reality shift somewhere between 1928 and 1929 which somehow led to one of the worst economic collapses in the history of the universe. (Perhaps it was a rip in the space-time continuum, or the result of a massive government conspiracy. Personally, I've always suspected it was a ploy to get more of us vaccinated.)

Or maybe – just *maybe* – the economic and political choices made in the 1920s laid the groundwork for the events of the 1930s and we just don't like to talk about it because (a) it's complicated and (b) capitalism is an American religion and we must never say or do anything to question its omnipotent grace. (I'm just speculating here. I assure you, my only biases are for red, white, and blue.)

Causes, Triggers, Events, Results

It's not unusual to see history presented in terms of "cause and effect." It's a rational, if simplified, method of trying to pull events together and understand the connections and interactions that make it all meaningful. Without cause and effect, history could only be taught as a series of unconnected occurrences – *this* happened, then *that* happened, then *another thing* happened, and probably some *other things*, until today. When events have causes and effects, however, history has some sort of order, even if it's occasionally imposed after the fact.

If we want to get a bit more specific, it's sometimes helpful to distinguish between "underlying causes" and "proximate causes" – which we're going to call "triggers." In this approach, "causes" are ongoing. They can be in place for days, weeks, months, or years without the event actually occurring as a result. The "trigger" is the thing that transforms those causes into action. The "event" occurs, and afterwards there are "results." Like "causes," these are ongoing and can last for days or decades. The "results" of one "event" often become "causes" of others. History's wacky that way.

For example, there were many ongoing *causes* for the American Revolution – Enlightenment ideals, "salutary neglect," the Proclamation of 1763, the Sugar Act, the Stamp Act, the Boston Massacre, Thomas Paine's "Common Sense," etc. All of these happened, however, without an actual revolution erupting – at least in the "shooting at one another" sense.

Then came Lexington and Concord – the "Shot Heard 'Round the World." All those *causes* suddenly became the *event* we know as the American Revolution. It was caused by many things, but the *trigger* was Lexington and Concord. The revolution (the *event*) lasted nearly a decade, and when it was finished there were many things which were very different than before – the *results*.

40,000+ men were dead who'd been alive before the war. The colonies were now independent. The United States was created. The "Articles of Confederation" were composed. George Washington was forever after known as the "Father of Our Country." These were all *results* of the *event*, and some of them would go on to become *causes* of new *events*.

You get the idea.

Causes of the Great Depression

Historians and economists still debate the details, but most agree on a few basic causes for the Great Depression – all of which occurred during the 1920s:

1. Unrestrained Stock Market Speculation

The 1920s are remembered as the "Roaring Twenties" for a reason. Life was good and getting better, everyone had a job (it seemed), technology was providing untold convenience and possibilities, and the economy was going only one direction – UP. This led to inflated (and unsustainable) stock prices, and people "playing the market" who had no business doing so. Banks loaned money far too easily, and it was not unusual for average families to go into debt in order to buy stock with the assumption they'd pay off the loan with their profits. This was called "buying on margin" and it's like hitting up your local payday loan shop so you can afford lottery tickets. It worked for a time, which only encouraged people to do it even more.

2. Consumer Debt / Failing Banks

This same optimism led many Americans to buy more than they could afford. This was possible thanks to the easy credit available to almost anyone, and debt quickly skyrocketed. When the economy began to tank, many families found themselves owing far more than they could possibly repay. Some historians blame banks for making it too easy to borrow money, chasing easy profits while ignoring the risks (even when it became increasingly difficult to do so). Either way, it was a lesson which would require relearning every generation or so – and still does, apparently.

Even customers careful with their savings weren't safe. When the economy began stumbling and customers attempted to withdraw their money, many banks collapsed, leaving hundreds of thousands of families destitute, their savings gone forever. What could have been a survivable rough period became bankruptcy and despair for millions of Americans all at once.

3. Overproduction

Manufacturing was still a major industry in the U.S., and productivity was up. Credit was easy to obtain, and people bought consumer goods at unprecedented rates. Eventually this had to slow (even the nicest homes can only use just so many washing machines or radios), and businesses found themselves grossly overstocked. Prices dropped. Workers were laid off and wages fell for those who remained. This resulted in even *less* demand for products, and the cycle continued.

4. Unequal Distribution of Wealth

The gap between rich and "not rich" grew dramatically in the early twentieth century. While there's nothing wrong with being wealthy, the man with ten times the net worth as his neighbor doesn't necessary spend ten times as much in the community. The man who makes a thousand times what his employees do may take more vacations and buy nicer things, but probably not a thousand-fold so. Instead, much of that wealth is tied up in long-term savings or investments, which aren't bad in and of themselves, but which effectively render those dollars *stagnant* in terms of their impact on the larger economy. Like water (or blood), money works best when circulating – flowing, rising, raining, repeat. When things get too out of balance between the top and bottom, it barely even trickles down.

5. Crop Prices Plummeted

Before it quit raining, farmers were producing a wider variety of crops more efficiently than ever before. That worked out well during WWI because soldiers gotta eat, and the U.S. served as the primary breadbasket for itself and many of its allies. When the war ended, however, prices dropped dramatically. Being hard-working, rugged individual-types, most farmers doubled down and worked harder, planted more land, or borrowed money to acquire even more machinery, fertilizer, etc. It worked – they grew even more food – and thanks to basic supply and demand, they made even less money as a result.

This should sound like a familiar pattern, by the way.

6. Over-Farming / Drought

The "Dust Bowl" was brought about by a combination of man's short-sightedness and nature's cruelty. The human portion was largely a result of those falling crop prices we just mentioned. In their efforts to reclaim solvency, farmers in the 1910s and 20s stripped away anything which might otherwise hold the soil together – grass, bushes, trees, weeds, etc. Every arable inch was planted with cash crops. Then it quit raining, almost entirely, for close to ten years.

Miles of unprotected, dry soil had nothing to hold it in place when the wind came sweeping down the plains. The result was a decade of raging, destructive, dark-sky dirt storms like nothing people had ever seen. It was terrifying.

7. The Federal Reserve (The Fed)

The Federal Reserve was still a relatively new concept. It was created by the Federal Reserve Act of 1913 in hopes it would provide the sort of national economic stability many felt had been lacking since Jackson "killed" the National Bank way back in the 1930s. The U.S. had maintained a federal bank of sorts since the Civil War, but it wasn't entirely sovereign and lacked the sort of "fiddling around" functions we associate with the Fed today. The new Federal Reserve not only managed the nation's money supply, it acted as a "lender of last resort" for banks across the nation, thus providing additional stability to the system (although in retrospect, perhaps not quite enough).

There are those who argue that the Fed did all the wrong things throughout the 1920s and then again after Black Tuesday, keeping interest rates low when they should have raised them and raising them when they should have lowered them. This "cause" is... *debatable* at best and primarily included here as an excuse to reference the Federal Reserve Act (1913). Besides, studies suggest that lists with seven items look *way* more complete than those with only six.

The *Trigger* – "Black Tuesday"

On October 29, 1929, the bottom fell out of the stock market. There'd been signs – the previous Thursday had almost been THE DAY, but a handful of big money types shored up confidence by buying shares in major industries at well-above market value. It didn't hold. "Black Tuesday" set off a domino effect of selling, panic, business failures, bank runs, and even a few suicides.

The *Event* And Its *Results*

Once the Great Depression itself was underway, a new chapter begins. The focus becomes FDR and the New Deal – super important stuff which impacts our expectations of government even today, but none of which is all that boring. (Well, maybe the Tennessee Valley Authority. Come to think of it, none of the "alphabet agencies" really make for riveting discussion.) The 1930s are well-covered elsewhere and generally quite engaging, if a bit dispiriting.

Note, however, that the *results* of the *event* in question (the Great Depression) were ongoing, at least for a time. (Many are still with us today.) Some became *causes* for new *events*, and the wacky web of history tangled on.

Making The Grade: What You're Most Likely To Be Asked

The most common multiple choice questions from the 1920s are variations of "What caused the Great Depression of the 1930s?" While several possible responses could be considered controversial, most test makers will stick with commonly accepted factors – consumer debt, borrowing to purchase stocks ("buying on margin"), and overproduction. The Dust Bowl itself may be treated as a cause, a result, or a complication of the larger Depression. It's generally attributed to some combination of over-farming and extended drought.

1. Which of the following contributed to rising unemployment in the late 1920s? (A) the Smoot-Hawley Tariff, (B) increased outsourcing of manufacturing jobs, (C) overproduction by many industries, or (D) the application of "scientific management" principles.

2. A government committed to laissez-faire economics is most likely to...? (A) restrict the buying and selling of land, (B) determine appropriate prices for essential consumer goods, (C) do nothing to restrict or regulate corporate mergers, or (D) publish reports on the relative safety of various workplaces and products without interfering with either.

3. One major problem faced by American farmers in the 1920s was...? (A) the failure of farmers' organizations to successfully stabilize prices, (B) drought and dust storms destroying their crops, (C) the excessive rates charged by railroads and grain storage facilities, or (D) overproduction of crops and reduced demand after the end of World War I.

4. Which of the following statements best describes the U.S. economy in the 1920s? (A) Mass production increased the supply of consumer goods. (B) The Stock Market struggled as post-war purchasing declined. (C) Congress pushed federal regulation of industries in order to combat more restrictive state legislative efforts. (D) For the first time in American history, prosperity was shared more or less equally across class, race, and region.

5. The Roaring Twenties were characterized by...? (A) brinkmanship, McCarthyism, and Levittowns, (B) internment camps, rationing, and the first atomic bomb, (C) installment plans, flappers, and prohibition, or (D) bread lines, unemployment, and dust storms.

6. Which of the following best describes how increased consumer investment in the Stock Market contributed to the onset of the Great Depression? (A) Corporate stock traders were able to purchase stock at lower rates than individual investors. (B) Individuals made poor choices about which stocks to buy. (C) Companies refused to pay regular dividends and instead reinvested in corporate growth. (D) Many people took out loans to finance their stock purchases then found themselves unable to repay those loans when the market slowed.

7. Much of the debt accumulated by consumers in the 1920s was due to…? (A) overproduction of agricultural goods, (B) <u>an increase in installment buying,</u> (C) extended strikes by labor unions, or (D) rising income taxes.

And on and on they go. In APUSH or other advanced coursework, you may get a few curveballs:

8. Complete this chain of events: First, consumers are unable to make payments on their installment plans. Second, demand for consumer goods declines. Third, manufacturers reduce production. Fourth…? (A) <u>companies begin laying off employees</u>. (B) Congress lowers tariff rates. (C) labor unions demand higher wages. (C) banks begin loaning money for stock market speculation.

9. Which of the following was a primary goal of the Federal Reserve Act (1913)? (A) Encouraging competition in the marketplace by breaking up trusts, (B) Raising money to finance World War I by selling war bonds and regulating prices, (C) <u>Providing stability in the national economy by creating a central banking system,</u> or (D) Encouraging American entrepreneurs by offers small business loans and other support.

Bank failures can be presented as both causes and results of the Depression. Think of them as the floor above you during an earthquake – its collapse could be a *result* of the same trembling you're experiencing, but when it crashes down on you it's also a primary *cause* of your injury and the destruction of the floor below you as well. (Sorry to be morbid, but it seemed an apt analogy.)

10. Which of the following statements best describes the role banks played in worsening the Great Depression? (A) Banks maintained high interest rates even when customers could no longer repay loans, (B) Bank owners chose to declare repeated "bank holidays" to prevent customers from accessing funds, (C) <u>The government did not insure deposits, so bank failures meant customers lost everything</u>, or (D) Foreign investment created an imbalance between loans and deposits.

You may even see questions about specific presidents of the era:

11. When Warren G. Harding said that "America's present need is not heroics, but healing… not revolution, but restoration… not submergence in internationality, but sustainment in triumphant nationality," he was promoting…? (A) <u>a "return to normalcy" after the turmoil and trials of WWI</u>, (B) restrictions on laissez-faire economics and corporate power, (C) the use of diplomacy to resolve disputes with other nations, or (D) a greater role for the U.S. across the globe.

12. Which of the following figures is remembered for insisting that "the chief business of the American people is business" and "the man who builds a factory, builds a temple"? (A) William McKinley, (B) <u>Calvin Coolidge</u>, (C) Andrew Carnegie, or (D) Cornelius Vanderbilt.

Short answer and essay prompts are likely to focus on one of two things –

why the 1920s were called the "Roaring Twenties" and stuff that in retrospect we think of as leading to the Great Depression. In APUSH or other advanced courses, you may even get something like this:

13. Compare and contrast the 1920s and 1950s in the United States with specific attention to changes in society and culture, economic policies, and the changing roles of women. (This one can come with pretty much any categories attached – race relations, foreign policy, consumerism, art and literature, etc.)

See? I told you the whole "preview of the 1950s" approach wasn't so crazy. You're welcome.

CHAPTER NINETEEN: THE 1950S
The Sixties Had to Come from Somewhere

Three Big Things:

1. The 1950s are largely remembered as a time of prosperity and "cultural homogeneity." Nevertheless, the major issues of the 1960s were poking through everywhere, if one thought to look.

2. An explosion of new "suburbs" (like Levittown) was facilitated by more highways and more automobiles. White families fled big cities for protected pockets of all-white schools, churches, and shopping, and green front lawns that all looked the same.

3. On a larger scale, workers and their families moved from the "Rust Belt" of the northeast to the "Sun Belt" of the south and west in pursuit of better employment opportunities. This move was facilitated by highways and cars as well, along with the miracle of better, cheaper air conditioning.

Introduction

The 1950s are an easily brushed-over decade, whether you're rushing to get through someone else's curriculum before "the test" or a lover of history browsing titles at your local bookstore or online.

As part of a formal curriculum, the fifties have the unenviable task of following World War II – which is kind of like booking Led Zeppelin as an opener and hoping the audience sticks around for your one-man banjo extravaganza. Even teachers who manage to get past "the last good war" before state testing or the AP Exam are anxious to get to the 1960s, where most of the important stuff is naturally engaging all on its own – sex, drugs, rock'n'roll, civil rights, hippies, war protests (and a war to go with them), MLK, JFK, LBJ, Malcolm X, Woodstock, "the pill," Brown Power, the American Indian Movement, women's rights – even men on the moon (yes, really).

Sure, we'd like to get to the Reagan Revolution and 9/11, but the Sixties managed to make sex safer and stage musicals blasphemous. Plus, there were Sea Monkeys. Why would we ever move on?

For adults simply interested in history, it's almost as bad. Browsing the shelves at your local bookstore or scrolling through Amazon search results, how often do you stop and exclaim, "Hey... post-war suburban development!" There are too many far more tantalizing topics to grab the eye, and no one wants to be the guy caught reading *The Rise of the Sunbelt: How the Interstate Highway System and Modern Air Conditioning Impacted Twentieth Century Migration Patterns* – as if your social life didn't have enough problems already.

The 1950s, however, have plenty of value to add to the conversation – and not just the interesting parts about the Cold War, the G.I. Bill, and the birth of rock'n'roll. Let's see if we can unborify a few of the most neglected or easily overlooked features of the decade before you eagerly plunge into all the violence, nudity, and social transformation of its successor.

The "Exciting" Parts of the 1950s

Despite its reputation (or lack thereof), there were plenty of important history-ish things going on in the 1950s which you probably already know about, even if you don't realize it.

The Cold War was certainly the biggest. This half-century staring contest between the U.S. and U.S.S.R. was already going strong by the time those post-WWII babies started to boom. With it came anticommunist hysteria topping even the "red scare" of the previous generation. All those Congressional committees investigating authors and filmmakers and McCarthy with his "list of known Communists" working for the State Department? That was all in the 1950s.

The Rosenbergs were executed in 1953 for (apparently) passing along U.S. atomic know-how to the Russians. Those same Russians launched *Sputnik* in 1957, prompting the creation of NASA in the U.S. and a national panic that American children didn't know enough math or science. (Sometimes it really *does* take a rocket scientist.)

Many of the less-dramatic-but-still-pretty-important results of the Cold War were rooted in the fifties – most notably the National Defense Education Act (1958). This provided financial aid for college students and boosted funding for math and science in high schools. It was the first meaningful foray of the federal government into public education and the basic approach proved so successful that it never went away: if Uncle Sam offers states enough money to do X, Y, or Z, he effectively becomes a controlling partner in what were previously state or local functions (at least according to the Constitution). If states want the money, they have to follow federal rules and adapt federal priorities.

Who's a good state? Does someone want federal funding? Hmmm? Heel, state – heel!

Speaking of "sharing" as a means of control, don't forget the Truman Doctrine (1947), under which the U.S. spends zillions of dollars every year propping up foreign "democracies" with American troops, money, and motivational posters. (The name is periodically updated to reflect whoever's in office, but its substance hasn't changed much in 75 years.) In 1954, President Eisenhower popularized the "domino theory" – the idea was that if communism were allowed to take hold anywhere in the world, the surrounding nations would soon fall to it as well. Capitalism and democracy, on the other hand, often required overwhelming military force to implement, as if they were for some reason less attractive to the rest of the world.

Weird, right?

American foreign policy was thus dramatically and forever altered. Rather than wait until U.S. interests were actually threatened, the military could now be sent anywhere in the world – locked, loaded, and overflowing with cash and lifestyle advice – to intervene wherever Uncle Sam thought it might be fun or profitable. It turned out to be surprisingly easy to justify just about *anything* in the name of someone else's "freedom" or "democracy" or "unrestricted oil supply." Besides, you wouldn't want the godless communists to win, would you?!

The same "domino theory" which would soon become one of the primary justifications for U.S. involvement in Vietnam was already being cited to explain the millions spent in the 1950s to finance the war against communism in Indochina. In the meantime, there was a Korean "conflict" to tie everyone over – like an extended trailer or complimentary appetizer. At least we got M*A*S*H out of the deal. (Rest in peace, Captain Tuttle.)

The modern Civil Rights Movement commonly associated with the 1960s actually started in the 1950s as well. The Supreme Court's decision in *Brown v. Board of Education* in 1954 and began the long, messy push towards school desegregation. (It's still possible we'll get there someday.) Rosa Parks refused to change seats on the bus in 1955, which in turn sparked the Montgomery Bus Boycott of 1956. A young reverend by the name of Martin Luther King, Jr., who pastored a church in the area, joined the protests and soon became the most recognizable face, name, and voice of the entire movement – all before New Year's Day, 1960.

There are a few other things we usually remember easily enough. The G.I. Bill, which helped returning soldiers go to school or start small businesses. The general economic prosperity of the postwar years. The explosion of modernity for normal people – kitchen appliances, automobiles, television, McDonald's, and Barbie. Finally, of course, there's that legendary "cultural homogeneity" of the 1950s – a collective sense of shared purpose lingering from WWII, now redirected into the brave struggle against alternative economic systems and political structures. There's great comfort in sameness, particularly when accompanied by common enemies and a newfound prosperity for those enemies to threaten.

In reality, the 1950s weren't quite as universally unified or prosperous as they appeared. Still, it was close enough to give the 1960s something to challenge – a lifestyle and presumed set of values for the youth of the era to reject. If nothing else, the 1950s made the 1960s possible. After all, how do you rebel against the mainstream unless there's a mainstream to rebel *against*?

So... what were the boring parts we should make sure we don't overlook?

Levittown and the Growth of the Suburbs

All those folks coming back from the war needed somewhere to live. Plus, there was that "Baby Boom" thing which began increasing the population. Dramatically. The name you should most remember in connection with all of this is William J. Levitt.

Levitt built entire neighborhoods of decent-but-affordable family homes. The most notable was his pilot project in Long Island, New York – Levittown. Disposable income was up, and while the 30-year mortgage so ubiquitous today wasn't yet standard, long-term financing was becoming increasingly common. The federal government played with ways to keep interest rates low to encourage home ownership and gave homeowners a big ol' tax deduction as well. (Remember the part above about using money to promote government-approved lifestyles?) It worked. Levitt sold nearly 17,000 homes in Long Island alone before moving into other markets. Needless to say, other developers quickly followed suit.

The ready availability of automobiles and the growth of highways made travel to and from work more convenient, even at a distance – and just look at all those freshly-mowed lawns that look exactly the same! Mass-produced suburban homes weren't always easy to tell apart. It became easy comedy to portray a husband coming home from work and entering the wrong home without ever noticing the difference. But this was the 50s – being the same as everyone else wasn't exactly a downside. For many, it was nirvana!

That homogeneity didn't end with the shingle choices on your Cape Cod. Levitt's suburbs, like many others, only sold to white families. This wasn't something subtle or implied by a close reading of the historical data; it was established policy. Part of the appeal of the suburbs was getting away from crowded cities and into affordable convenience, but the "white flight" element was a driving factor as well. White neighborhoods meant your kids could go to all-white schools and you could attend all-white churches and shop at all-white stores, etc.

Which brings us to an uncomfortable topic:

It's important to avoid creating the impression that racism in America was always planned, systematic, and intentional across the board and by everyone involved. History is generally far more complex than such easy talking points suggest, and as scholars we must seek truth over dogma. In reality, racism is only *usually* planned, systematic, and intentional across the board by *almost* everyone involved.

Other than that, though, the suburbs were (and are) swell.

Prosperity Doctrines

The federal government had poured major stimulation into the economy during WWII, and they were in no hurry to dial it back just because the bad guys had finally surrendered. Tax dollars both collected and anticipated were funneled into education, social programs, highways and other infrastructure, the aforementioned G.I. Bill, mortgage protection for all those new suburban homeowners, and anything else Congress could think of. While federal spending in the 1950s may have been humble by the standards of subsequent decades, the idea that it was a time of pure self-sufficiency or any version of laissez-faire economics is just silly. As with railroads, homesteading, and the New Deal, the "general welfare" often requires government support and encouragement.

Nothing against the "invisible hand," but it's terrible at land grants, national defense, affordable mail service, funding higher education, or promoting interstate travel.

In the 1950s, at least, all that government stimulation turned out to be quite effective. Americans whipped themselves into a consumerist frenzy, purchasing homes, cars, appliances, entertainment, and anything else they could think of. All that buying and wanting meant higher demand for pretty much everything, which in turn meant good wages and low unemployment – all while somehow keeping inflation manageable. It was truly a marvelous time to be alive. The growth of the suburbs nicely encapsulates all of these things.

Including the part where much of it only applied if you were white.

Let's Get Moving (Rust Belt ➡ Sun Belt)

For more than a century, manufacturing was central to the American economy. While the image of the north as universally industrialized and the south as endlessly agricultural is far too simplistic, a definable "Manufacturing Belt" *was* easily traceable from New York through Pennsylvania, Ohio, Indiana, Michigan, and eastern Illinois. Some sources would add St. Louis or other noncontiguous pockets, using the description less as a geographical marker than as an economic indicator – which it was.

Thousands of families throughout the "Manufacturing Belt" relied for generations on the solid blue-collar incomes available there. Workers produced steel, weapons, and automobiles, buoyed by a strong economy and periodic government contracts. Until, one day, they didn't.

The term "Rust Belt" didn't take hold until the late 1970s, by which time many factories were closed (or closing) and their structures left to decay. As with the more positive moniker, the term was less about specific location and more about economic changes – changes which took place unevenly and over an extended period. The decline of the "Manufacturing Belt" had been delayed by World War II, during which government defense needs brought a massive infusion of cash and energy to the region. Once peace ruined everything, however, the writing was on the factory wall. The party wasn't entirely over, but the DJ had switched to slow dances and the host was out of punch.

History teachers like to talk about "push-pull" factors whenever people migrate. There's usually at least one good reason to *leave* a place and a different good reason for one's chosen *destination*. In the mid-twentieth century, changes in the economy and dramatic technological improvements began chipping away at blue collar jobs across the "Manufacturing Belt" (aka "Rust Belt"). At the same time, high-tech industries and defense plants were beginning to flourish in parts of the south and along the west coast. The "push" was the loss of opportunity up north; the "pull" was the need for skilled and semi-skilled labor in the south and west.

The "Sun Belt" migration didn't happen overnight, and it wasn't monolithic. A "Second Great Migration" occurred at much the same time as Black workers left the south in search of greater economic opportunity and less racial oppression. Some headed north, but many headed west in search of the same jobs drawing white laborers from the north. (Side Note: "white" by this time had largely expanded to include descendants of numerous immigrant groups reviled by Anglos – and one another – only a few generations before.) Skilled or semi-skilled workers could find reliable employment and good wages in Los Angeles, Portland, Phoenix, and the like, as well as in select cities scattered across the south – locations not previously known for their manufacturing prowess.

Remember the Missouri Compromise way back in 1820? Picture that same general line reaching both directions to each coast. Once we get to the 1950s, everything below that line (minus Oklahoma, because... *Oklahoma*) becomes collectively known as the "Sun Belt." "Sun" because it's hot down there, but also "Sun" like "Here Comes the ____." The Sun Belt was the new land of opportunity for workers in the fifties and thereafter.

The 1950s were still a pretty good time to be a blue-collar worker, but that was beginning to change. Republicans were already successfully limiting worker protections and weakening labor unions. President Truman had vetoed the Taft-Hartley Act in 1947, but Congress passed it anyway. Depending on your point of view, this act and others like it either reined in union abuses and suppressed communist influences in the workplace or began rolling back worker protections and working conditions to something more akin to the Gilded Age.

Politicians still like to promise select regions of the nation that, if elected, they'll restore the great age of manufacturing and bring back all those textile mills, coal mining jobs, and other 1950s era factory gigs. They'll eliminate all manufacturing technology developed over the past half-century and ensure a glorious new age of sweaty uneducated labor for outrageously high wages. This absurd campaign strategy works far more often than it should, proving once again that democracy may have been a huge mistake after all.

On The Road Again...

All the moving about described above was made much easier by the interstate highway system. The Eisenhower Administration championed the passage of the Federal Aid Highway Act (1956) which dramatically increased the number and quality of freeways across the U.S. (Henry Clay and the Whigs would have been thrilled.) States often contributed funding to the segments within their borders, but federal money and planning was key – and that's what was new and *almost* exciting about the whole thing.

Much of the infrastructure was paid for through taxes on vehicles and gasoline and justified as essential for national defense. (If the Commies landed on our shores, we'd need to be able to get our soldiers, tanks, and boom-sticks to wherever they needed to be, quickly and efficiently.) It was tolerated because most people were feeling pretty prosperous and didn't want those "reds" coming after their nifty new black and white television sets or hi-tech frozen dinners. The trucking industry loved it, as did white families shifting to the suburbs and pretty much anyone moving from the "Rust Belt" to the "Sun Belt."

Not everyone was thrilled. New construction often meant moving or elim-inating older neighborhoods and relocating residents. Railroads were under-standably dismayed. Urban residents who relied on public transportation – often the elderly or poor – soon found their lives becoming more difficult. The environmentalists wouldn't have loved it either, but that really wasn't a thing yet. They'd make up for lost time come 1970, however.

Whatever their downsides, interstate highways have become an essential element of state and federal cooperation and are considered critical in-frastructure today. They make excellent metaphors for freedom and oppor-tunity and adventure ("If you're going my way, I wanna drive it all night long..."). They're also powerful symbols of environmental destruction, the loss of humanity and individuality, and a future rushing madly forward with unstoppable force ("I didn't hear nobody pray, dear brother... I heard the crash on the highway, but I didn't hear nobody pray...").

Highways aren't particularly helpful without automobiles, of course. Once World War II ended, Americans who'd saved up money during the war (partly because there were so few big-ticket items available) were ready to spend. In-dustries which had been fully committed to wartime production shifted back into making consumer goods, including automobiles. It was a perfect match of supply and demand.

No wonder the communists were so jealous. They didn't even have toaster ovens.

The other major technological evolution smoothing this massive migration was air conditioning. The underlying technology had been around for several decades, but it was in the post-war years that air conditioning was first con-sidered indispensable. If you want people to be productive during the day and tolerably comfortable and well-rested at night anywhere south of Nebraska, you need affordable, effective, artificial air-cooling. Now it was possible – even *practical*. When combined with neat stuff like refrigerators, washers and dryers, vacuum cleaners, and the like, Americans in the 1950s had arguably the highest quality of living in the known universe.

Even without Sea Monkeys (which were coming soon).

The Writing (and Painting) On The Wall

Not everything was as idyllic as it may have seemed in the 1950s – at least, not for everyone. Poverty still existed and racial disparities were glaring in many parts of the nation. Even among mainstream white folks, there were hints of discontent.

Some of the art, for example, started to get a bit challenging. Abstract expressionism was just coming into its own, while guys like Edward Hopper or George Tooker utilized new forms of realism (Hopper) and surrealism (Tooker) to explore the universality of human isolation. Jack Kerouac violated sexual taboos and experimented with drugs while writing it all down (often in no particular order). Allen Ginsberg broke poetry howling about broken people and a broken society, echoing the chaos around and within by writing in new and provocative forms. J.D. Salinger's *Catcher in the Rye* explored teenage disillusionment through the eyes of a young man who failed his classes and was diagnosed as mentally ill because of how he felt about the world around him.

Also, he cussed. A lot.

Abstract art and the Beatniks may seem tame compared to what came next, but at the time... well, what came next hadn't happened yet.

Making The Grade: What You're Most Likely To Be Asked

Expect at least one generic multiple choice question about Levittown or the growth of suburbs in general. These may be presented in conjunction with the Baby Boom, soldiers returning from the war, the interstate highway system, the increase in automobile ownership, or general post-war prosperity. All of these are by themselves fair game as well:

1. The 1950s saw a dramatic expansion of the middle class, the development of an interstate highway system, and the introduction and explosive growth of suburbs. These trends were largely the result of...? (A) the increase in federal bureaucracy and oversight after the war, (B) reduced spending and lower taxes after the war, (C) widespread economic prosperity after WWII, or (D) the "open borders" policies of the Truman and Eisenhower administrations.

2. One prominent result of the "Baby Boom" after World War II was... (A) the growth of suburbs like Levittown (NY), (B) a growing dissatisfaction of women with modern conveniences and motherhood, (C) greater restrictions on immigration, or (D) a large-scale migration from the "Rust Belt" to the "Sun Belt."

3. The rapid development of suburban areas across the U.S. during the 1950s was largely a result of...? (A) the lower cost of building materials after the war, (B) the increased supply of skilled labor as soldiers returned home, (C) the rapid deterioration of urban areas, or (D) the growth of a national highway system.

The shift from the Rust Belt to the Sun Belt will usually get at least one question either identifying the movement itself or specifying the underlying causes. Don't be surprised if there's a map included – meaning you might not get helpful cues like "Rust Belt" or "Sun Belt" in the actual prompt. For that matter, the "map" might not even be a map, but a chart or graph demonstrating the population shift in some other way – changes in electoral votes for select states, growth of some cities and population decline in others, etc. If it's the 1950s, picture arrows coming out of the northeast and heading south and/or west. (And don't forget some "Second Great Migration" arrows coming out of the south as well.)

4. Which of the following was NOT a major factor in the migration patterns shown above? (A) The decline of employment opportunities in the northeast. (B) <u>The expansion of voting rights and political participation for Black Americans in the South</u>. (C) Improved air conditioning technology available at lower costs. (D) The growth of an interstate highway system.

APUSH and other advanced classes are likely to ask about ways in which "postwar economic and demographic changes had far-reaching consequences for American society, politics, and culture." Specific prompts will usually narrow things down in some way or ask you to make specific connections – tying the development of the suburbs to the Reagan Revolution a generation later, for example, or comparing reactions to *Brown v. Board* with resistance to bussing efforts of the 1970s or the explosion of private schools and voucher programs still being debated today. The powers-that-be get particularly giddy when you're able to identify specific technological improvements (automobiles, air conditioning, etc.) as driving forces behind major migration patterns.

APUSH also loves primary sources and visuals, so look for ads related to Levittown or similar endeavors. It's not unheard of for them to ask you to compare some aspect of the 1950s (the culture, the economy, the politics) with a similar decade (like the 1920s) or other forgotten decade (like the 1970s).

None of this means you can ignore all the expected stuff – the Truman Doctrine, the Fair Deal, the Taft-Hartley Act, *Brown v. Board*, Rosa Parks, the bus boycott, MLK, McCarthyism, NATO, the Marshall Plan, and curriculum writers' bizarre fascination with John Foster Dulles. If it seems like a lot to keep up with, just wait until you get into the 1960s.

CHAPTER TWENTY: THE CARTER ADMINISTRATION (1977-1981)

Good Men Don't Always Make Good Leaders

Three Big Things:

1. The 1970s were a time of continued social upheaval, political mistrust, and economic quagmire. Jimmy Carter was a Washington outsider voters hoped could bring a fresh, new approach to leadership and turn things around.

2. President Carter's foreign policy was more concerned with human rights and "doing the right thing" than with cold, pragmatic calculations about American's best interests. He hosted the historic Camp David Accords between Egypt and Israel (major win), boycotted the 1980 Olympics in Moscow (unpopular), gave the Panama Canal to Panama (*very* unpopular), and ended his presidency crippled by the Iran Hostage Crisis (the nadir of a generation).

3. At home, Carter was unable to end the energy crisis or restore economic growth and confidence during his time in office. While many of the problems he faced began long before his inauguration, he is the president most closely associated with gas shortages and "stagflation." Along the way, he blamed Americans for not having pluckier attitudes about it all.

Introduction

President Jimmy Carter served one term, from 1977 to 1981. While quite memorable at the time (for better or worse), the Carter Administration is easy to overlook when reviewing the twentieth century. In a classroom setting, end-of-the-year examinations are rapidly approaching by the time the 1970s arrive, and even for the informal student of history the decade was surrounded by far more appetizing topics. The 1960s were packed with provocative people, issues, and events – the Cold War, the modern Civil Rights Movement, JFK, MLK, LBJ's "Great Society," Vietnam, Woodstock, Hippies, War Protests, Malcolm X, the Pill... even man landing on the moon. Then came the Nixon Administration, with even *more* Vietnam, the "silent majority," the Plumbers, CREEP, and of course Watergate – the scandal we all thought was as bad as things could realistically get without complete and total collapse of our little adventure in representative government.

Silly us.

Immediately following Carter's time in office came the Reagan Revolution and the birth of the modern conservative movement, as well as their new apocalyptic, us-or-them, heaven-or-hell approach to *everything*, be it political, economic, cultural, or spiritual. The pendulum which had swung so far left during the 1960s and early 1970s came back like a righteous wrecking ball, full of fury and zeal. We're still navigating the dynamics of that one today.

And yet, in the middle of all this came four years deserving at least a *little* attention. If nothing else, the Carter Administration provides handy examples what the 1980s were reacting *against*. So let everyone else zero in on the exciting topics, the brand name players, and events so memorable they've been brought to life in movies and television a dozen times over. We're going to talk about national malaise, the Camp David Accords, and what *not* to do when attacked by aquatic bunnies.

Early Political Lessons

Whatever one thinks of his politics, most folks agree that Jimmy Carter was (and as of this writing, *is*) a good man. He was born on a small farm in Georgia and raised in a home without electricity or indoor plumbing. His mother defied local law and custom by crossing over into "Negro" territory to counsel Black women on issues related to pregnancy or general health and nutrition. He served his country in the Navy before coming back to Georgia to become a peanut farmer. He taught Sunday School and served on various local boards working to improve the lives of his neighbors. He was a good ol' boy, minus the gun fetish or "Don't Tread On Me" flag on the back of his truck.

Carter served in the Georgia state Senate, then ran for Governor in 1966. He was quite vocal about his opposition to segregation and his support of voting rights for Black Americans, which for some reason didn't play well across much of the state. When he ran again four years later, he dialed back his rhetoric on racial issues substantially; that seemed to do the trick. Carter became governor of Georgia in 1971 and (despite his shift in campaign strategy) declared segregation in the state *over* – a laudable goal, no doubt, but perhaps a tad premature.

Why he didn't pronounce poverty ended and Mars conquered as well remains uncertain.

Carter had even higher ambitions, however – and with the way things were going in D.C., it was beginning to look like he just might have a shot at attaining them.

Watergate

Watergate is *not* boring history. It's been well-covered plenty of other places and there's no need to go into it here. What matters for our purposes is that the corruption of Nixon and his cronies cast a serious pall over all things GOP. Congressional Republicans had defended Nixon almost to the bitter end, but after the release of secret recordings made in the Oval Office ("So John, how's the massive illegal coverup going?"), most felt they had no choice but to vote for impeachment. The American public felt lied to, not only by their President but by the party who had repeatedly assured them all was well until they just couldn't pull it off anymore.

Nixon's Vice President, Spiro Agnew, had already resigned by the time impeachment was looming. (He faced a variety of charges which included tax evasion, bribery, extortion, and all sorts of other naughty-sounding things.) Agnew was replaced by Gerald Ford, a solid Republican insider with limited charisma and a bad habit of losing his balance while cameras were rolling. When Nixon, too, resigned, Ford became president. Ford promptly pardoned Nixon, claiming it was necessary to bring America's "long, national nightmare" to a close.

Most Americans weren't convinced.

So, as the Election of 1976 approached, Democrats knew they had a grand opportunity. One of those Democrats was Governor James Earl Carter, Jr., of Georgia. His friends just called him "Jimmy."

The Election of 1976

Carter had several advantages going into the Democratic primaries:

* He was a relative "outsider" at a time when many voters were dissatisfied and suspicious of politicians – whatever their party affiliations.

* The Democratic field was unusually chaotic, with over a dozen maor candidates running. Figures who'd normally have captured news time or who might already be familiar to voters were often lost in the shuffle. That left campaign stops, one-on-one conversations, and the periodic unplanned news event to boost or destroy you.

* Party rules had recently changed so that primaries had become the determining factor in choosing a candidate – not the party bosses meeting in back rooms during the convetion. Many candidates hadn't yet adjusted to this and saw no reason to enter *every* state primary contest, let alone *visit* every single state. Carter was considered an oddball when he decided to do just that.

* Primary season was a mess (it was still the 1970s, after all), and many of the extreme personalities and mini-melodramas kinda cancelled one another out. When candidates first began withdrawing from the race, Carter was a safe option to throw their support behind. He'd largely avoided extremes and had only minimal gaffs. Most importantly, he didn't seem to be the polar opposite of anyone else in the race – you might not have loved him, but you probably didn't hate him, either. He was the Applebee's of the Democratic Party dinner options that year.

Former governor of California Ronald Reagan challenged sitting president Gerald Ford for the Republican nomination, but the party was hesitant to unseat their own incumbent, however unexciting he may have been. Reagan's concession speech at the Republican Convention left many thinking perhaps they'd made the wrong choice, but it might not have mattered either way. Democrats won strong majorities in both the House and Senate in the 1976 elections and would likely have taken the presidency no matter who they ran that year. Jimmy "Who?!" Carter became the thirty-ninth President of the United States.

The Outsider

Some of the same characteristics which made Carter such an appealing candidate nearly crippled him as an executive. Congress (including many from his own party) viewed this squeaky-clean outsider with skepticism, and Carter did himself no favors by shunning the face-to-face discussions and political give-and-take typically required to move one's agenda through the legislature. He came across as either arrogant or ignorant, depending on the moment, and opposed even his own party's spending priorities when he found them wasteful or unnecessary. Republicans nevertheless managed to portray him as an out-of-control tax-and-spend liberal, a strategy which would prove quite effective no matter what the reality of any given administration for the next half-century.

Whatever voters had expected from Carter, in practice they found themselves wanting more "leader" and less "manager." Whereas some men see the forest, and others the individual trees, Carter was aptly described as more of a "leaf man" – so focused on minutia and daily details that he often missed both the big picture and the essentials of the moment. America wanted to be inspired, not audited. Before long, it didn't really matter what he did or didn't accomplish – the public's perception was that they'd elected a dud.

The Energy Crisis

The details of the "Energy Crisis" of the 1970s can get a bit daunting. An accurate breakdown involves economics, politics, world history, cultural geography, religion, and strong emotions. It was that very complexity that prevented most voters from caring much about the technicalities. What *was* clear was that gas prices went *up*, and eventually lines got so long you couldn't even fill your tank without it taking half the day. *That* part people understood: Gas lines bad! Energy crisis bad! Want car gas good! Maybe grab Slushee!

The roots of the crisis arguably trace back to the story of Jacob and Esau (see Genesis 25–33), but for our purposes we'll start a few thousand years after that in 1973 C.E. You've probably heard of OPEC, a group of oil-producing states in the Middle East who coordinate production and pricing to maintain profits and their own long-term supplies. OPEC was annoyed with Uncle Sam because during the Arab-Israeli War of 1973, the U.S. jumped in and supported Israel with resources and encouraging words ("Go get 'em, Izzy! You got this! Shalom! Torah Torah Torah!"). In retaliation, OPEC imposed an embargo – no one in their cartel would sell oil to the U.S. or other allies of Israel *at any price.*

Naturally this drove gas prices up considerably. Open any American History textbook to the chapter on the 1970s and you'll find a black-and-white photo of long lines of cars waiting to get gas. It was depressing. The embargo lasted for less than six months, but the economic (and emotional) fallout would linger far longer. The freedom of the open road had by that time become a foundational American value, and no one appreciated having it stripped away from them in such humbling fashion.

To his credit, Nixon made token efforts to decrease U.S. dependence on foreign oil. Even Ford pushed fuel economy standards for new vehicles. Neither accomplished much. If the U.S. continued to support Israel, they were going to pay for it (literally) at the pump.

Economists will tell you it's more complicated than that, and they're probably right – but we don't care. What matters here is that when Jimmy Carter took office, he knew that energy policy would be central to his success or failure... not to mention the well-being of the nation. It would take bold leadership and decisive action to ensure America's energy independence! So, Carter promptly had solar panels installed on the roof of the White House and raised taxes on gasoline to discourage consumption.

Done! On to cultural decay and unemployment!

OK, that's not entirely fair – but it does reflect how much of the public perceived Carter's response to the crisis. In reality, Carter pushed through an Emergency Natural Gas Act which allowed the federal government to manage the national supply of natural gas. He created the Department of Energy to support and regulate the entire industry in hopes of increasing efficiency while promoting innovation and conservation. He pushed for greater deregulation of fuel prices in order to lower consumer prices at the pump and promoted alternative energy sources (particularly nuclear power).

The alternative energy thing remained hit-and-miss over the years, but the rest of Carter's efforts were generally successful. By the early 1980s, gas prices were under control. Supplies were up and the nation was merrily revving its collective engines again... and thanking Carter's successor.

The Panama Canal "Giveaway"

Since 1914 or so, the Panama Canal had symbolized either American engineering prowess and economic might or the worst elements of white imperialism, depending on one's point of view. The U.S. had gone to a great deal of trouble to secure the area (it's not always easy starting revolutions in other folks' countries) and then to complete the actual canal (over 25,000 workers died in the effort), and there was absolutely no way they were going to give it up without—

What's that? He did? Are you sure? Well, then, um...

Carter gave it away. Because it seemed like the right thing to do.

In September of 1977, less than a year after his inauguration, President Carter signed a treaty with Panama's dictator, a fellow named Omar Torrijos, transferring control of the canal to Panama by the end of the century. The U.S. also agreed to give up ownership of the "Canal Zone" around the actual waterway. Carter hoped the gesture would help reduce tensions between the U.S. and many South American countries by demonstrating a new level of respect for their autonomy – a kind of "sorry about the whole imperialism thing" or "new besties forever!" type gesture.

Whatever the reaction in South America, the decision didn't go over well with everyone back home. Carter played his one and only "hey-I'm-the-brand-new-president-and-I'm-from-your-party" card in order to eke through Senate ratification by a single vote. He'd find it increasingly difficult to duplicate this success moving forward.

The Camp David Accords

Any discussion of foreign policy under President Carter has to start with the phrase "human rights." It should end with the phrase "human rights" as well. And you'll probably want to stick it in the middle seven or eight times just to be clear.

Even if we assume most presidents are good people genuinely trying to do what's best for the country (don't roll your eyes like that – it's rude), Carter's insistence on morality as a foundation for policy was disruptive, and not always popular. A fervent Christian, Carter had the wacky idea that Biblical values (as opposed to the right-wing dogma which would mesmerize the faith community less than a decade later) should shape every major decision he made. That meant he was big on compromise, peace, and the-other-cheek-turning – no matter whose cheek might be involved.

The crowning achievement of the Carter presidency was series of compromises made between Egypt and Israel in September of 1978. Carter brought Egyptian President Anwar Sadat (pronounced AN-war seh-DOT) and Israeli Prime Minister Menachem Begin (pronounced meh-NOCK-em BAY-gin)** together at Camp David (Maryland), typically utilized as a sort of vacation campgrounds for presidents and their guests. The details of the agreements involve far more Middle Eastern history than necessary here, but the short version was that the Arab world (as represented by Egypt) recognized Israel's right to exist, while Israel agreed to begin withdrawing from the West Bank, thus making room for a Palestinian state there.

If you watch the news at all, you've probably noticed that things in that part of the world aren't exactly settled nearly a half-century later. Not everyone impacted was thrilled even at the time. Still, the Camp David Accords were the first formal negotiations between Israel and any of its Arab neighbors. They showed that compromises were possible and that peace was a mutual goal, at least most of the time. The next major negotiations producing positive results in the Middle East were fifteen years later and modeled very closely after what happened at Camp David. Most subsequent efforts have followed the same basic recipe. Whatever else Carter did or didn't manage, he set a high bar for future presidents and their role in facilitating peace in that part of the world while protecting Israel, a treasured ally.

At the risk of sounding cynical, the Accords also laid the groundwork for another proud American peace strategy – paying everyone involved billions of dollars every year as long as they keep playing nicely with one another. And here you thought we were going all positive and rose-colored for once. Sorry – it's still history.

The Rest Of The World

Carter's record was mixed (at least in terms of public perception) dealing with rest of the world. During his time in office, U.S. foreign policy moved away from the *realpolitik* and détente of the Nixon era and began prioritizing human rights instead (or did we mention that already...?) Nations who subscribed to Uncle Sam's concept of playing nicely with their populace and with one another might get a little help from time to time. Those who didn't, well...

This wasn't an outright rejection of the progress Nixon had made reducing tensions between the U.S. and Soviet Union – just a shift in focus. In June of 1979, Carter and Soviet president Leonid Brezhnev signed the SALT-II Treaty which limited nuclear proliferation and otherwise attempted to reduce the likelihood of ending life on the planet as we know it – at least for another decade or two. The first treaty (now called "SALT-I") was signed during the Nixon administration with the same basic goals but left many important details unresolved. As the years went by, the U.S. worried that the U.S.S.R. was pulling ahead in the arms race while the Russians didn't like how well Uncle Sam was getting along with the Chinese. Both hoped to slow down the other a bit and regroup.

In reality, the new treaty wouldn't actually have changed much, but it still couldn't muster enough support back home to secure Senate approval. Conservatives saw it as another example of traitorous liberal concessions to the Commies while those genuinely interested in arms control were upset that it failed to take serious steps to control the growth of nuclear weapons on either side. After the Soviets invaded Afghanistan in December of 1979, Carter realized it just wasn't going to happen and pulled the treaty from Senate consideration. (Both sides nevertheless agreed in principle to try to follow it until they could come up with something better... so that's something.)

Once the Russians were in Afghanistan, Carter allowed his administration to return to more of a "Cold War" mindset, supporting "containment" and increased military spending. Carter cut off food exports to the Soviets and instituted an American boycott of the 1980 Olympics, which were being held in Moscow that year. For a president with a tougher public persona, these actions might have been perceived as taking a hard stand against Soviet aggression. For voters who'd already largely made their minds up about their chief executive, it appeared the president was punishing American farmers and athletes more than he was Leonid Brezhnev.

Carter was slightly more successful elsewhere. He built on the progress made during the Nixon administration and granted China (still proudly communist) formal diplomatic recognition as of New Years' Day 1979, further reducing tensions between the two nations and eventually leading to an active trading relationship which continues today. At the same time, Carter insisted the U.S. cease sending aid to totalitarian governments in South America who abused their power and rejected democratic reforms.

A president can try, yes?

The Malaise Speech

In July of 1979, President Carter asked for TV time to address the nation. (In the 1970s, there were still only three major networks plus PBS in most regions; when a president had something important to say, they asked those three networks if they could have a slot. Usually, all three said yes.) After boring viewers with what felt like *hundreds* of anecdotes about his discussions with various voters and their perceptions of him and of government, Carter told the nation the <u>real</u> problem was a "crisis of confidence":

> It is a crisis that strikes at the very heart and soul and spirit of our national will. We can see this crisis in the growing doubt about the meaning of our own lives and in the loss of a unity of purpose for our nation. The erosion of our confidence in the future is threatening to destroy the social and the political fabric of America.

Rather than inspire, encourage, or energize, Carter lectured the nation on why they were depressed and told them they should try harder *not* to be depressed. The president then segued into his new energy policy and insisted that Americans try to use less oil and more public transportation. He also told them to eat more leafy vegetables and to stop provoking their sister when she's trying to do her homework. And would it kill you to put your clothes *in the hamper* once in a while? They're not going to crawl there by themselves, you know.

Needless to say, the nation was instantly revitalized and things begin turning around dramatically almost overnight. Wait – that's a typo. It should read, "In retrospect, this was a horrible idea."

The moment is remembered in history as Carter's "malaise" speech (although he never actually used that term in his remarks). It would stand in sharp contrast to his successor's ability to persuade voters that it was "morning again in America" and things were going nowhere but up. There's something to be said for the "say it until it's true" approach – and I'm not even being sarcastic this time.

The Iran Hostage Crisis (Part One)

Iranian revolutionaries spent most of 1978 and the first few months of 1979 overthrowing the hereditary monarchy which had ruled Iran since the 1920s and replacing it with an Islamic republic. It's tricky in the western world to be both succinct and accurate when it comes to Islamic affairs; we simply have too much baggage and too many stereotypes when it comes to that part of the world and its sociopolitical dynamics. Suffice it to say that in this case, the net result was replacing someone relatively moderate (at least in all the ways that mattered to the U.S.) with someone not particularly moderate (and who didn't care for the U.S. at all). His name was Ayatollah Khomeini.

"Ayatollah" is a title indicating religious leadership. It's typically pronounced "EYE-uh-TOLL-uh.". Khomeini was his actual name. It's pronounced "co-MAIN-ee" by us western types.**

The guy he usurped was Mohammad Reza Pahlavi, the final (as it turned out) shah of the Pahlavi Dynasty. It doesn't matter how *his* name is pronounced because no one in the U.S. history biz ever uses it. He is simply remembered as "the Shah." If you want to be especially fancy, you can add "of Iran." (Make sure you rhyme it with "I fawn," not "I ran.")

Initially, Carter took a hands-off approach. The Shah had a poor record when it came to human rights which trumped even many practical concerns in the minds of the president. In October of 1979, however, the Shah was allowed to come to the U.S. to receive medical treatment (he had cancer). That was the trigger that sparked what became known as the Iran Hostage Crisis.

There were plenty of underlying causes already in place, of course. The U.S. and the Middle East have never played all that well together – religious, historical, and political divisions run deep on both sides. Many Iranians had long resented American "interference" in their affairs. Great Britain and the U.S. had controlled much of Iran's oil supplies for decades and freely inserted themselves in local elections and policymaking by way of protecting those interests.

It's easy to forget that while Khomeini was the "bad guy" in the story from a western standpoint, he was the "hero" to many Iranians. Even for those less religiously fundamentalist, the Ayatollah was a substantial improvement over the Shah. Pahlavi was one of those U.S. allies who tortured and murdered thousands of his own people, but who Uncle Sam thought was a swell fellow because, well... oil and influence and schmoozing with the red, white, and blue. (You know, the usual.) The Ayatollah was a militant fundamentalist, but at least he wasn't buying weapons from western devils to use against his own kind.

Intermission: The Killer Rabbit

In the middle of this madness, one of those stupid little side events occurred which didn't have to become a thing, let alone secure a place on the cover of "How Not To President." But, as luck would have it...

In August of 1979, Carter was fishing near his home in Georgia, alone in a canoe in the middle of a lake. A rabbit appeared, swimming madly towards the president's boat. Carter was enough of a sportsman to recognize an animal on the run (it was being chased by hounds, although that wasn't immediately obvious) and wasn't even all that surprised to see a rabbit swimming. (Most wild animals can, in a pinch.) He used his paddle to push the creature away, knowing that it's generally unwise to tempt fate by allowing yourself to become trapped in a canoe with a panicked wild animal of *any* sort – even a rabbit. It wasn't fear, just experience and caution.

The incident would probably been quickly forgotten except for two things. First, an official presidential photographer happened to get a few shots of the event. Second, several people close to the president thought it made for a humorous story – the kind where you're laughing *with* someone you like and think well of. They didn't consider how the story might play to people who already considered the president to be a bit of a buffoon – weak and embarrassing and such. It wasn't long before reporters and editorial cartoonists were having a field day with the image of Carter "warding off a killer rabbit" from his canoe. It didn't help that most people didn't even believe rabbits could swim, let alone that there was ever a situation in which you might need to bat them away. Caricature subsumed reality almost immediately and the event became one of the most crippling metaphors of Carter's presidency.

The Iran Hostage Crisis (Part Two)

In early November of 1979, less than a month after the Shah arrived in the U.S., a group of revolutionaries (who also happened to be Iranian college students) breached the walls of the American embassy in Tehran and took 66 hostages. 14 were released shortly afterwards – women, people of color, or citizens of other nations who Khomeini considered "oppressed" by the U.S. That left 52 hostages at the embassy, where they'd remain for a long, long, *long* time.

Diplomatic efforts didn't seem to go anywhere and before long the nightly news was opening with "America Held Hostage, Day XX!" It wasn't very encouraging. In April of 1980, Carter authorized a rescue mission with a dramatic code name – "Operation Eagle Claw!" (The exclamation point wasn't actually in the official title, but it certainly feels implied, doesn't it?) An unscheduled desert sandstorm brought down several military helicopters essential to the operation, one of which crashed into a transport plane and killed eight American soldiers. As commander-in-chief, Carter took the blame and once again appeared both weak and incompetent as a result.

The president didn't do much campaigning during the 1980 election cycle, choosing to focus on the ongoing hostage crisis instead. He was still in the news every evening, but it wasn't the kind of coverage that gets you reelected. Carter had been caricatured as something of a tragic buffoon before, but now it felt like he'd taken the rest of the country down with him. Impotent and in over his head, he floundered while voters prayed for a savior.

The 1980 elections were held a few days after the one year anniversary of the embassy takeover. Ronald Reagan won in one of the most lopsided victories in American history. The Iranian revolutionaries kept their hostages until the inauguration, releasing them a few hours after Reagan took the oath of office. Whether this was a coincidence (negotiations had been going on behind the scenes through various intermediaries for months) or a strategic decision by the revolutionaries for reasons of their own, it baptized Reagan's presidency with a sense of strength and renewal he'd as of yet done little, if anything, to earn. It nevertheless served as a fitting preview for the rest of the Reagan administration and its priorities – the U.S. was back, and Uncle Sam wasn't playing any longer.

Stagflation & Societal Decay

The many shortcomings, both real and perceived, of Carter's administration might have been forgiven – or at least mitigated – if the economy had been strong or people felt secure in their communities. But the 1970s were in many ways microwaved leftovers of the 1960s, minus the revolutionary fervor of young activists or the naïve optimism of "flower power." Also, the music wasn't as good – which didn't help.

Marriage rates were down, illegitimate births were up, and drugs weren't that fun anymore (not that they'd ever been a *great* idea). Crime of all sorts was on the rise and optimism was on the skids as the last remnants of American manufacturing seemed to be turning to rust with little hint what might take its place. Income inequality grew more extreme and the "generation gap" became less about eye-rolling and more about fear and hostility between demographics. Political divisions seemed increasingly insurmountable. Half the nation longed for the good ol' days while the other half fought for a better future.

Economically, the nation experienced what would become known as "stagflation." Production and employment fell while prices rose – the worst of both worlds. It was easily the bleakest economic era since the Great Depression.

In short, Americans saw themselves failing as a world power, decaying as a society, and collapsing as an economy. Watergate had ruined any sense of political superiority, leaving the nation without much to feel good about. The setting was ripe for anyone able to make America feel good about itself again. As it turned out, someone did.

Making The Grade: What You're Most Likely To Be Asked

Multiple choice questions over the Carter administration are annoyingly unpredictable. There will almost always be a few, but the events on which they'll focus and the depth of knowledge required to successfully respond are inconsistent to say the least. If you're lucky, you'll encounter questions centered around three basic things – Carter's focus on human rights, the Camp David Accords, and the energy crisis of the 1970s.

1. What priority or principle formed the foundation of President Carter's foreign policy? (A) human rights, (B) free trade, (C) compromise and diplomacy before military action, or (D) *realpolitik*.

2. How did the boycott of the 1980 Olympics, the Panama Canal Treaty, and the Camp David Accords reflect the foreign policy priorities of President Jimmy Carter? (A) They demonstrated Carter's willingness to compromise with unpopular or oppressive leaders. (B) They showed Carter's focus on

human rights and respect for the sovereignty of other nations. (C) They manifested Carter's conviction that a strong military was there to be used in peacetime as well as war. (D) They're examples of Carter using "dollar diplomacy" to secure the cooperation of other nations.

3. Which of the following resulted from President Carter's efforts to bring greater stability to the Middle East while still protecting the interests of Israel? (A) The Paris Peace Accords, (B) The Panama Canal Treaty, (C) The Camp David Accords, or (D) The Nuclear Test Ban Treaty.

4. Which of the following do most historians agree constituted President Carter's greatest foreign policy achievement? (A) He effective resolved the Suez Crisis, (B) He withdrew U.S. troops from Vietnam, (C) he helped open up diplomatic relations with Iran, or (D) he mediated the Camp David Accords between Israel and Egypt.

5. Why did gasoline prices rise dramatically in the 1970s? (A) Congress imposed new regulations on foreign energy imports. (B) Middle Eastern nations limited American access to petroleum for nations supporting Israel. (C) Natural disasters impeded offshore drilling. (D) Congress imposed punitive gas taxes to encourage the development of alternative fuel sources.

Sometimes OPEC will be referred to by name; other times the reference to oil-producing nations is more general. Questions asking about domestic "solutions" are almost always looking for "alternative fuel sources." Many, *many* questions related to gas shortages will include pictures of cars waiting to get fuel...

6. How did the federal government attempt to address fuel shortages and long lines at the pump? (A) Congress reduced the maximum speed limit on national highways. (B) The president assigned citizens to specific days of the week on which they could get gas. (C) The government supported the development of alternative power sources. (D) Congress approved tapping into national emergency petroleum reserves. (This same question may have a picture and ask how the government addressed "the situation show in this photograph" or something similar.)

Outside of these big three topics, however, it's difficult to predict what might come up. For such an easily overlooked one-term presidency, it sure seemed to cover a lot of ground:

7. President Carter declared that the U.S. had a "crisis of confidence." What was his proposed solution? (A) More energy conservation and the development of alternative fuel sources. (B) Greater federal investment in counseling services – especially for families. (C) A renewed focus on the space program. (D) Everyone turn to the person to your left and tell them something you *really* like about them.

8. The SALT I and SALT II treaties of the 1970s attempted to reduce tensions with the Soviet Union by... (A) reducing tariffs and eliminating trade barriers, (B) formalizing relations and establishing permanent embassies in one

another's capitals, (C) blending parts of each nation's space exploration pro-grams, or (D) <u>limiting each side's supply of nuclear weapons.</u>

Short answer or essay prompts specifically about the Carter Administration or events therein are rare. You'll want to be prepared, however, to bring it up yourself in response to prompts covering more general topics from the latter half of the twentieth century – foreign policy, the economy, the energy crisis (which was a combination of the two), perceived cultural decay, or the larger evolution of events leading up to the conservative revolution of the 1980s.

9. How did the relationship between the U.S. and U.S.S.R. change over the sec-ond half of the twentieth century? (This is rather broad; specific prompts will likely narrow the topic down a bit. The same idea may be expressed simply as the "Cold War" without naming the major players or time period. In add-ition to the major events of the Carter Administration, remember that Nixon began thawing relations with China, Carter boycotted the Olympics after the Soviets invaded Afghanistan, and Reagan was, well... *Reagan*.)

10. Discuss the economic and social changes which led to the Reagan Revo-lution of the 1980s. (Again, specific prompts may narrow this down a bit, but the topic itself is quite popular – especially in APUSH or other advanced courses.)

11. How did the U.S. attempt to resist the expansion of Communism in South America in the latter decades of the twentieth century? (This gets into some stuff not covered here, but the Panama "giveaway" would be relevant, as would Carter's prioritization of human rights in making foreign policy deci-sions. Obviously Nixon and Reagan could be relevant here as well.)

12. What options should be considered when a rabbit unexpectedly appears to be attacking your canoe? Discuss the potential symbolic impact of each choice in your response.

That last one probably isn't all that likely. Then again... it's a tough topic to predict. I'd be ready just in case.

**Like most foreign names or other terms, accurate vocalization in the original tongue sounds way cooler and more legit. Pronunciation guides inserted here refer to the most common "Ameri-canized" versions you'd have heard on the evening news or in academic discussions.

HISTORY SURVIVAL SKILLS: WHAT IF I STILL DON'T CARE ABOUT ANY OF THIS?

Faking It Until You Fall In Love (With History)

Excellence is an art won by training and habituation. We do not act rightly because we have virtue or excellence, but we rather have those because we have acted rightly. We are what we repeatedly do. Excellence, then, is not an act but a habit.

(Aristotle, sort of – but maybe historian Will Durant... because why should *anything* be easy?)

Choose Your Tingle

There's a common misconception among students that subjects are either interesting, or they're not. That you either care about them, or you don't. That you're either good at them, or you're not. This is simply not so.

We may not have *total* control over how we feel about certain people, subjects, or tasks, but we have far more ability to shape our mindsets about such things than many of us realize.

You've probably seen at least one movie in which people pretend to be in love with one another. Maybe it's to win a bet. Maybe it's to secure a green card. Maybe one of them is just being a jerk at the other's expense. Whatever the motivation, what almost *always* happens by two-thirds of the way through the movie?

It turns out they're "really in love." They've been faking it so well and for so long, that something clicks.

But hey, that's only in movies, right? Not necessarily. The success rate of arranged marriages throughout history and across cultures is astronomical – something in the mid-nineties, percentagewise. Sure, some of that's cultural, or because your spouse's family will light you on fire if you try to leave, but much of it, I respectfully suggest, is because two people simply *choose* to be in love. Maybe they have to fake it at first, but over time...

It becomes real. Or, real enough.

Compare this to the American system of love and marriage: I get a tingly feeling for you... you get a tingly feeling for me... at some point, we decide to mingle our tingles. It's great for a few ~~weeks~~ years, but eventually the tingle starts to fade. Oh no! We must not be "in love" anymore! These suspicions are verified when I discover I'm beginning to tingle for your sister or my co-worker or that sweet young thing at the deli instead. We divorce so we can each tingle with someone new. As a result, American marriages have something like a fifty percent long-term success rate.

But wait! Maybe we don't give up that easily. Maybe we go to tingle counseling where an expert suggests we must do a better job of pretending to tingle even when we're not quite feeling it. When you're telling me about your day (in excruciating detail), for example, I'm told to practice reflective listening:

* "Isn't that what you suggested last week?"

* "Do you think she put it that way on purpose?"

* "That sounds exhausting (or exciting or promising or potentially problematic)."

* Or even just "Oh my god... seriously?!?"

Maybe you're encouraged at tingle counseling to rephrase things as "I" statements so your partner doesn't feel attacked or criticized quite so often:

* "I realize she can be difficult, but she's still my mother. I'd like to find a way she can still visit while still respecting your right to walk naked and unashamed in your own house."

* "When you don't remember my birthday, I feels like I must not be as important to you as National Donut Week – I mean, you put up *decorations* every year for that one."

Relationship counselors don't teach such things so that we can both hide our misery and fake it until we die. They push these approaches on us because they know that if we practice them, they'll become less and less *forced* and more and more how we *naturally enjoy interacting* with one another. We may even end up with something deeper and more trustworthy than those original tingles.

So, what does this have to do with the "boring" stuff in history?

It's Not History; It's You

All history is inherently fascinating. Some parts are more accessible or more naturally engaging than others, but none of it's actually *boring* once you start paying attention.

In other words, the entire premise of this book is a lie. Sorry about that. But you've made it this far, right? No sense taking it back now. Besides, you've already bent the cover and smudged some of the pages – might was well keep reading and not hurt my sales totals by doing anything foolish.

That doesn't mean every teacher is a master storyteller. It doesn't mean every documentary or hot new non-fiction text is a barnburner. There are people and events here and there that may require a little context to give them life. And there may be a few issues or eras in history that we drag through less for their intrinsic yippies and more because they set up the *really* good stuff – the *Harry Potter and the Order of the Phoenix* installments, as it were. But none are truly *boring* when you love history.

But I *Don't* Love History

You're breaking my heart, friend. I may need a moment. Also, shut up – yes, you do. At least that's what you're going to start telling yourself. Every day. Like you mean it.

Here are a few simple ways to get started:

* When you're scrolling through Netflix or whatever streaming service you prefer, looking for something to watch, try one of those historical fiction shows recommended on the main screen. It doesn't have to be a documentary (although those have gotten SO much better in the past few years) - even something completely fictional but in a historical setting can help spark your interest in real history.

* If you already like a show or movie set in another time or place, take ten minutes before the next time you watch it and look up something about that time or place. Creative types love getting all detailed about their craft with stuff like this and you might be surprised how it enriches the viewing experience to know some basics from real history.

* If you play video games and come across something using a historical setting or making a historical reference, take that same ten minutes to look up whatever it is. It's even OK to use Wikipedia! Having at least a basic overview of the place, people, or issue being used by your game can make the game more fun (game designers love getting all clever about that sort of thing) and it's one more thing you now know something about.

* This same idea works for song lyrics, books or short stories, clever t-shirts, or whatever. If the song you're listening to says something about shipwrecks and Sirens, take five minutes and find out what that means (granted, that allusion is to fiction – but let's not nitpick). If that weird guy in class who sometimes lets you copy his homework has on a Che Guevara t-shirt, take five minutes to gather enough basics that you can fake your way through a brief conversation if necessary.

* Find some weird or wacky historical podcast and try a few episodes. If you're up when everyone else is asleep, this is a great headphones activity. If you have a long drive back and forth to work or anywhere else on a regular basis, you can listen in the car. If the first one doesn't do anything for you, try another. There are hundreds out there – with even a little effort, you'll find something that grabs you.

* If you prefer text to audio, subscribe to a few "weird history" or "forgotten history" type blogs. There are dozens (maybe hundreds) out there, and quality varies widely, but that just means there are at least a few which could potentially give you the tingles.

* If you're a student, time yourself to see how long you can maintain eye contact with your instructor while they're talking or explaining something.

Nod a little here and there to make it less creepy, and consider taking a few notes along the way to help yourself focus. Bonus points if you remember half of what they said once time is up.

* When reading about history stuff, focus less on memorization and more on visualizing what's being described. What would people experiencing the moment likely have been thinking, feeling, hoping, or fearing? How were their lives similar to yours and how were they different? How does this event or issue compare to something you've experienced in your own life, or to current events in the world around you? You may have amazing insights or be way off in your assumptions about other times and places, but that's OK – the more you learn, the richer your understanding will become.

* If ten minutes is all you can stand, then do ten minutes and move on. Don't belittle yourself (or the subject matter) if you're not able to maintain your interest longer than that at first. It's the regularity more than the endurance that most matters when you're trying to develop new habits and new mindsets.

* If you're an "all or nothing" type, you'll need to shake that off right now if you're going to get anywhere with history. There's simply too much out there for you to ever know *everything*, even about the tiniest subject or time frame. Pick something and build from there. A lot or a little, it's OK.

* Above all else, regularly *choose* to be excited. Say it out loud if necessary – "I can't wait to learn more about THIS!" "Holy Moses in a leaky basket... WHO KNEW THAT WAS A THING?!?" or even "Huh. I guess I'm a tiny bit smarter than I realized after all!"

* Finally, buy more copies of this book and give them as gifts to all of your friends and loved ones. Tell them how much you look forward to discussing it together and how those conversations will strengthen your relationship. If you're a student, emphasize to family members that their participation might be the only way you'll even graduate. They might want to get additional copies for grandparents, cousins, or even casual acquaintances from the grocery store or hair salon – you know, if they really care about your success and happiness.

You may not always have control over how you *feel*, but you have plenty of control over your *choices*. You determine your own *mindset*, your own *focus*. That doesn't mean it's always easy or fun, but it's not some insurmountable task – the thirteenth labor of Hercules. Once you've committed to at least *pretending* you care about history, you may be surprised how often "feeling it" and "caring about it" come right along behind.

If it helps, you can feel a tiny bit martyred for making the effort. You're so noble like that.